Effective Hiring
&
ADA Compliance

Effective Hiring & ADA Compliance

Arlene Vernon-Oehmke

American Management Association

New York • Atlanta • Boston • Chicago • Kansas City • San Francisco • Washington, D.C.
Brussels • Mexico City • Tokyo • Toronto

This book is available at a special
discount when ordered in bulk quantities.
For information, contact Special Sales Department,
AMACOM, a division of American Management Association,
135 West 50th Street, New York, NY 10020.

This publication is designed to provide accurate and authoritative information in regard to the subject matter covered. It is sold with the
understanding that the publisher is not engaged in rendering legal,
accounting, or other professional service. If legal advice or other ex-
pert assistance is required, the services of a competent professional
person should be sought.

Library of Congress Cataloging-in-Publication Data

Vernon-Oehmke, Arlene.
    Effective hiring & ADA compliance / Arlene Vernon-Oehmke.
        p.   cm.
    Includes bibliogrpahical references and index.
    ISBN 0-8144-0246-1
    1. Handicapped—Employment—Unitgged States.   2. Employee selection—
United States.   3. Handicapped—Employment—Law and legislation—
United States.   I. Title.   II. Title: Effective hiring and ADA
compliance.
HD7256.U5V47   1994
658.3'045—dc20   94-16783
                                                            CIP

© 1994 Arlene Vernon-Oehmke.
American Management Association, New York.
All rights reserved.
Printed in the United States of America.

This publication may not be reproduced,
stored in a retrieval system,
or transmitted in whole or in part,
in any form or by any means, electronic,
mechanical, photocopying, recording, or otherwise,
without the prior written permission of AMACOM,
a division of American Management Association,
135 West 50th Street, New York, NY 10020.

Printing number

10   9   8   7   6   5   4   3   2   1

Contents

Introduction

The objective of the Employment Title of the Americans with Disabilities Act of 1990 is to ensure that businesses do not discriminate against applicants and employees with disabilities.

The Employment Title is implemented in two stages. Employers with twenty-five or more employees were required to comply on July 26, 1992. Two years later, on July 26, 1994, employers with fifteen or more employees were required to comply. Since ADA legislation affects a significant percentage of American businesses and a more significant percentage of American workers, employers in all industries are changing how they select and hire their workforce.

The Impact of ADA

The changes in employment policy and procedures stimulated by the ADA are positive steps for both employers and employees. Businesses will now recognize qualified individuals with disabilities as viable candidates for their workforce. With the changing demographics of our population, and especially the workforce, business will benefit from the new pool of qualified applicants with disabilities. From an operational perspective, the ADA will motivate employers to audit their current employment practices to ensure compliance. This audit and thorough revision of policies and practices will increase the overall effectiveness of human resources management efforts.

Employers' fears of discrimination suits, with their related legal fees and potential financial penalties, are a prime motivating factor for ADA compliance. But this fear is unwarranted for businesses that participate in good hiring and employment practices. Those with less consistent employment practices may need to audit their management operations to determine areas where noncompliance may be an issue.

As businesses become more aware of ADA requirements and as the courts make more ADA rulings, the appropriate legal and operational steps to avoid discrimination will become more apparent. Until the courts determine the practical applications of the ADA, businesses need to determine independently how best to treat all employees and applicants equitably. Whether fear or proactive efforts initiate these actions, employers will learn how complying with the ADA and employing people with disabilities can benefit us all. These changes for improved operations, fine-tuning of policies, and consistent treatment of employees throughout an organization will have long-term benefits for both employers and employees.

How This Book Can Help You

Effective Hiring & ADA Compliance accomplishes multiple objectives for readers who want to ensure that their business complies with the ADA in selecting and hiring practices. The book presents an understandable and practical explanation of the ADA's Title I—Employment. It explains the ADA's employee selection requirements and helps you understand ADA compliance in the workplace.

For employers, managers, interviewers, and employees, here are the practical tools, methods, and examples to help simplify ADA compliance in the selection process. After reading these chapters you will understand how every facet of employment must consistently meet ADA standards to ensure such compliance. However, the greatest benefit of this book will be in demonstrating how consistency in practice and policy improves your employment operation and employee selection.

The book discusses current selection processes and creates a selection system. This system begins with identifying the essential functions of a job and using an ADA-compliant job description as the core of the hiring process. Presented here are sample employment advertisements that focus on a job's essential functions. Sample compliant and noncompliant employment application language is also included. The book presents effective, compliant screening methods for job applications and resumés as well.

The employment interview plays a pivotal role in ADA compliance. *Effective Hiring & ADA Compliance* describes in detail how to interview in accordance with the ADA. It simplifies the process and experience of interviewing by structuring the interview process, and it provides examples of incorrect and correct interviews to help you understand how common interview techniques can be discriminatory. You will also learn how to interview people with disabilities, and you will increase your comfort level in the interview by learning how to address people with disabilities, both in the interview and in the work environment.

With its overview of selection decision making, the information here will help you ensure that medical examinations and other screening methods comply with the ADA. You'll also find an employment accessibility checklist to help you ensure that people with disabilities can access all the employment services available to people without disabilities.

Upon completing this book you will have a tool to help you and the other interviewers in your company interview and select employees more effectively. In following the book's methodology, you'll be complying with the Americans with Disabilities Act as a routine aspect of your company's employment practices.

Part One

The Basics of The ADA and Employee Selection

Chapter 1

Today's Selection Process

There is no guarantee that you will always find or identify the perfect employee. There's no guarantee that you won't make mistakes in your hiring decisions. However, there are steps you can take to improve your end results. Let's analyze how you currently select employees and how effective your methods are. Then you can evaluate and redesign your selection process, particularly as it relates to ADA compliance.

What is the full sequence of events in the selection process? First, a manager identifies the need to fill a vacant position. Next, he or she performs the following steps on a formal or informal basis:

1. Documents the position's responsibilities
2. Advertises the job
3. Screens resumés and applications
4. Interviews candidates
5. Makes the hiring decision
6. Extends the job offer

Each of these functions must now comply with the Americans with Disabilities Act. However, before we get into the legalities of these processes, let's examine how an organization performs each of these steps.

Documenting the Responsibilities of the Vacant Position

The bottom line for documenting job responsibilities is to determine the tasks performed on the job. To do that, you need a complete picture of the vacant job. This picture should be in a usable format for all participants in the hiring process. When the job picture is incomplete or not user-friendly, new-employee selection is more likely to fail.

An interviewer must thoroughly understand the job responsibilities and the required job skills in order to make an effective selection decision. Think about the quality and quantity of job information currently available at your company to help interviewers make hiring decisions. Consider how the level of job documentation directly affects the caliber of job-relevant information acquired from the applicant during the interview.

Ask yourself the following questions to help you evaluate how well your company documents jobs, how these methods fit your organization's culture, how to identify those documentation areas needing improvement, and how to implement these operational changes.

1. What is your company's philosophy regarding documentation of job responsibilities? Is this activity a human resources department responsibility or a line function? (This response may be predicated on the size and resources of your company.)

2. Does your organization document the responsibilities and requirements of each position? Is this documentation in a standardized job-description format? Is job documentation handled informally, manager by manager?

3. Are there job descriptions for every position? For most positions? For certain positions? For few positions?

4. How frequently is each job description updated? Is it ongoing with every responsibility change? Annually with performance appraisals? When each position turns over to a new employee? Rarely? How many years has it been since your company conducted a major job-description update effort?

5. Who is responsible for writing new job descriptions or updating older descriptions? Human resources staff? Managers? Employees?

6. Are the individuals who write job descriptions trained in how to write effective descriptions, the purpose and benefits of the descriptions, and how to apply the descriptions in the workplace?

7. How do the human resources staff, management, and employees use formal job descriptions? Are they used to determine salary levels? To explain to incumbents their job responsibilities? To train new employees? To evaluate employee performance? To advertise job openings? To keep documents on file just in case?

8. Do applicants receive a copy of the job documentation before, during, or after their interview to help them decide whether to accept the job?
9. Are job descriptions in the computer and easily accessible to those responsible for revising the documents?
10. What format are your descriptions in? Are they written as paragraphs or as an outline? Do they give an overview of responsibilities or do they get into the details of each task?
11. Do your job descriptions comply with the ADA?

Fantasize about how you would change your current job-documentation methods if given the opportunity and unlimited resources. Consider how you can develop a plan of action to improve current methods. Compare these ideas with the guidelines in this book. In Chapter 4, I explore the details of job descriptions and ADA compliance, and explain how to ensure that each description complies with the ADA requirements.

Advertising the Job Opening

Every company uses a different method to inform the public it is seeking qualified job candidates. Companies base these methods on the company's demographics, applicant pool, business location, job skill requirements, and available internal financial and staffing resources. Review the following partial list of recruitment options. Consider whom you are trying to bring into your organization and how effective you are in reaching your targeted applicants.

1. Do you advertise job openings inside your company? Are your selection criteria the same for internal as for external candidates?
2. Do you advertise in local or national publications? Newspapers? Newsletters? Trade magazines?
3. Do you contact schools, public employment centers, or other agencies that have placement or training services?
4. What responses do you typically get from advertising? Do you track applicants by type of advertising method? Does one method attract a different caliber of applicant than another?
5. Who is responsible for writing the job advertisement? Human resources staff? Management? Incumbents? Is it a joint responsibility?

6. Does your company have an employment and selection philosophy? How is the philosophy communicated to applicants and employees?
7. Do your advertising methods comply with the ADA?

Consider how much thought your company gives to its current job-advertising methods. Many companies have been using the same practices for years with varying success while others have mastered the process of attracting new employees. Is it time to take a fresh look at how you advertise for applicants in order to attract better candidates? If you were looking for a job, would you find your company's job advertisements attractive? If you had free rein over this responsibility, how would you improve the current ads?

Screening Resumés and Employment Applications

The third step in filling a vacant position focuses on the written information you receive from job applicants concerning their skills and background. First, your company must determine whether your application form complies with the ADA and other Equal Employment Opportunity (EEO) requirements. Second, your company must review its current methods for screening job applicants. The ADA specifies the questions you can and cannot ask on an application form. These details are provided in Chapter 6. However, consider when you last updated your application form. Ask yourself whether its organization and design are useful for your screeners and interviewers. If the application needs updating for ADA compliance, this may be the time to take a fresh look at the overall effectiveness of the employment application.

Your company's technique for screening job applicants relates to the application design, but actually is a separate employment issue. Most companies review job applications and resumés informally; few develop formal systems and methods, and documentation of the results of these reviews is almost nonexistent. Thus, proof of nondiscriminatory screening practices would be difficult for most organizations to show. So review these questions and consider potential improvements in your current methods.

1. Who is responsible for screening the applications and resumés? The human resources staff? Hiring managers? Clerical staff? Employees?
2. Who determines the criteria for each position?

3. Are participants trained in screening techniques?
4. Do those who do the screening prepare in advance for each task? How do they learn the details of the job in question?
5. After someone has reviewed a particular application, what methods are used to explain why it was rejected?
6. Is there a double-check of reviewed and rejected applications?
7. Is there a system for tracking and organizing the applications that have been reviewed?
8. How do you file and store the rejected applications?
9. Who selects the acceptable applicants who are interviewed for the job?

A poorly reviewed pile of applications and resumés can be costly for employers. "The one that got away" shouldn't happen at your company. ADA legislation does not directly discuss the ADA-compliant screening of job applicants. However, screening techniques, potential screener bias, inconsistent efforts, and the absence of documentation that results in discrimination against people with disabilities will oblige employers to formalize this process.

Interviewing the Candidates

There are right and wrong ways to interview; there are effective and ineffective interview methods. But if you ask people who interview whether their interviews are effective and legal, most will answer yes. As an employer or manager, are you truly comfortable with this automatic response? The time has come to rethink the employment interview.

Ask yourself the following questions about how the interview process takes place in your company:

1. Does your company have a philosophy to interviewing? Is it an informal philosophy or is it in writing? Are interviewers aware of this philosophy?
2. Who in your company conducts the interviews? The human resources staff? Managers? Nonmanagement employees?
3. Does the company conduct interview training? Are all interviewers trained? When did the last interview training session take place? Has training been updated for recent legislation or to refresh interviewing styles?
4. What information is provided to the interviewers in advance

of actual interviews regarding the job, job qualifications, departmental operations, and the applicant?

5. How do interviewers know what questions elicit the best information for making a hiring decision?
6. Are candidates interviewed by more than one person to obtain a second opinion?
7. What criteria does each interviewer use to determine the best candidate for the job?
8. Is there a procedure for documenting and evaluating each interview?
9. Is there an evaluation of the interview process itself?

The most worrisome aspect of employment interviewing is the fact that the interview occurs behind closed doors. Typically, there are no observers to the interview discussion. Unless you have direct feedback from an applicant, you don't know what your interviewers say about the company and the job or what illegal questions are being asked, subtly or directly. Yet many times illegal questions are still being asked. When you receive an interview evaluation from an applicant, the feedback typically is unsolicited and negative.

There are simple solutions that address the issue of effective and compliant interviewing. Employers and managers can take steps to ensure that the employment process is effective and does not discriminate against protected groups. These steps take time and effort, but they provide multiple benefits, including more comfortable interviewers, satisfied applicants, and more qualified new employees.

Making the Hiring Decision

Another area employers need to consider from a legal perspective is the hiring decision itself. Many people consider the hiring decision to be the final step of the interview process; however, this is not true. Do we participate in the interviewing process or the selection process? The interview is more appropriately seen as a process rather than the end result, which is the hiring decision.

Consider how much time your organization spends finding the best applicants and how much more time it spends making the final decision on whom to hire.

1. What systems are in place in your company to evaluate the results of each interview?

2. Which (or how many) interviewers provide input on the candidate's skills, interview performance, and potential job success?

3. Who has final responsibility for making the selection decision? The manager? The human resources department?

4. After the hiring decision is made, is there any documentation of how the best candidate was identified?

5. Is there any documentation supporting reasons why other interviewed candidates were not hired?

6. Is there a method for reviewing how hiring decisions are made in your company?

The objective is to identify a new employee. Think about how many new employees your company (or department) hired this past year. How many of these individuals are still on the job? How many perform satisfactorily or better? Determine your company's (or department's) ratio of successful new employees to its number of new hires. How small a ratio is it?

For the remainder of this book, you'll use the answers to these questions to learn how effective selection methodology can improve your hiring processes and meet ADA requirements. All the questions posed in this chapter lead to this text's theme: consistency, thoroughness, and documentation in the hiring process. Your company will meet its selection objectives when these three processes are in place.

Chapter 2

Understanding the Americans With Disabilities Act

Before we discuss specific disabilities and employment issues, let's look at disability in the United States. Right now, there are an estimated 43 million people with disabilities. Those disabling conditions stretch across a broad spectrum of types and severity. Some individuals have multiple disabilities; others have single disabilities. The largest group of people with disabilities are those with hearing impairments. Twenty-two million people have hearing impairments. Only 9 percent, or 2 million of the 22 million, are totally deaf.

There are over 9 million people with developmental disabilities such as cerebral palsy and mental retardation. There are approximately 2.5 million individuals who have mental retardation. Ninety percent of these individuals have mild mental retardation; this constitutes a large group of individuals who have the potential to work at low-skill jobs.

There are 5 million people with mental illness. Mental illness is not the same as mental retardation or developmental disabilities. Mental illness refers to people who may have experienced depression or a type of breakdown. Many of these individuals have work skills; mental illness may not impair development, job skills, or abilities.

Approximately 3 million people have diabetes. Over 2 million people have speech impairments, such as stuttering or lisping. Two million people have epilepsy; 80 percent of individuals with epilepsy control their seizures by medication.

Over 1 million people have partial or complete paralysis. One million people use wheelchairs. One hundred twenty thousand people are totally blind and 60,000 people are legally blind, meaning that they have some vision.

Why We Need the ADA

To address each employment issue effectively, we must have a basic understanding of:

- Why we need the ADA
- What the ADA is
- What the ADA's objectives are
- How employers must comply with the ADA
- How the ADA relates to the selection process

The Rehabilitation Act of 1973 was the first legislation designed to protect people with disabilities against discrimination in employment. Federal contractors and subcontractors—those businesses with federal contracts and subcontracts exceeding certain dollar amounts—must meet Rehabilitation Act requirements. The proponents of this law had the objective of changing the way *all* businesses addressed the employment of people with disabilities. They hoped that nondiscriminatory practices performed by federal contractors and subcontractors would spread to other employers. However, the law functioned only in its literal sense. The larger business sector did not adopt nondiscrimination practices for people with disabilities, and it took nearly twenty years and diligent lobbying by disability advocates to implement broader legislation.

As mentioned, there are 43 million people with disabilities in the United States. In the past, our society has not included people with disabilities as an identified and protected minority group. However, these people have the highest unemployment rate of *any* minority group in our country—more than three times the unemployment rate for nondisabled people. The result of this extremely high unemployment is that people with disabilities constitute the poorest segment of our population. The U.S. government spends $300 billion each year to support people with disabilities. Financial support is not a solution, however. By providing people with disabilities with equal opportunity for employment and the chance to live a more complete life, the ADA is a more effective solution to the problems of unemployment and poverty.

Discrimination against people with disabilities occurs in many different ways. Some of the discrimination is intentional, some is unintentional. Some forms of discrimination are subtle, some are not so subtle. We have been taught to view and treat people with disabilities as being different from people without disabilities. The media have portrayed people with disabilities at varying extremes—

as extremely dependent (in the home or in the streets), as villains (Captain Hook), or as superheroes (Ironside, Longstreet). These extremes are unrealistic and do not help us see people with disabilities as our peers. In the past, our education system segregated people with disabilities. As children, many of us were not given the opportunity to learn and work side by side with people with disabilities. Thus, this discrimination by separation increased our unawareness of people with disabilities. It emphasized our differences and ignored our similarities. The separation increased our unfounded fear and discomfort in dealing with people with disabilities.

Implementing the Americans with Disabilities Act gives us the opportunity to modify these historical behavioral patterns. The ADA's objective is to put people with disabilities into mainstream society and to offer them opportunities that nondisabled people take for granted. These efforts will integrate our workplaces, public places, and lives. Through increased visibility and personal contact, our misconceptions about people with disabilities will be eliminated. The separateness will be eliminated.

What Is the ADA?

The Americans with Disabilities Act is broader in scope than many of us realize. It addresses accessibility, service, and employment issues, as well as providing opportunities and decreasing discrimination for people with disabilities. The act divides into five titles for easier understanding and implementation.

Title I is the Employment Title. It defines and describes how employers are prohibited from discriminating against qualified individuals with disabilities in all terms and conditions of employment. This title is of greatest relevance to the employee selection process.

Title II is the Public Service Title. It prohibits discrimination and increases accessibility to programs run by public agencies, such as state and local governments. This title requires that public transportation become more accessible to people with disabilities. This benefits employers. Due to increasing access to public transportation (increasing the number of buses, subways, trains), people with disabilities are able to reach more businesses and expand their opportunity for employment into different communities. This gives employers a larger pool of applicants with independent, reliable transportation to and from the workplace.

Title III addresses Public Accommodations. It requires that private businesses serving the public make their goods and services available to people with disabilities. For example, all retail establishments must provide full service and their goods must be accessible to people with disabilities.

Title III also requires that buildings be accessible to people with disabilities. The ADA developed elaborate criteria for new construction and modification of existing buildings to ensure accessibility. You may have noticed such changes in the form of an increased frequency of ramped sidewalks, additional accessible parking spaces, motorized shopping carts in grocery and department stores, public telephones with hearing amplifiers, or commercials including people with disabilities. All of these efforts help people with disabilities acquire the services and products nondisabled people have always obtained. From a business perspective, the benefit of increased accessibility is a larger customer base and increased sales.

Title IV, the Telecommunications Title, requires that telephone services be accessible to people with hearing and speech impairments by providing relay services. The relay service uses an operator as an intermediary communicator between the speaking or hearing person and the individual needing assistance. For example, the operator may type one party's spoken message into a telecommunication device for the deaf (TDD) so that a person with a hearing impairment can read it and type back a response.

Title V contains miscellaneous technical information relating to such areas as ADA implementation, the Rehabilitation Act, and state laws.

The two titles that have the greatest impact on the business environment are Titles I, Employment, and III, Public Accommodations. These two titles require that employers not discriminate (1) in any aspect of employment and (2) when servicing customers with disabilities. For example, Title I states that when an applicant is the most qualified person for a job, an employer cannot refuse to hire him or her because of a disability. Title III requires that all customers, regardless of disability, receive all the services available at that business.

Title I was effective on July 26, 1992, for employers with twenty-five or more employees. Employers with fifteen or more employees were required to comply with Title I on July 26, 1994. The primary effective date of Title III was January 26, 1992. There are separate provisions and effective dates for businesses in existing buildings and for those constructing new buildings.

Title I: Employment

To comply with Title I throughout the employee selection process, a company must understand how the ADA has defined its requirements. ADA legislators recognized that they could not predict every possible discriminatory employment circumstance, so they created legislation that is broad and open to interpretation. The key to Title I implementation and compliance is in how the ADA defines who is protected and how it describes basic employer responsibilities.

The core of Title I is the provision of:

equal employment opportunities for qualified individuals with disabilities.

For businesses to implement Title I, they must understand who is a qualified individual with a disability. The ADA states further that Title I protects someone who is:

disabled and *qualified* to perform the *essential functions* of the job in question with or without *reasonable accommodation(s)*, unless the accommodation(s) present an *undue hardship* to the employer. [Italics added.]

The ADA provides more in-depth definitions to help businesses further recognize their obligations. The following explanations will help you understand the intent and the application of the ADA's key terms.

How Does the ADA Define *Disabled*?

Congress intentionally defined *disability* broadly. It wants to protect as many people with different disabilities and disabling conditions as possible. According to the ADA, a person has a disability if he or she falls under one or more of the following four categories:

1. *Has a physical or mental impairment that substantially limits one or more major life activity.* For example, a person who is hearing impaired, visually impaired, or mobility impaired has a limitation in the major life activities of hearing, seeing, or walking.
2. *Has a record of such an impairment.* This protects someone who has had heart surgery but no longer has a heart condition,

or someone who has recovered from cancer. These individuals have a history of disability but are no longer impaired.

3. *Is regarded as having an impairment.* Some individuals are discriminated against because people perceive them to have a disability. For example, someone with a facial scar, burns, or a limp is now protected from discrimination.

4. *Associates with someone with a disability.* For example, someone whose spouse or child has a disability cannot be discriminated against because of his or her relationship with the spouse or child.

Chapter 8 provides further information on disabilities covered by the ADA.

Who is *not* considered disabled and therefore is not protected under the ADA? The regulations have an extensive list of those individuals excluded from ADA protection, including someone with a temporary disability (such as a routine broken arm) or who currently uses drugs illegally.

What Is *Qualified* according to the ADA?

One major misconception people have regarding the ADA is that employers must hire a person with a disability regardless of that person's ability to perform the job. This is not Congress's intent. The ADA protects only people with disabilities who are qualified to perform the job. For example, a qualified person would have to meet all or some of the following job qualifications:

- Education requirements
- Work experience
- Training levels
- Job skills
- Licensing requirements
- Certification
- Other job-related requirements determined by the employer

The ADA gives employers the right to determine the qualifying standards that all candidates must satisfy. If an employer establishes hiring criteria, the employer must apply them consistently in evaluating all applicants; thus the criteria apply to candidates with and without disabilities. If a person with a disability is the most qualified person for the job, the employer should offer that person the job. If a person without a disability is the most qualified, the employer should offer that person the job. Again, the ADA reinforces an employer's right to hire the most qualified applicant for a job, regardless of disability.

What Is an *Essential Function* of the Job?

An *essential function* is a fundamental duty of the job. To be the most qualified applicant for the job, the person must meet the job-related requirements listed above and must also be able to perform the fundamental duties of the job. The essential functions, then, are the primary responsibilities of a position. Any position has key duties easily identified as essential to the objective of that job. The ADA does not expect employers to eliminate or make changes to these core job duties when hiring people with disabilities. In contrast, every job typically has a few tasks that are not vital to the overall purpose. The ADA refers to these tasks as *nonessential functions*. Under the ADA, a company cannot refuse to hire a person with a disability because of his or her inability to perform a *non*essential job function.

The ADA's emphasis on hiring the most qualified person for a job merely implements good hiring practice. It is logical that the most qualified person is the one who can perform the job's essential functions, with or without accommodation.

According to the ADA, it is the employer's responsibility to determine what is essential to each job. The task of identifying essential functions is pivotal to business operation and must remain within the employer's rights. Every aspect of how a business manages and complies with the ADA relates to essential functions. Chapter 3 focuses on this topic and its relation to the job description.

What Is a *Reasonable Accommodation*?

A *reasonable accommodation* is a modification or adjustment to the job, the work environment, or the way the job is typically performed, which helps a qualified individual with a disability perform that job. Employers can accommodate either or both the essential functions and the nonessential functions of a job.

The ADA describes the circumstances under which employers can make reasonable accommodations:

1. To the job application and interview process
2. To the performance of the job's essential functions
3. To enable an employee with a disability to enjoy equal benefits and privileges of employment

Reasonable accommodation may be made to the *job application process* to ensure equal opportunity. For example, you can help a visually impaired person complete an employment application form. The ability or inability to read the print on a job application should not prohibit individuals from applying for a job for which they qualify.

Reasonable accommodation to the way someone *performs a job function* may include:

- *Making facilities used by employees readily accessible to and usable by people with disabilities.* For example, a person in a wheelchair may need to have his workstation rearranged or the desktop height adjusted to help make all the objects on the desk or in the files reachable.
- *Restructuring a job by reassigning nonessential functions.* For example, a nonessential function for a clerical position may be the physical distribution of memos within the office building. This responsibility may be eliminated or exchanged with another employee for other nonessential responsibilities if the clerk has a disability that prohibits her from performing this nonessential duty.
- *Modifying how an essential job function is performed.* For example, an employer could accommodate an individual with a hand mobility impairment to use a calculator or a computer keyboard by purchasing equipment or a device to make this task easier.
- *Modifying work schedules or hiring qualified individuals on a part-time basis.* For example, an employer could accommodate a disabled employee with a weekly doctor's appointment by allowing the employee time off without pay. Another option could be to reschedule the employee to make up the missed time during another day.
- *Modifying examinations, training materials, or policies.* For example, make video training more effective for a hearing-impaired employee by providing her with a written script that corresponds to the video. Read written examinations to a visually impaired employee. Allow a person with a learning disability a longer period to complete a job training program.

- *Ensuring equal accessibility to employee benefits and other privileges of employment.* For example, review medical insurance benefits for equitable treatment of disabling conditions. Ensure that company-sponsored events are at accessible locations.

There is an infinite number of accommodation options depending on the job, the individual, and the circumstances. To make this process easier and more effective, remember these tips:

1. *There is no one solution for every disability.* Treat each person as a unique individual in all aspects of employment and especially when considering accommodations.

2. *Involve the applicant or employee when making an accommodation.* The individual generally has a better understanding of her circumstances and needs, and should participate in selecting the appropriate accommodation.

3. *Find experts and external resources to help research and select the best accommodation for applicants and employees.* Requesting assistance and documentation from the individual's treating physician can make accommodation selection more effective. Additionally, there are organizations in the country familiar with job accommodation options and assistive devices for people with disabilities. Call them for assistance. Many provide these services at no or minimal cost.

4. *Recognize that it is the individual's responsibility to request an accommodation from the employer.* The employer has the responsibility to inform job applicants and employees of their right to request an accommodation. Employers are not expected to know instinctively when the need for an accommodation exists. However, once an employee requests an accommodation, the employer should make every effort to provide one.

5. *The employer has the right to select the accommodation used.* Take, for example, the scenario in which three effective accommodation options are available, priced at $10, $50, and $350. The employer can select any one of the options. The employee can state a preference, and the employer should take this preference under consideration. However, it is the employer who chooses the accommodation option.

What Is *Undue Hardship*?

There is only one circumstance whereby an employer can refuse to hire or promote an otherwise qualified individual with a disability.

That occurs when the required accommodation would create undue hardship for the company, making the accommodation unreasonable. This is an unusual circumstance that employers should consider carefully and use infrequently.

An *undue hardship* is an action that requires significant difficulty or expense to the employer when considering:

- The nature and net cost of the accommodation, taking into account potential tax credits and alternative funding
- The financial resources of the facility, the number of people employed at that facility, and the effect on expenses and resources
- If the facility is part of a larger entity, the overall size and resources of the larger entity (i.e., a parent company) with respect to number of employees, and the number, type, and location of its facilities
- The type of operation of the larger entity including the structure and functions of the workforce, the geographic separateness, and the administrative or fiscal relationship to the facility
- The impact of the accommodation on the operation of the facility, including the impact on the other employees' ability to perform their duties and on the facility's ability to conduct business.

The larger the company and the greater its financial resources, the more difficult it will be to prove undue hardship. Any company that pursues undue hardship following an accommodation request should consult an attorney and accountant before informing the requester.

What Are the *Terms and Conditions of Employment?*

The ADA states that it is unlawful for an employer to discriminate on the basis of a disability against a qualified individual relating to any term, condition, and privilege of employment. Simply put, this means that the ADA prohibits discrimination throughout the employment process, including every part of the relationship between the employer and the employee. The ADA provides a partial list of the employment areas, including the following as well as any other term, condition, and privilege of employment.

1. The recruitment process: job advertising, applications, interviewing selection, and hiring
2. Internal employment issues: transfer, promotion, demotion, layoff, termination, and rehiring
3. Compensation issues: pay equity, pay increases, and other changes in compensation
4. Organizational issues: job assignment, structure, position descriptions, and succession planning
5. Absenteeism issues and policies: leaves of absence, sick leave, personal leaves, and other leaves
6. Employee benefits: insurance benefits, fringe benefits, employee relations activities, credit unions, and exercise facilities
7. Selection and financial support for training programs: apprenticeships, professional meetings, associations, and conferences
8. Employer-sponsored social and recreational activities: bowling or other recreational teams, company picnics, and parties

The prohibited discrimination issue includes physical accessibility to business locations as well as access to services and benefits. For example, employers cannot segregate people with disabilities from other employees. They also cannot exclude employees with disabilities intentionally or unintentionally from the opportunities available to other employees.

Chapter 3

The Essential Functions
Of the Job: The Core
Of the ADA

The key to ADA compliance is its requirement that employers identify the essential functions of a job. The essential functions of the job affect every aspect of the employment process. As such, an organization that identifies and documents the essential functions of each job and applies essential functions in every aspect of management will find ADA compliance an easier task.

The first step is to teach managers that identifying and recognizing essential functions is the basis for successful selection, decision making, and supervision. Managers must learn to view essential job functions as the foundation for managing employees. Once we all begin practicing this theory consistently, our operational systems and our employees will benefit because the manager's responsibilities will be easier and employees will know the performance expected of them.

Figure 3-1 depicts a simplified diagram of the life cycle of an employee. Managers and employees can use essential functions as the basis for:

- Making selection decisions
- Working together to understand the purpose of each job
- Assessing general and employee-specific training needs
- Setting job performance expectations
- Evaluating individual employee performance levels
- Determining the necessary skills to place or promote people in the position

Figure 3-1. The life cycle of an employee.

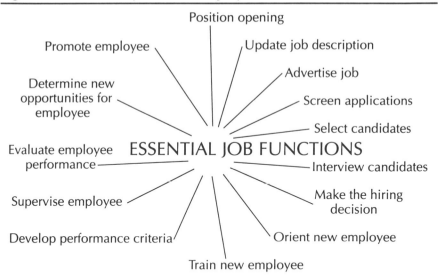

Companies that thoroughly document job responsibilities are more likely to have managers who base their decisions and activities on job functions, referring to job descriptions and other job documentation methods on an informal basis. However, companies should move to a more formal utilization of this documentation to ensure consistency and nondiscrimination in managerial efforts.

Employment

The need to document job functions and relate management efforts to the essential functions of each job is greatest during the employment process. The risk of and opportunity to discriminate peak during the selection process. When businesses hire new employees, the public evaluates them as employers. For example, when advertising their job vacancies to the community, companies generate attention and interest. During this period of high visibility, any public perception of unfair hiring practices can expose a company to possible discrimination charges.

When an external job applicant perceives discrimination, there is only one discrimination settlement mechanism: litigation in the courts or before a discrimination agency such as the Equal Employment Opportunity Commission. On the other hand, when a current employee perceives discrimination in the hiring process, companies have the opportunity to handle any charges through internal, employee relations methods. Discriminatory employment practices against internal and external applicants cannot be allowed. Consequently, businesses develop good employment practices to avoid the potential for discrimination. Figure 3-2 outlines the employment steps to identifying the essential functions of the job.

The ADA states that employers must identify the essential functions of a job before advertising a vacant position. This means that as soon as employers identify the need to fill an employment vacancy, they must identify the job's essential functions *in writing*. No recruitment efforts can begin until this task is completed, regardless of whether recruiting involves internal job posting or external advertising. Even if an organization has identified an internal candidate for the position, it must identify the essential functions before formal recruiting and interviewing can take place.

There are many advantages to identifying essential functions and skill requirements as a position becomes vacant. For example, it ensures that everyone involved in the selection process views the job in the same way. How often have you seen outdated job descriptions used in hiring, only to realize later that the description omitted a particular skill or job requirement? And how often has an old job description included outdated responsibilities? Often a company will add tasks based on the skills of the incumbent when previously

Figure 3-2. Key employment steps benefiting from essential function identification.

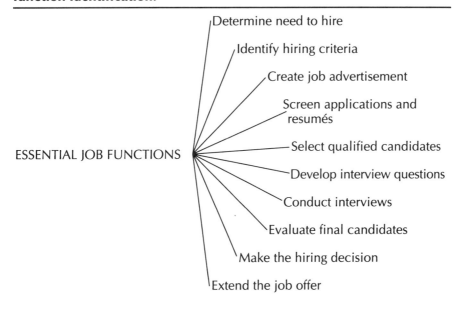

the tasks weren't part of the job. But by effectively identifying the essential functions, you can provide all selection participants with a clear, accurate description of the position to be filled.

Thus, the essential functions details provide the basis for the first step in recruiting: to write the job posting or help wanted advertisement. A good job advertisement helps the individuals screening the applications to better understand the position's key responsibilities and skills. Additionally, it provides applicants with a clear understanding of whether they qualify for and can perform the job.

Interviewers who thoroughly understand the job's primary duties are more effective. They can focus their questions on the job's primary qualifications and abilities, thus acquiring more information on each applicant's ability and making a better hiring decision. A hiring manager can make the *selection decision* by matching applicant skills, abilities, and background to the job's essential functions. They can hire the candidate who best meets the criteria. And if the most qualified person has a disability that needs a job accommodation, the detail in the description of essential functions will make the accommodation process easier.

A new employee who attends a *training* program that covers each of the essential job components can more effectively learn the details of each task. During training, the manager can develop a checklist of essential function descriptions to evaluate the employee's task comprehension and performance, and to gauge the success of each employee who completes the training program.

It is the manager's responsibility to determine a standard of performance and output for each job, based on the essential functions of the job. You need to present these standards to all employees, introducing the information when an employee starts the job and reinforcing it throughout the employee's tenure.

When the manager conducts an employee's performance evaluation, there should be no questions regarding expected level of performance. If an employee's performance falls below the standard, the manager can refer to the essential functions to identify problem areas, compare actual and target performance levels, determine the assistance (retraining, education, motivation) needed, and correct the problem.

For employees seeking advancement opportunities, the well-documented essential function information makes it easier to know the skills, responsibilities, and expectations required for promotion. Employees can use this information to develop the skills required for future opportunities.

How to Identify Essential Functions

The ADA offers eight criteria to help you determine whether a particular job function is essential. If the answer is yes to any of the following questions, then the function most likely is essential. It is important to note, however, that the ADA's list is not all inclusive. The ADA gives employers the right to identify unique circumstances and to determine what is truly essential to their business operation.

Essential-Function Criteria

1. *Are employees in the job performing the task?* If no one actually performs a task, clearly it is not an essential function of the job. Frequently, duties become outdated and remain on job documentation only in case the need arises. Eliminate these tasks from the job description and other job documentation.

2. *Did people who held the position in the past perform the task?* Job responsibilities change frequently. Some changes are due to business needs and others to staffing changes. When there is a staff change, managers should compare current and previous job descriptions, looking for task changes. The manager then determines whether operational or personnel circumstances created the change. If an operational change resulted in a shifting or elimination of essential functions, there is probably no essential function involved. However, if essential functions changed owing to an individual's interests or skills, the manager must decide whether this change should continue. In this circumstance, you should compare the primary objective of the job to the task in question to determine if the task is essential.

3. *Does the position exist to perform the function?* Many jobs revolve around several primary responsibilities. If you eliminated these responsibilities, the job would not exist or it would serve an entirely different purpose. As a result, these tasks are essential because the job's objective is based on performing those tasks. For example, a data entry position exists for a person to enter data into the computer; entering data is an essential function. A cashier's primary responsibilities include totaling a shopper's purchases using a cash register, collecting payment from the customer, and generating change; these are essential functions of the cashier's job.

4. *How much time does the employee spend performing the function?* Record the percentage of time an employee spends doing each job component. Generally, the more time spent performing the task, the more essential it is to the job. For example, a telephone sales-

person spends 60 percent of the day making sales calls and 30 percent of the day creating sales reports. Each of these functions constitutes the majority of the workday and would be considered essential.

Certain tasks are exceptions to the time issue. In some jobs, employees spend relatively little time performing a task, however the task is still essential to the job objective. In these circumstances, the employer determines whether the task is essential. For example, a company has one copy machine clerk who spends 90 percent of the workday making copies; copying is an essential function. The clerk spends 5 percent of the day maintaining the copy machine and performing minor machine repairs. While machine upkeep takes only a small percentage of the workday, the company determines that machine upkeep is an essential function of the job. By not performing the task the machine becomes inoperable and no further copying can take place.

5a. *Are there a limited number of other employees available to perform the function or among whom to distribute the function?* According to the ADA's definition of reasonable accommodation, employers can reassign nonessential job functions to other employees. To determine whether a task is essential or nonessential, an employer must consider each workplace, department, or office separately. The employer must ask whether other people are available to assume the responsibilities in question. If no one else is available to assume a task, then it may be considered essential according to the ADA. However, if there are other employees available to perform the task, then the employer may determine that the function is nonessential to the job.

For example, a small office has one secretary to support a branch sales force of twenty-five. One of the secretary's duties is maintaining the office files and client records. Since the sales staff travels, there are no other employees available to file, and therefore filing is an essential function of the secretary position. However, in another company a pool of six secretaries works in the marketing department. Each secretary performs related filing functions; as a result, the other secretaries are available to share the filing responsibilities. In this circumstance, filing may be a nonessential function.

5b. *Are there peak work periods that would prevent the transfer of responsibilities to others in the department?* In some positions, there are two work paces. During regular times, everyone works at a steady pace to get assignments completed. Under these circumstances, the employer can transfer or exchange nonessential tasks as a reasonable accommodation. For example, in a production facility, a team of eight workers is cross-trained to perform all eight job functions. One employee's accommodation might be being relieved from performing a task that requires standing for long periods.

This same company has one major client who routinely demands additional merchandise in a time frame that exceeds regular production levels. During these periods, overtime is required of all employees and there is no flexibility in who can perform specific job duties. Everyone must be able to perform all tasks upon demand. In this scenario, each of the eight tasks is an essential function of the job. Accommodation requiring the transfer of responsibilities to another individual in the work group would not be feasible.

6. *Is the function so highly specialized that the person is hired for her special expertise or ability to perform the function?* Some job duties require a high level of skill or a particular accreditation. These duties may or may not make up a large part of the individual's job, but in either case they may be essential to overall job function. For example, an employer may not require CPA certification for an accountant who performs routine accounting tasks. However, if an accountant is responsible for completing and auditing annual reports, the company may require a CPA as part of its hiring criteria. The special expertise required to perform this function makes auditing and completing annual reports an essential function of this accountant position.

7. *Would there be serious consequences if the employee is not required to perform the function?* In some circumstances, if an employer eliminates a job function, legal, safety, or service problems could result. You need to thoroughly review each job task to determine whether serious consequences for the employee, customers, or business could result from eliminating a particular task.

For example, a security guard is routinely responsible for checking and locking doors in an office complex. These tasks require the ability to travel to and access all locations in the buildings. Also, if an intruder breaks into the complex, the security guard is responsible for apprehending the intruder. This task requires the guard to move at great speed on foot. Though the latter event may be rare, if an employee could not chase the intruder, serious consequences might result. Therefore, the ability to move at fast speeds in case of emergency is an essential function of this security guard's job.

8. *Does the current collective bargaining agreement require that a particular job function be performed only by the incumbent in this position?* Employers should review each collective bargaining agreement to

determine whether there are contractual differences between how the union defines a job and how the ADA defines the job. In some collective bargaining agreements, employers may not exchange job responsibilities between employees with different titles or grades. If the agreement limits job tasks from being moved to another employee as an attempt to accommodate a person with a disability, the task may be an essential function for the position. On the other hand, the ADA's authors intended that employers and unions would revisit such collective bargaining restrictions to help open up more opportunities to people with disabilities.

The checklist that follows will help you determine whether a job function is essential.

ESSENTIAL FUNCTION CHECKLIST

For each job task in your company, answer the questions below to determine whether it is essential to the job.

____Yes ____No   1. Are employees in the job performing the task?
                         [If yes, continue. If no, STOP. The task is nonessential.]

____Yes ____No   2. Did other people who held the position in the past perform the task?
                         [If yes, continue. If no, consider whether the task is still required.]

____Yes ____No   3. Does the position exist for an employee to perform the function?
                         [If yes, STOP. The task is essential. If no, continue.]

____Lots ____Little   4. How much time does the employee spend performing the function?
                         [If lots of time is spent, the function may be essential. If little time is spent, continue for further clarification.]

____Yes ____No   5a. Are there a limited number of other employees available to perform the function or among whom to distribute the function?
                         [If yes, the function may be essential. If no, go to 5b.]

____Yes ____No   5b. Are there peak work periods that prevent the transfer of responsibilities to others in the department?
                         [If yes, the function may be essential. If no, the function may be nonessential. Continue.]

___Yes ___No   6. Is the function so highly specialized that the person is hired for her special expertise or ability to perform the function?
[If yes, STOP. The task is essential. If no, continue.]

___Yes ___No   7. Would there be serious consequences if the employee is not required to perform the function?
[If yes, STOP. The task is essential. If no, continue.]

___Yes ___No   8. Does the current collective bargaining agreement require that a particular job function be performed only by the incumbent in this position?
[If yes, the task may be essential. Discuss further with union representatives. If no, the function is nonessential.]

When determining essential functions, remember this important point: Even if a function is essential, the employer is responsible for making a job accommodation if requested. But the employer has the right to select the accommodation and to request medical details from the employee and the employee's treating physician in order to select the best accommodation. When the function to be accommodated is essential, the employer is not required to eliminate or transfer the task. There are few circumstances when an employer can deny an accommodation request; the primary one is if, after considerable research, the employer determines the accommodation creates an undue hardship.

Documentation of Essential Functions of a Job

Companies use a variety of documents that list or describe the essential functions for their jobs. The most common documentation tool is the job description. If your company doesn't use job descriptions, note that the ADA does *not* require job descriptions. In lieu of such job descriptions, the courts will accept other written evidence showing that essential functions were identified. The ADA states that the courts will accept a job description prepared in advance of advertising an opening as such evidence.

Employers often forget about the numerous other documents that list a position's key responsibilities. For example, job functions are described in performance evaluations and objective-setting tools, internal telephone directories, job postings, and organization charts. These can be excellent resources to help you determine the functions that are essential to a particular job. Investigate what documents are available in your company to start you on this task.

Remember, the ADA gives employers the right to determine what is an essential function of a particular job. If more than one document in your company lists such essential functions, make sure that all relevant documents are on file and describe the function consistently. If you use job descriptions, make them thorough and timely so that it is easier to develop consistency in related documents.

Part Two

The Recruitment And Hiring Process

Chapter 4

The ADA-Compliant
Job Description

There is no singular, universal method or format for writing job descriptions. Many companies' job description designs already comply with ADA requirements. Each style can vary from company to company, from manager to manager, and even from employee to employee. However, there are specific items to include in any job description that simplify ADA compliance and improve employee selection and management.

In this chapter I outline the components of a job description, review several job descriptions, and revise them to meet ADA and employment objectives.

Preliminary Considerations

The job description is multifunctional. One company may use its job descriptions to help managers tell employees what tasks to perform. Another might use job descriptions to determine whether employees have performed their assigned tasks. When an employee leaves a job, the employer may use the job description as a tool for selecting a new employee. Another might take this one step further and use it as a basis for training new employees.

Since companies use job descriptions differently, what really *is* a job description? The basic job description is a statement of the tasks, duties, and responsibilities of a position. To comply with the ADA, job descriptions should include job-specification information, with a description of both job duties and the skills and qualifications needed to perform those duties.

How were the first job descriptions created? By observation. As employees performed their jobs, someone recorded their actions. What were the tasks? What were the steps involved in performing each task? How much time did the employee spend at each activity? What skills did the employee need to perform those tasks? Job documentation was the result of asking these questions and more.

How do companies create their job descriptions now? Each business decides the method best for it. Some companies still use observers to document work as it is performed. Sometimes employees record their tasks in a diary or log as they perform them. Businesses often have managers write the job descriptions for persons reporting to them. Another method is to use job-analysis questionnaires to help writers document the functions. Employees can be interviewed to extract job data. Employers can also film their employees performing their jobs and then have a person review the film and write the job descriptions. Many companies use a combination of methods. In short, there is no one right method.

Once the job descriptions are written, how are they recorded and stored? Some companies retain the information on computers for easy retrieval and updating. Others document the tasks in writing. There are also software packages offering job descriptions for benchmark or general positions; from these tasks you build your company's own job descriptions.

The employer or manager usually determines how to collect and record the details of each job. Whatever the choice, it must be:

- Accurate
- Complete
- Thorough
- Appropriate
- Consistent
- Timely

An *accurate* job description correctly portrays the tasks performed. A *complete* description includes every aspect of the job. A *thorough* description details how to perform the job. An *appropriate* description suits the business environment it represents, matching the corporate culture. A *consistent* description matches other company job descriptions in format, language, and detail. A *timely* description is updated regularly and serves as a reference for management and employees.

If you wish your company's job descriptions to comply with the ADA, then don't discriminate in how you develop or use the descriptions. Make sure a job description exists for every position. If managers complete job descriptions for the people reporting to them, those descriptions should be consistent in format, content, and quality across departmental lines. If your current method works well, make sure it works well for everyone.

Now is the time to change writing methods or format, since most job descriptions do not have the detail required by the ADA. So whether you're auditing all job descriptions for compliance or only updating descriptions as positions become vacant, start using an ADA-compliant format.

If you are reviewing the status of your descriptions (how many are missing, incomplete, and for which positions), try to gain consistency as quickly as possible. Look for major information gaps, or possible trends and problem areas. Identify the departments or job classes where descriptions are missing. Also, avoid the scenario where descriptions exist for nondisabled employees but none exist for employees with disabilities, or vice versa. You don't want to find yourself in the predicament of having an employee with a disability request an accommodation and you don't have sufficient job documentation to make a fair accommodation. After an accommodation request is not the time to be scrambling. Determine the best approach for achieving ADA-compliant job descriptions in your company, develop a plan to achieve them, and proceed with it.

Since the ADA does not require that employers have job descriptions, you do not have to have job descriptions. There is other documentation that can serve as evidence of essential functions. However, the ADA states that if you *do* use job descriptions, they must comply, so consider the following steps toward compliance:

1. Update each description to be compliant with the ADA regulations before advertising a job vacancy.
2. Develop a company-wide job description format to use for all positions.
3. Have management sign, date, and centrally file a copy of each job description as it is revised.
4. Assign someone the responsibility of reviewing job descriptions, tracking previous updates, and implementing a regular schedule for job description revision.
5. Hold managers and other job-description writers accountable for completing timely, accurate descriptions according to company policy or as requested.

Some companies are so thorough in their job documentation that their existing information already complies with the ADA. Their sole task may be to identify and classify essential and nonessential job functions. Federal contractors who comply with the Rehabilitation Act of 1973 may have descriptions that meet ADA standards. But most companies will need to revisit their format and ensure they have the detail the ADA suggests.

The ADA does not require that companies revise every job description at once. Those companies who elect to redo all their job descriptions are ahead of the game; however, they will still need to review relevant job descriptions before advertising vacant positions to verify that the list of essential functions is valid.

Those companies bringing their job descriptions into compliance at a slower pace should identify the job descriptions whose revision is a high priority and update these first. Examples of high-priority descriptions include entry-level positions, high-turnover jobs, or those with demanding physical requirements. Since managers deal with entry-level and high-turnover positions regularly, you only make your work easier by addressing these first. On an ongoing basis, update each job description as the position becomes vacant and before any advertising or interviewing takes place. It is more difficult to analyze and quantify the skill and ability requirements of the more physical jobs, so address these early. Then you won't delay timely hiring when the positions become vacant.

Remember, the ADA requires identification of essential functions before you can advertise an opening. Have an authorized person sign and date each reviewed job description. This will serve as evidence that you updated or checked the job description. And be sure to record the authorization even when the job description is not changed.

The Components of a Job Description

Most job descriptions consist primarily of task descriptions and skill requirements. Some companies explore these in great detail; others contend that a brief list of job requirements is sufficient. It is noteworthy that either extreme in documentation may not comply with the ADA. In short, be careful however you approach the matter of job descriptions.

If the job description is too brief, you may not provide enough information for the interviewer or candidate to truly understand the position's requirements. A shallow description won't allow the interviewer to explore whether the candidate can perform the essential functions, with or without accommodation. On the other hand, if your job description is detailed, you will help applicants and employees to better understand job-performance expectations.

There are cautions against writing an excessively detailed job description. For instance, you want to avoid limiting how the employee performs the job. The description should be open to other methods of accomplishing a task. It should not limit potential accommodations. Also, in adding detail, don't add extraneous or rarely performed tasks and don't include tasks that the incumbent performs because of a special expertise. Ask yourself: If someone else performed the job, would the task be included in the description? If not, exclude it.

Take the *ACTions* (Accurate, Complete, Thorough) approach presented earlier to write job descriptions. A comprehensive job description takes more time and adds challenge to the task; however, it also makes the job description a powerful tool for the company. Its usefulness will carry through from employment and selection to orientation, training, and performance.

Some possible components of a job description are:

- Job identification header
- Job function statement
- Job summary
- Major tasks
- Work conditions
- Job qualifications
- Attendance and other work requirements

Businesses use various terminology for description headings. Also, many companies use more complicated formats than what we consider here. Use whatever style or format that fits your work environment, so long as it meets ADA compliance. To determine this, check the ADA text for clues to the job description puzzle. If you pull these clues together, you will consolidate your job documentation into an effective, ADA-compliant tool.

Let's look at several excerpts from the text of the ADA in light of job-description efforts.

Clue 1:
[A] qualified individual with a disability means an individual . . . who can perform the essential functions of such position.

Does your current job format differentiate essential functions from marginal functions or are all your functions listed in one job duties section? The pivotal step toward ADA compliance is to identify and document the essential functions of each job. Study the format of your current job descriptions. Determine the best method for identifying the essential functions. Develop a long-term plan to repair your job descriptions or redesign them to incorporate ADA-update requirements.

If you need a quick fix to fill a vacant position, be creative. For example, you can code the job description with "EF and NEF," initialing and dating the change. You can also attach a sheet filling in the compliance gaps, identifying nonessential tasks, and clarifying the qualification requirements. These efforts will comply as long as you have evidence that you identified the essential functions of the job prior to the hiring process. Be sure that these abbreviated efforts accurately represent the job.

To determine whether a job responsibility is essential to the position, refer to the Essential Function Checklist in Chapter 3. Take the time to ask *all* the questions for each task, so as to determine whether the task is truly essential. Beware of circumstances in which a job description groups several different tasks as a single responsibility; some of those tasks may be essential and some may not.

Clue 2:
Evidence of whether a function is essential includes . . . the amount of time spent on the job performing the function.

Estimate the percentage of time an employee spends performing each task and record this figure in the job description. The time figure does not have to be formally timed or tracked and the total doesn't need to add up to 100 percent. Most jobs are not so predictable that the employee spends the same amount of time every day or every week performing a task. However, a good-faith estimate helps determine whether the function is essential. It also helps employees understand the importance of each function.

The ADA maintains that documenting the time spent performing a task can be evidence of whether the task is essential. Include the time spent in every updated job description.

Clue 3:
    Qualification standards mean the personal and professional attributes including the skill, experience, education, physical, medical, safety and other [job-related] requirements . . . [of the position].

Include a qualification or job specification section in every job description. The core defense for selecting the most qualified candidate for a job is your written identification of these qualifications. Be thorough in this documentation and include every qualification. Don't assume that others know the qualification requirements.

You'll have to identify the ideal format for listing these qualifications in the job description. For example, consider separating the qualifications into subsections for easy reference. You could group skill, experience, education, and licenses together as one qualification, and physical and mental requirements as another section. Group safety and work conditions could be a third section. Whatever approach you choose, be complete and consistent in identifying the requirements of each job compared to similar jobs.

There is another key to properly determining job qualifications: Be sure each job specification corresponds to a particular task. Consider each duty individually, then ask yourself, "What education, skills, or knowledge is required to perform this task?" Record the requirements, then consolidate duplicate requirements after you have analyzed each task.

In the past, job descriptions often included preferred but not required job skills and education levels. ADA-compliant descriptions focus on *required* qualifications that match *essential functions*. If you choose to include preferred requirements, you should identify them as such. Consider these preferred requirements the same as you would consider nonessential functions. Do not use preferred qualifications to screen out otherwise qualified candidates. Lack of preferred qualifications cannot be the basis for making a hiring rejection.

For example, an employer cannot require a college degree when equivalent experience has equal value. Even if every incumbent has a college degree, if it is not truly a prerequisite to perform the essential job functions, it cannot be a required qualification. Thus all candidates who meet the basic requirements of the job have equal opportunity in the selection process.

There are two "new" qualifications to include in the job description. To make job documentation ADA-compliant, you need to include the physical and mental requirements of the job. Some job descriptions include an overview of these requirements, but it is now important to describe these qualifications more specifically. This compliance requirement provides all applicants sufficient information to determine whether they can meet the job standards. A person with a disability who understands the job's physical and mental requirements can recognize and suggest the need for accommodation. The information eliminates any surprises once the person begins the job.

The more specific the qualifications, the more complete the job description. For example, in one company, unloading trucks is an essential function for a warehouse position. The job description's qualification section states, "incumbent must be able to lift and unload large boxes weighing 50–75 pounds and carry them 10 feet." It is insufficient to merely state that lifting boxes is a job requirement; the ADA requires more detail such as in this description. Document the requirement, even if you can accommodate for this task.

The same level of specificity is required for other job qualifications, such as formal education, training requirements, type and amount of relevant job experience or background required, technical or administrative complexity, mental abilities, physical requirements, responsibility for dollar results, responsibility for supervision, or other such working conditions.

Determining the Job Qualifications

To determine job specifications and requirements, study each task separately. List the skills, education, experience, physical, mental, and other criteria the task requires. Include special job-related items such as unique scheduling (overtime, nights, weekends), special certifications, attendance requirements, and travel. Mention any special feature of the work environment, especially if it is unique. For example, list safety issues, excessive noise levels, and outdoor work. Verify these requirements with the incumbent and other experts who know the specifics of the position.

The ADA's evidence requirement is not the only reason to provide this detail. This documentation provides comprehensive data on what you seek in a qualified candidate. The level of detail offers essential support for your selection team. The person developing the job advertisement can better describe the opportunity; the person screening the applicant and reviewing the resumés can match specific work experience to need; the person interviewing the candidates can focus the questions on specific areas.

The qualification detail also helps avoid misunderstandings of job requirements. Don't assume that every applicant understands all facets of the job. An applicant not told of the overtime required, the working conditions, travel, or safety issues cannot truly tell you whether he will perform the essential functions of the job with or without accommodation. So providing this level of detail helps a candidate decide whether to pursue the job, considering the working conditions. Businesses need applicants and employees who understand all components of the job.

Make sure your job requirements are reasonable. They should be consistent with how the job currently operates and how it has operated in the past. Be sure not to overstate any skill requirements. Likewise, don't feel obligated to list criteria that are too basic. The description need not be excessive, just thorough. For example, a BA in accounting is not a legitimate requirement for a payroll clerk. On the other hand, you can use a generic requirement of good mathematical skills, rather than describe what figures are added or subtracted.

The ADA makes an important point regarding determination of qualifications. It does not intend to "second-guess an employer's business judgment with regard to production standards" or other similar requirements. A business can establish any output level for a given job. The ADA will not question its validity as long as consistent output requirements are required of all employees and standards are not intentionally discriminatory. For example, in a manufacturing environment a conveyor belt moves at a specified speed for employees to assemble parts. The ADA will not challenge the speed of the belt or the quota of assembled parts. It will not require that the employer change these levels to accommodate a person with a disability. The employer has the right to determine all production levels.

Bringing the Three Main Components into Compliance

If your job-description format includes most of the components required by the ADA, it is unlikely you will develop entirely new job descriptions for every position. The simplest method, mentioned earlier, is to work off the centralized job-description copy and manually identify essential functions. Make sure that an authorized person signs and dates all changes made. These notations serve as evidence that management identified the essential functions prior to advertising or interviewing for the position.

Another option is to attach an addendum to each description. This sheet can identify which functions are essential and which are nonessential. Some job descriptions list tasks in numerical order. In this case, the addendum could say, "Tasks 1, 3, 5, and 7 are essential. Tasks 2, 4, 6, and 8 are nonessential." This effort is not time-consuming; job descriptions written in paragraph format, however, are more difficult to update in this way. The addendum sheet can also include a list of additional job requirements or qualifications. It is likely that the original description omitted qualifications that now need to be added. If this is the primary problem with your current job descriptions, attach separate sheets listing new job specifications.

Probably new to most employers is the detail the ADA requires on the job's physical and mental requirements. Job descriptions for industries such as manufacturing and construction are more likely than service or office-oriented settings to include such physical requirements. However, few companies include mental requirements in their job descriptions.

Again, consider the best method for adding these physical and mental requirements to the job descriptions. Some companies add a checklist of physical and mental attributes to each description, using observation and incumbent input to determine the physical requirements. In any event, the descriptions should include abilities such as lifting (weigh items and describe their size), mobility and motion (walking, sitting, bending, stretching), or dexterity (keyboard or calculator use, manipulation of controls, part assembly). Refer to Appendix B for a sample physical and mental checklist.

Direct observation is a more difficult way of identifying mental job requirements. Consider how to determine factors such as decision-making ability, work pace, job stress, or written and verbal communication skills. Incorporate some of these directly in the qualifications list and put others in a paragraph description as appropriate. Be careful to stick to core job requirements when identifying physical and mental requirements.

There are experts such as occupational therapists who can assist you in identifying physical and mental job requirements. Their expertise is most useful when trying to describe a physically difficult job, during accommodation evaluations, and when handling workers' compensation situations. As a rule, however, most employers can determine their job requirements without help from an external consultant.

Examples of Job Descriptions and Their Revisions

In this section I show how to revise actual job descriptions from a variety of businesses and industries to meet ADA compliance. The basic format of each job description is similar, though some descriptions are more complete and provide more detail. Some are better organized. Some use outline or numerical formats rather than description paragraphs. Since no one format is right for every business, select the components and organization best suited to your industry, operation, and resources. Compliance in any format is the objective. To revise the examples, follow this checklist.

THE ADA JOB-DESCRIPTION CHECKLIST

Critique the job descriptions in Figures 4-1, 4-3, and 4-5, using the components presented below. Consider how complete or incomplete the job description is for each task. Then make the appropriate corrections to the job descriptions using the checklist.

Job Identification Header: Does the job description include all of the following information? For ADA compliance, supply any missing data.

- [ ] Job title
- [ ] Division or department
- [ ] Location
- [ ] Employment status (full-time, part-time, temporary)
- [ ] Salary grade
- [ ] Salary range
- [ ] Work hours or shift
- [ ] Job code number
- [ ] Reports to . . .
- [ ] Supervises . . .
- [ ] Date of last revision
- [ ] Who revised the description
- [ ] Signature of the approving supervisor and/or human resources professional

Job Function Statement/Job Purpose

- [ ] Does it describe why the position exists?
- [ ] Is it too general or too repetitive of the tasks and duties of the job?
- [ ] Does it focus on the essential functions of the job?
- [ ] Does it include requirements that may be nonessential or discriminatory?

Accountabilities/Job Summary: Some job descriptions include a section describing the overall accomplishments of the position, the outcome of the person's activities, or the results of the work. Other job descriptions go directly to the next section listing duties and tasks. Determine whether this section is an important job-description component. If you include this section in your descriptions, check the following:

☐ Does it focus on the essential functions of the job?
☐ Is it repetitive of other areas of the job description (tasks, knowledge, or skill requirements)?
☐ Is it well organized?

Major Tasks/Duties and Responsibilities/Major Areas of Accountability/Scope of Responsibility/Essential Job Duties: Whatever you decide to call this section, it is the core of the job description. It identifies the tasks a person must perform to accomplish the job objectives. Depending on the level of detail, this section may include steps to accomplish each task. For ADA compliance, revise the list of duties and check for the following:

☐ Determine whether each task statement does and should include what is done, to what it is done, why it is done, when it is done, how many times it is done, and how long it is done.
☐ Sequence the job responsibilities in order of priority or in terms of the amount of time required to perform each function.
☐ Include an estimated percentage of time required to do each task.
☐ Determine how to identify essential and nonessential functions in the description format. For example, separate essential and nonessential functions as subsections of this category or mark nonessential functions with an asterisk.
☐ Duties as assigned generally are nonessential functions. If certain "duties as assigned" tasks are essential to the job, specify each activity as a major function.
☐ Review the language describing the tasks. Avoid specifying ways to perform the job when accommodations or other methods may work equally well.
☐ Be sure each task description is complete. Don't assume the reader understands the steps or tools needed to accomplish the task.
☐ Read each task statement to determine whether something is missing. Do the terms accurately portray the responsibilities? Are they too vague or too specific?

Work Environment/Work Conditions: Some jobs and industries require elaboration of the physical work conditions. Include these facts to describe the conditions for performing the job. If all of your company's jobs are office related and nonphysical, this effort may be brief; however, physical jobs, outdoor jobs, and factory or warehouse jobs should include a complete description of the work environment. Tie each factor to an essential function of the job. Verify whether the description includes:

☐ Safety and hazards (i.e., chemicals, machinery, electrical hazards, weather conditions)
☐ Work site layout (i.e., office, warehouse, customer traffic, visiting other businesses)
☐ Other miscellaneous conditions (i.e., noise, lighting)

Job Qualifications/Knowledge, Skills, Education, and Abilities: Many job descriptions include job-specification information. Some job descriptions group these attributes together; others separate them by category. Some of this information may overlap with the working conditions section. Since there is no formatting rule of thumb, apply these sections to best suit your needs.

From an ADA perspective, the requirement to describe accurate and detailed qualifications has increased. In the past companies wrote more generic portrayals of qualifications. As a result of the ADA, this change may create more work for the job-description writer. When developing these specifications, make sure each requirement is necessary to perform the essential functions of the job.

- ☐ Physical requirements (i.e., lifting, bending, long periods of standing, carrying, being sedentary)
- ☐ Mental and emotional requirements (i.e., decision making, prioritizing, withstanding excess stress)
- ☐ Tools and equipment (i.e., calculator, personal computer, copier, telephone, lathe, forklift, conveyor belt)
- ☐ Education (i.e., school, training, certification, degree or equivalent requirements)
- ☐ Experience (i.e., quantify years, type of work performed)

To determine the list of job qualifications, review each duty and responsibility. List the specific requirements of each essential function. Consider:

- ☐ The knowledge required of each task
- ☐ How that knowledge is acquired (on the job, schooling, specified training)
- ☐ What skills and abilities are required to perform the task

Phrase these items using minimums, such as the lowest education level or the minimum number of years experience. Include any licenses or legally required certification. List required knowledge of particular laws, systems, or other technical areas. Specify whether you require particular job experience.

List preferred (nonessential) attributes separately from required (essential) attributes. Remember that you cannot use preferred attributes as criteria to disqualify a candidate with a disability.

Some companies format their job descriptions creatively. In certain formats the job qualifications directly correspond with the duty described. For example, some descriptions contain job duties and qualifications in side-by-side columns, in matrix format, or by numbering the qualifications according to the duty each describes. These designs help ensure that each qualification requirement directly matches an essential function, and also help incumbents understand the skills required to perform the tasks of a job.

Review each qualification to make sure each skill, experience, and education level truly represents the job performance requirement. Don't overstate requirements based on wishful thinking or on an incumbent who has acquired extensive experience.

Attendance and Other Work Requirements: The length of this section depends on company policy or the restrictions and requirements of the job. Be sure to describe these requirements consistently across similar positions. Include:

- ☐ Work hours
- ☐ Required or periodic overtime or weekend work
- ☐ Applicable policies regarding attendance and absenteeism
- ☐ Travel, whether local or long-distance
- ☐ Personal contacts
- ☐ Miscellaneous requirements unique to the essential functions of this job

Discussion of Example Job Description 1

Using the ADA Job-Description Checklist, let's study each component of the External Custodian job description (Figure 4-1) for thoroughness and ADA compliance.

Job Identification Header: In this job-description format, several of the information pieces suggested for the header are located elsewhere in the job description. This company chose to separate "Working Relationships" from the header. The preparation date of this description is at the end of the description. Remember, there are no rules for locating information. The important point is to include the details in the description.

The Job Identification Header notes the department, salary grade, job code, and FLSA status. It excludes employment status, salary range (which is a common exclusion), who revised the description, and who authorized the description. To complete the header, this company may choose "Employment Status: Full-time." If it wishes to keep the preparation date at the end of the description, I recommend it write the name of the person who completed the description and have a signature line for approval of the description. The latter components are most relevant to ADA compliance. They serve as documented evidence that the employer reviewed and edited the job description prior to beginning the employment process. All preparation and approval dates should predate the job advertisement.

Job Purpose: This statement clearly states that the incumbent is responsible for maintaining and cleaning the external areas of the facility. This is an essential function of the job. However, the pur-

Figure 4-1. Example job description 1.

TITLE: External Custodian

DEPARTMENT: Maintenance

JOB CODE: GA 404

PAY GRADE: 06

FLSA* STATUS: Nonexempt

Working Relationships

> Reports to: Maintenance Supervisor
> Subordinate staff: None
> Other internal contacts: Facility staff
> External contacts: None, possibly facility guests

Purpose: This position is mainly accountable for the maintenance and cleanliness of exterior areas of the facility, but will assist in maintaining the appearance and cleanliness of other areas as needed.

Duties and Responsibilities: Incumbent may perform some or all of the following:

1. Sweeps, cleans, and picks up trash in landscaped areas, parking lots, docks, entrance areas, and sidewalks.
2. Performs landscape maintenance duties such as mowing, trimming, and watering.
3. Performs snow removal duties using tractor with plow, snowblower, or shovel.
4. Empties ash and trash containers and removes waste to appropriate area.
5. Provides directions and assistance to facility guests when asked.
6. Provides support and assistance to team members and other departments as requested.
7. Provides duties as assigned.

Preferred Skills, Knowledge, and Abilities

1. Three months' experience using outdoor maintenance equipment (i.e., tractors, mowers, weed trimmers) preferred.
2. Working knowledge of the safe handling and operation of equipment and materials used in landscape maintenance and custodial duties.
3. Ability to work variable and/or rotating shifts including nights, weekends, and holidays.
4. Ability to work outdoors in all weather conditions.
5. Ability to understand simple verbal and/or written instructions.
6. Ability to perform some or all of the physical tasks involved in lifting, driving, sweeping, mowing, and related exterior custodial maintenance duties.

Date Prepared: 5/92

---

*FLSA = Fair Labor Standards Act.

pose adds a secondary statement that the employer needs to clarify for ADA compliance. This second component of the job function— to clean other areas of the facility as needed—must be specified as essential or nonessential duties to the External Custodian job. The employer must consider each of the essential function criteria for these responsibilities. If the backup custodial services are essential, then the employer needs to include the job skills and requirements of the Internal Custodian as part of the criteria for selecting the External Custodian. If the backup Internal Custodial responsibilities are not essential to the job, then the employer should list them as such on the job description. This separate identification of essential and nonessential functions is vital to employee-selection efforts. Employers must not categorize as unqualified for the job those candidates who cannot perform the nonessential duties.

Let us assume that the employer determined that both responsibility statements are essential to the external custodian position, because there was a limited number of custodial staff available to service this large facility. When an Internal Custodian is absent, an External Custodian is temporarily placed indoors to perform higher priority cleaning. These indoor tasks are essential to the smooth operation of the facility, so the tasks must be added to the job description of the External Custodian as essential.

Duties and Responsibilities: This list of duties is complete in presenting the position's overall activities. The duties appear to be listed in sequence of importance and are worded clearly. The incumbent and the interviewer can easily understand tasks such as sweeping and cleaning. However, more detailed information is missing.

The first omission is a quantification of these responsibilities. The description does not provide a typical percentage of time spent performing each task. For example, does the incumbent spend 25 or 50 percent of the work week cleaning the outside areas? The description also does not provide a maintenance schedule for landscaping. For example, how frequently should the employee mow grassy areas? How frequently should the employee empty trash receptacles? The description should include criteria vital to determining the job's physical requirements.

In some circumstances it is difficult to pinpoint how much time the incumbent should spend landscaping versus cleaning. These percentages do not have to be exact; one option is to present the percentages in ranges. For example, there could be a statement in the description that in the spring and fall the External Custodian spends 30 to 40 percent of the time on landscaping; this increases to 50 percent in the summer and decreases to 5 percent in the winter.

Another ADA-compliance change is recommended. The Duties and Responsibilities section begins with the statement, "Incumbent may perform some or all of the following." Without further documentation, an incumbent would not know which tasks to eliminate. The employer could change this sentence to include "based on seasonal requirements," which would exchange landscaping responsibilities for snowplowing. Otherwise, the statement confuses the reader regarding what is essential and nonessential to the job.

The third recommended change is more significant. To help incumbents understand specific job requirements, the employer must expand the description of each task. While the overall concept of sweeping is recognized, the description should include the tools used (machine sweeper or 12-inch broom?). It should detail the task description for mowing and trimming to include the type of tools. For example, "perform mowing activities with a tractor and/or push mower. Perform trimming activities using clippers or an electric string trimmer." Additional detail should include the completion of tasks. For example, the External Custodian may be responsible for emptying grass from mower attachments, cleaning the mower when the task is complete, or performing minor maintenance or machine adjustment as applicable. This level of detail helps the interviewer better understand the applicant's abilities and helps the incumbent understand the full scope of the position.

Preferred Skills, Knowledge, and Abilities: The External Custodian position has specific physical job requirements. The description generalizes these requirements; it does not detail requirements to the necessary level. For example, the position includes the ability to lift. However, it does not tell the incumbent what is lifted, how frequently to perform the lifting task, and how much weight to lift.

The employer must also be more specific in other ability descriptions. For example, the position requires three months' experience with outdoor equipment. Is a homeowner who takes care of a large yard in the summer qualified for this position? Or should the qualified person have three months' full-time experience using equipment for a professional landscaping service? Does the custodian need to have a valid driver's license in order to drive a tractor and plow the parking lots? These generalities must be clarified to reach the level of detail required by the ADA. The clarification will help determine the best qualified person for the job.

The requirement section included the need for an employee to work a flexible schedule and to work outdoors in all weather conditions. These two criteria are vital to a complete description. Include work conditions, especially when they are as important to the job as these are. The interviewer needs to be able to discuss these requirements with each candidate. Someone who is unable to perform physical labor in the extreme heat or cold would not meet the essential criteria for this job. Although an employer may be able to accommodate some things in this area, it is unlikely the employer can change weather conditions.

This section requires the most revision because of the gaps in abilities and skill information. The employer needs to thoroughly analyze the job's physical requirements, measure weights, and observe the frequency of tasks. The employer should state each requirement to include every piece of equipment and every unique condition of employment.

The employer also titles this section using the term *preferred*. This implies that not all candidates are required to possess these skills and abilities. The employer must determine whether to require each of these skills and abilities as a job prerequisite. In Figure 4-2, the term *preferred* is eliminated, instead requiring all required skills and abilities to be listed for each position.

Discussion of Example Job Description 2

Now let's use the ADA Job-Description Checklist to study each component of the Records Clerk job description (Figure 4-3) for thoroughness and ADA compliance.

Job Identification Header: This provides the basic information regarding the job. It includes a section for incumbent signatures. This shows when the employee reviewed her updated job description. It does not include employment status as nonexempt, or any salary-related information such as grade or range. These are not required by ADA; it is an employer's choice whether to include wage-related information. The section also does not include any work relationships, although it does include the supervisor's title in the Job Function statement.

Function Statement: Included here are the supervisor's title, the primary filing responsibility, and the objective activity of maintaining group records. It has the *what*, the *why*, and the *for whom*.

Job Summary: The statement presented here is more of a job requirement than a summarization of responsibilities. The advantage of this section is that it introduces performance levels for the incumbent's skills. For example, it mentions a working knowledge

(Text continues on page 58.)

Figure 4-2. ADA revision of example job description 1.

TITLE: External Custodian

DEPARTMENT: Maintenance

JOB CODE: GA 404

PAY GRADE: 06

FLSA STATUS: Nonexempt

Employment Status: Full-time, 40 hours per week

Working Relationships

> Reports to: Maintenance Supervisor
> Subordinate staff: None
> Other internal contacts: Facility staff
> External contacts: None, possibly facility guests

Purpose: This position is mainly accountable for the maintenance and cleanliness of exterior areas of the facility. The incumbent will assist in maintaining the appearance and cleanliness of other areas **on an as-needed basis as directed by the Maintenance Supervisor.**

Duties and Responsibilities: Incumbent may perform some or all of the following, **depending on seasonal job requirements:**

1. Sweeps, cleans, and picks up trash in landscaped areas, parking lots, docks, entrance areas, and sidewalks, **covering assigned area two times each day (40–45%)**

   1.1. **Uses 12-inch push broom and gas-powered blowers to clean paved surfaces.**

   1.2. **Brings portable trash containers to centralized custodial areas as cleaning of assigned areas is completed.**

2. Performs landscape maintenance duties **(0% winter–30% summer)**

   2.1. **Mows lawn twice per week using tractor and/or push mower, emptying grass from mower attachments, cleaning mower when task is completed, and performing minor maintenance or machine adjustments as needed.**

   2.2. **Waters lawn twice per week, setting automatic sprinkler systems, placing hoses and sprinklers where required, and manually watering individual planters.**

(continues)

Figure 4-2. Continued.

    2.3. Trims shrubs and flowers weekly using hand trimmers or gas-powered string trimmer and cleans garden beds.

3. Performs snow removal duties (5% **spring and fall–20% winter)**

    3.1. Uses tractor with plow in parking lots, snowblower or shovel on sidewalks and ramps.

    3.2. Ensures public access to all primary facility entrances.

4. Empties ash and trash containers and removes waste **three times per day (10%)**

    4.1. Moves small portable dumpster to each container for trash consolidation.

    4.2. Brings dumpster to centralized custodial area for emptying.

5. Provides directions and assistance to facility guests when asked **(1%)**
6. Provides support and assistance to team members and other departments as **assigned by Maintenance Supervisor (3%)**
7. Provides duties as assigned **(nonessential job functions)**

(Delete the term *Preferred) Skills, Knowledge, and Abilities*

1. Three months' **professional** experience **with landscaper** using outdoor maintenance equipment (i.e., tractors, mowers, weed trimmers, **hand clippers**). **(Delete** *preferred* **from requirement.)**
2. Working knowledge of the safe handling and operation of equipment and materials used in landscape maintenance and custodial duties.
3. Ability to work variable and/or rotating shifts including nights, weekends, and holidays.
4. Ability to work outdoors in all weather conditions.
5. Ability to understand simple verbal and/or written instructions.
6. Ability to perform some or all of the physical tasks involved:

    6.1. Lifting **trash receptacles weighing 25–50 pounds three feet high into dumpster,** driving **tractor or mower, valid driver's license required.**

    6.2. Sweeping **walkways for one- to two-hour periods; shoveling walkways and pushing snowblower for one- to three-hour periods; lifting and removing 10–20 pounds of snow; bending, kneeling, and grasping to pick up trash from ground surfaces,** and related exterior custodial maintenance duties.

Date Prepared: 5/92

Job Description Updated By _____ **Date** _____

Job Description Approved By _____ **Date** _____

Figure 4-3. Example job description 2.

Job Title:	Records Clerk	Job No.:	21.4
Department:	Central Records	Division:	Group Administration
Analyst:	Beth Martin	Interview Date:	3/92

Reviewed by Incumbent: _____ Date: _____

Reviewed by Supervisor: _____ Date: _____

Function

Under the supervision of the Supervisor, Central Records, performs filing activities to maintain the group records.

Job Summary

Requires a working knowledge of the filing system and procedures of the Central Records section. Requires attention to detail to accurately locate and replace records filed under alphabetical and numeric systems in a prompt manner. Must be able to operate microfiche reader to review newly microfiched records for completeness and accuracy.

Principal Activities

1. Sorts and files correspondence and other materials into proper files in chronological order.
2. Pulls and delivers file folders for users as requested and refiles folders upon return to unit.
3. Creates and maintains temporary correspondence files and inactive files.
4. Maintains orderliness and accuracy of files.
   a. Repairs and replaces damaged file folders as necessary.
   b. Separates file materials when file folders are too full.
   c. Audits files to ensure that materials are in proper files.
   d. Rearranges files as expansion is needed.
5. Retrieves and transfers files from users as necessary.
6. Provides backup for the Correspondence and Records Clerk; answers and processes telephone file requests and makes photocopies of contracts and other documents for requesters.
7. Performs other tasks as directed and as time permits.

of the system. It requires prompt filing and file location. It calls for completeness and accuracy in job performance.

This section includes some of the skills, abilities, and job knowledge required of the incumbent, such as attention to detail, knowledge of alphabetical and numerical systems, and the ability to use a microfiche reader. But these requirements are insufficient. Also, its location before the Principal Activities of the job makes it difficult for the reader to determine whether the requirements match the job's essential functions. The reader must first read ahead, then determine whether the required qualifications correspond to the Principal Activities.

Principal Activities: The duties listed in this section provide a good task overview but the section is missing details. Tasks are not presented in order of importance, therefore not identifying what is essential. The section lacks the percentage of time spent performing each task. It also doesn't present the quantity of documents to file, pull, or create. When quantified, this information helps the candidate or incumbent understand the priority and importance of each activity. Quantification also helps the candidate understand the volume of paperwork to be completed each day.

What are the essential functions of this job? Clearly, all filing, file maintenance, and correspondence sorting are essential to the job. The volume of work for each task, the number of Records Clerks, and the availability of other support staff would determine whether other functions are essential. For example, if the volume of files to be delivered to users throughout the company is considerable and others are not available to perform this function, that will be an essential task. If the delivery takes only a minor portion of the Record Clerk's day and other employees are available to perform this function, it may not be essential.

Another job responsibility to study is that of providing backup for the Correspondence and Records Clerk. Are there other employees available to perform this task? Consider that the skills required for this backup responsibility (telephone and photocopying) require skills different from the routine responsibilities of the Records Clerk. Are these backup skills essential to the true function of the Records Clerk? Do work flow, scheduling, meals, and breaks make these duties essential? The employer needs to study each component to ensure that each listed function is truly essential.

The brief description of the Correspondence and Records Clerk responsibilities are cause for questioning another aspect of the Records Clerk's responsibilities. This description does not tell the incumbent how work is assigned. The user requests appear to be from internal employees wanting file information. Who receives these requests? Are user requests for files telephoned directly to the Records Clerk? Does someone else take the requests and delegate them to the Records Clerk? This information gap may create an incomplete listing of job qualifications. The document should include who initiates the filing efforts and user requests.

As alluded to above, the Job Qualification section is incomplete. The job description omits several physical and mental job requirements. For example, requirements may include use of the telephone; quick response to employee file and information requests; use of photocopier equipment; manual dexterity for developing, maintaining, and repairing files; basic decision making to determine when to expand or rearrange files; and sufficient department knowledge to check for accurate microfiching efforts. Creating file folder labels may require minimal typing skills. The job may also require mobility throughout the office complex.

Depending on the physical organization of the files, the retrieval and replacement of files may require reaching or bending and pulling out files. File delivery to others may also require mobility throughout the office complex. An analysis of the job and other support services could determine whether interoffice delivery systems can handle the deliveries made by the clerk, making parts of this function nonessential. The description also fails to present internal and external contacts; however, these appear to be important since the incumbent is delivering and retrieving files throughout the company. Add contacts as well as interpersonal skills related to telephone file requests and meeting with employees.

The description does not include experience or education requirements. The employer should establish minimum background requirements to ensure consistent selection of qualified employees. If this is an entry-level position, then the description should include a statement that no experience is necessary. If the quantity and performance speed required of the incumbent are higher than average, then the employer needs to state something to the effect of one to three years' filing experience is required. Take the same position regarding education. The entry-level position may require numeric and alphabetic knowledge gained at a tenth-grade level. Perhaps the output level requires a speed based on a high school graduate's or equivalent experience. The important point here is to make a fair determination and to be consistent with other positions in the same pay grade or with similar job requirements. See Figure 4-4 for a re-

Figure 4-4. ADA revision of example job description 2.

Job Title: Records Clerk   Job No.:   21.4
Department: Central Recods   Division: Group Administration
Analyst: Beth Martin   Interview Date: 3/92

Reviewed by Incumbent: —————————————— Date: —————————

Reviewed by Supervisor: —————————————— Date: —————————

Function

Under the supervision of the Supervisor, Central Records, performs filing
activities to maintain the group records.

Job Summary

Requires a working knowledge of the filing system and procedures of the
Central Records section. Requires attention to detail to accurately locate
and replace records filed under alphabetical and numeric systems in a
prompt manner. Must be able to operate microfiche reader to review
newly microfiched records for completeness and accuracy.

% of Time	Principal Activities
40%	1. Sorts **1,500 pieces** of correspondence and other materials **daily and places documents** into proper files in chronological order.
20%	2. **Implements users' requests for files.** a. **Retrieves file request forms from Correspondence Clerk.** b. Pulls **400** file folders **daily** for users as requested. c. Follows Records Department procedures for logging file removal and tracking location of files. d. Delivers **folders to user departments in office complex.** e. Refiles folders upon return to Records unit.
20%	3. Maintains orderliness and accuracy of files. a. Repairs and replaces damaged file folders as necessary. b. Separates file materials when file folders are too full. c. Audits files to ensure that materials are in proper files. d. Rearranges files as expansion is needed.
5%	4. Retrieves and transfers files from users as necessary. a. **Contacts user of second request for file.** b. **Schedules retrieval and delivery of file to second user.**
5%	5. Creates and maintains temporary correspondence files and inactive files.

10%   6. Provides back up for the Correspondence and Records Clerk.
   a. Answers and processes telephone file requests.
   b. Makes photocopies of contracts and other documents for requesters.
7. Performs other tasks as directed and as time permits **(non-essential function).**

Job Qualifications

Equipment: Microfiche machine, photocopier, telephone
Education: High school diploma or equivalent required
Experience: 1–3 years experience in alphabetical and numerical filing required
Skills and Abilities:
1. **Basic interpersonal skills for internal contact with file users on telephone and in person**
2. **Manual dexterity to maintain files, file documents in folders, place file folders into multishelf units, and pull file folders out of shelves**
3. **Ability to climb a step stool to retrieve files on top shelves**
4. **Ability to bend or stoop to retrieve lower shelf files**
5. **Mobility to deliver files to users located throughout office complex; ability to work on feet for $1/2$–$2/3$ of day**
6. **Basic decision-making skills to detemine when file maintenance is required and when users should be notified to return files**
7. **Organizational skills to organize delivery of files in most time-effective manner**

---

vision of this example. Note that changes are shown in boldface type.

Discussion of Example Job Description 3

The employer's use of Essential Job Functions in the job description (Figure 4-5) shows its efforts to comply with the Americans with Disabilities Act. While there are some steps still recommended for ADA compliance, the reader can see the steps the employer took to comply.

Job Identification Header: This section includes the basic job information. The description applies to all sales floor personnel in multiple locations. Because the description is generic, it need not include incumbent information, employment status, work hours or shift, or supervisor approval of the description. The employer could

Figure 4-5. Example job description 3.

Title: Sales Associate
Department: All Departments   Regular Location: Stores
Reports To: Department Manager   Job Code: 1086
Revision Date: 6/12/92

Purpose

To acknowledge customers and assist in their merchandise selection and to process transactions at the point-of-sale terminal, while maintaining an organized and efficient department through merchandise presentation, stock fill-ins, and paperwork processing.

Essential Job Functions

Maintain productivity standards within company guidelines by:
- Acknowledging and approaching customers courteously, conversationally, and in a timely manner.
- Assisting the customer in locating desired merchandise and communicating to the customer basic knowledge of the merchandise including features and benefits, trend information, and availability.
- Processing point-of-sale transactions by interpreting merchandise information tickets and entering the information into a point-of-sale system and packaging merchandise, verifying credit information, and counting back change for the customer.
- Developing and maintaining personal clientele by taking steps to follow up on future customer needs and fostering repeat business.

Responsible for timely stock fill-ins and merchandise movement for area of responsibility. This may include moving merchandise from stockroom to the selling floor and moving merchandise from rolling racks to appropriate selling floor fixtures.
Participate in floor moves and set-up and take-down of merchandise, fixtures, signing, and other related items for sales events.
Maintain all company merchandising and visual presentation standards.
Perform accurate paperwork processing. This includes interpreting merchandise ticket information and completing required paperwork for markdowns, holds, transfers, counts, defective merchandise ticketing, etc.

Additional Job Functions

Work cooperatively with other coworkers and management.
Process telephone orders and sends, including gift wrap when necessary.
Participate in housekeeping duties for assigned area and stockrooms,

which includes cleaning, dusting, arranging, and sizing merchandise.

Relationship

Communicate to and work cooperatively with store management team and other employees and coworkers.

Supervision

Number of employees: Not applicable
Supervisory duties required: Not applicable

Skills/Abilities Required

Professional communication skills
Problem-solving abilities
Interactive social skills
Reading, writing, and math skills
Operate a point-of-sale terminal and ticket scanner
Operate a telephone

Education/Training/Certification/License Required

Not applicable

---

add pay grade information, FLSA status, and the signature or initials of the staff person who revised the description.

Job Purpose: The statement is thorough. It is a broad overview of the essential job functions and includes tasks that are secondary to sales but primary to the Sales Associate job. Some employers would omit the required support functions from the statement; however, this employer showed their importance by including them.

Essential Job Functions: The list explains each task clearly. Each statement walks the incumbent through the steps to perform the task. It includes the physical tasks involved in the sales position, the required knowledge, and the reason or end result of the task being performed. To ensure compliance with the ADA, the employer should prioritize these duties and estimate how much time is spent performing each function.

Additional Job Functions: The section is an excellent approach to listing secondary functions not regularly required of all associates. The employer should add a "duties as assigned" statement. This lets incumbents know that they are expected to perform tasks on an as-needed basis and protects the employer when assigning nonroutine duties.

In this section, the employer includes "work cooperatively with other coworkers and management." The statement is not truly a job function and should be put in the Relationships section.

Relationships: Here is an important segment for a position that requires interaction with the public. This employer included the importance of the Sales Associate's working cooperatively with coworkers. Interestingly, the employer failed to mention the important relationship between the customer and the Sales Associate. Add this relationship.

Supervision: Responsibilities as noted are also important to the job description. For this entry-level position, there are no supervisory requirements.

Skills/Abilities Required: A good effort, the list includes cognitive abilities such as problem solving. It also mentions education-based skills such as reading, writing, and math. The employer specifies two of the primary tools that the incumbent must be able to use: POS equipment and the telephone. The employer phrases these requirements well, not specifying how the incumbent must operate the telephone. This allows for flexibility and accommodation.

The employer omits several physical job requirements that match tasks included in the Essential Functions list. For example, moving the merchandise from the stock room to the selling floor may require pulling rolling racks with a strength of x pounds. Hanging and moving merchandise from one fixture to another and changing signage may require lifting a weight of x pounds and reaching a height of x feet. The job is not sedentary and requires standing and walking or active servicing of a retail department area for periods up to x number of hours (the majority of a work shift). List these physical requirements in the Skills/Abilities section.

Figure 4-6. ADA revision of example job description 3.

Title: Sales Associate
Department: All Departments   Regular Location: Stores
Reports To: Department Manager   Job Code: 5.6
Pay Grade: **5**   **FLSA Status:**   **Nonexempt**
Revision Date: 6/12/92   **Revised By:**

Purpose

To acknowledge customers and assist in their merchandise selection and to process transactions at the point-of-sale terminal, while maintaining an organized and efficient department through merchandise presentation, stock fill-ins, and paperwork processing.

Essential Job Functions

The Sales Associate must maintain productivity standards within company guidelines by **performing the following essential functions:**

1. Provide effective customer service **(35%)**
   1.1 Acknowledge and approach customers courteously, conversationally, and in a timely manner.
   1.2 Assist the customer in locating desired merchandise.
   1.3 Communicate to the customer basic knowledge of the merchandise including features and benefits, trend information, and availability.
2. Process point-of-sale transactions **(30%)**
   2.1 Interpret merchandise information tickets.
   2.2 Enter the information into a point-of-sale system.
   2.3 Package merchandise.
   2.4 Verify credit information.
   2.5 Count back change for the customer.
3. Responsible for timely stock fill-ins and merchandise movement for area of responsibility **(20%)**
   3.1 Move merchandise from stockroom to the selling floor.
   3.2 Move merchandise from rolling racks to appropriate selling floor fixtures.
   3.3 Participate in floor moves and set-up and take-down of merchandise, fixtures, signing, and other related items for sales events.
   3.4 Maintain all company merchandising and visual presentation standards.
4. Perform accurate paperwork processing **(10%)**
   4.1 Interpret merchandise ticket information.
   4.2 Complete required paperwork for markdowns, holds, transfers, counts, defective merchandise ticketing, etc.

(continues)

Figure 4-6. Continued.

5. Develop and maintain personal clientele by taking steps to follow up on future customer needs and fostering repeat business **(5%)**

Additional Job Functions

1. Process telephone orders and sends.
2. Gift wrap merchandise when necessary.
3. Participate in housekeeping duties for assigned area and stockrooms, which includes cleaning, dusting, arranging, and sizing merchandise.
4. **Perform duties as assigned.**

Relationships

1. Communicate to and work cooperatively with store management team and other employees and coworkers.
2. **Provide quality service to customers to foster repeat business.**

Supervision

Number of employees: Not applicable
Supervisory duties required: Not applicable

Skills/Abilities Required

Professional communication skills
Problem-solving abilities
Interactive social skills
Reading, writing, and math skills
Operate a point-of-sale terminal and ticket scanner
Operate a telephone
Ability to lift and hang merchandise to a maximum height of 6 feet
Ability to move merchandise from stockrooms on rolling racks
Ability to service sales floor for up to an 8-hour work shift

Education/Training/Certification/License Required

Not applicable

Education/Training: The Sales Associate position is an entry-level position. The employer does not state a minimum education requirement. This omission implies that the employer does not require incumbents to have specific schooling, and consequently the employer cannot use education as a criterion for screening out applicants. Nevertheless, the ability to read, write, and perform math

Figure 4-7. ADA revision of example job description 3 (alternative format).

Title:	Sales Associate		
Department:	All Departments	Regular Location:	Stores
Reports To:	Department Manager	Job Code:	5.6
Pay Grade:	**5**	**FLSA Status:**	**Nonexempt**
Revision Date:	6/12/92	**Revised By:**	

Purpose

To acknowledge customers and assist in their merchandise selection and to process transactions at the point-of-sale terminal, while maintaining an organized and efficient department through merchandise presentation, stock fill-ins, and paperwork processing.

Essential Job Functions

1. Provide effective customer service (35%)
   1.1 Acknowledge and approach customers courteously, conversationally, and in a timely manner.
   1.2 Assist the customer in locating desired merchandise.
   1.3 Communicate to the customer basic knowledge of the merchandise including features and benefits, trend information, and availability.
2. Process point-of-sale transactions (30%)
   2.1 Interpret merchandise information tickets.
   2.2 Enter the information into a point-of-sale system.
   2.3 Package merchandise.
   2.4 Verify credit information.
   2.5 Count back change for the customer.
3. Responsible for timely stock fill-ins and merchandise movement for area of responsibility (20%)
   3.1 Move merchandise from stockroom to the selling floor.
   3.2 Move merchandise from rolling racks to appropriate selling floor fixtures.
   3.3 Participate in floor moves and set-up and take-down of merchandise, fixtures, signing, and other related items for sales events.
   3.4 Maintain all company merchandising and visual presentation standards.
4. Perform accurate paperwork processing (10%)
   4.1 Interpet merchandise ticket information.
   4.2 Complete required paperwork for markdowns, holds, transfers, counts, defective merchandise ticketing, etc.
5. Develop and maintain personal clientele by taking steps to follow up on future customer needs and fostering repeat business (5%)

Skills/Abilities Required

1. **Professional communication skills**
   Interactive social skills
   Reading skills

2. Operate a point-of-sale terminal and ticket scanner
   Operate a telephone
   Math skills
   Writing skills

3. Lift and hang merchandise to a maximum height of 6 feet
   Move merchandise from stockrooms on rolling racks
   Push or pull a maximum weight of 60 pounds
   Service sales floor for up to an 8-hour work shift

4. Problem-solving abilities
   Reading, writing, and math skills

5. Operate a telephone
   Professional communication skills

are job requirements. To determine who can perform these tasks, the employer should conduct a basic skills test of every candidate. This will help the employer determine whether candidates have the level of skills required to read tickets, perform markdowns, calculate discounts, and give change.

This job description is one that an employer could format more creatively than in the traditional way. For example, the employer could use a two-column format. The left column would list the job functions and the percentage of time spent performing each function; the right column could show the physical and mental skills required for the job. Because there is such a close correlation between tasks and requirements in this job, the structure would be quite effective.

See Figures 4-6 and 4-7 for revised versions of this job description. Note that the revisions are in bold print.

Chapter 5

Job Posting and Advertising

In the employment cycle, once a job becomes vacant management determines whether to refill the position. If business needs require a replacement employee, the ADA now provides the employer with the next step: to update the job description (or other documentation), identifying the job's essential functions. If the job description already complies with the ADA, then management must ensure that the functions classified as essential are still valid. With each clarification, management signs and dates the review. At this point, management can determine how to recruit and advertise for qualified job candidates.

We now recognize that each employment component should focus on the essential functions of a job. Job advertising is one of those complying components, so all job advertising must focus on the essential job functions. This is true whether the solicitation method is formal or informal, whether you use an internal posting system or external newspaper classifieds.

Remember, the ADA tells us that the qualified applicant is the person who can perform the essential functions of the job. Employers cannot consider nonessential functions when determining whether a person has the qualifications to perform the job. Thus, one solution is to avoid any reference to nonessential functions in the job advertisement. This helps ensure that you do not use nonessential functions as criteria to screen out otherwise qualified people with disabilities.

What is the risk of including nonessential requirements? Let's look at this scenario. A potential applicant with a disability reads an advertisement in a local newspaper. The first part of the ad lists the essential functions of the job, which the applicant can perform. She reads further and sees listed nonessential functions that she cannot perform, and she therefore does not apply for the job. This person has no way of knowing that she would still be a qualified candidate because she can perform the first part of the job description. Should she later learn that the job did not require the performance of the latter duties, because they were nonessential, she could file a discrimination suit on grounds that the advertisement was misleading and resulted in discrimination against a qualified person with a disability. Just as hiring decisions focus on a person's qualifications to perform essential functions, so too should other components of the hiring process.

Sometimes employers prefer to attract applicants who have extra qualifications, although these qualifications are not required. In that case, they should use wording that tells the reader that the nonessential skill or experience is desired or preferred, but not required.

Some Typical Ads

Let's look at some examples of job advertisements, taken directly from local newspapers. Because of the compactness of want ads, it is difficult to determine whether the qualifications and requirements described are truly essential to the job. However, it is useful to analyze and critique different ads. Study the ads' components, effectiveness, and whether their wording needs changing to comply with the ADA.

Example 1

Element Testing and Fabrication

Long-term position open for individual with good mechanical background and reading comprehension (you will be tested). Must be able to follow written and oral instructions in the element testing, packaging, and fabrication of water purification products. Must be able to stand 8 hours and lift 35–50 lbs. Two years previous manufacturing background needed. Good learning opportunity.

Discussion: This ad includes several pieces of important information to help it comply with the ADA. It focuses on key physical, mental, and experiential job qualifications. First, inclusion of a reading test requirement acknowledges the importance of reading comprehension to the outcome of the job. The ADA allows selection testing as long as employers administer and interpret the test consistently and the test is relevant to the essential job functions. This employer appears to meet these ADA factors. Also, inclusion of this test requirement can be beneficial information to someone with a disability who needs a testing accommodation during the interview process.

The specific standing and lifting requirements are clear and measurable. This inclusion of physical requirements provides a more complete picture of the work required on the job. It screens out those who do not want to perform that type of labor, and prepares those who may need accommodation. This detail serves the ADA's intent.

Example 2

Printing: Mail Sorting/Bindery

Growing company needs dependable FT bindery employees to sort mail 1st and 2nd shifts. Frequent standing, bending, repetitive movements with hands and wrists and lifting to 50 lbs. No previous experience required.

Discussion: This ad includes the hours worked as one of its first selection qualifications. Include work schedule requirements in any advertisement where scheduling may be a unique function of the job. The ad lists the variety of physical requirements of the position. This effort is likely a function of the ADA. There are disabilities that directly affect a person's ability to perform repetitive movements with hands and wrists. Describing this task is key to the selection effort. Although the employer may accommodate these requirements, the level of detail provided emphasizes the physical stress placed on employees.

Example 3

Mechanic

One of the nation's leading truck leasing firms has an opening for a mechanic. Qualifications include certificate from diesel mechanic school or 3 years' experience. Must have valid CDL, pass physical and drug screen. Must be able to perform essential job functions and work all shifts as needed.

Discussion: This ad has both strengths and weaknesses. The strengths include listing two options to qualify for the job: certification or experience. In reviewing the job description, this company determined that qualified candidates can acquire the expertise in multiple ways; qualified applicants are not limited to one method of training. The ad also includes licensing requirements. These are performance standards allowed by the ADA. They display the skill level of the employee and reinforce the fact that licensing supports an essential function of the job.

Another issue relates to the statement that candidates must pass physical and drug screening. According to the ADA, physical screening is legal only if it is conducted after a job offer has been made. If the company uses a test to screen out candidates, the screening criteria must relate directly to the job's essential functions. The drug screening is not legislated by the ADA. The ADA allows drug tests to be administered before employment or interviewing or during employment, and it offers no drug testing restrictions. However, employers who conduct drug testing should review relevant state laws and, if drug testing is permitted, have a corresponding policy and administer the tests consistently.

The most interesting part of the ad is the statement that qualified applicants "must be able to perform essential job functions." I believe that this company took the ADA too literally. By doing so, the company gives no information to potential applicants as to what these functions may be. It would have been better if it included a sampling of the mechanic's actual essential duties.

Inclusion of the requirement that employees must be available for all shifts does offer pertinent information on the job. Applicants need to be aware of such criteria that relate to the business necessity of the work environment, such as rotational scheduling.

Example 4

Office: Staffing Coordinator

National nursing service has an opening for a FT Staffing Coordinator who lives near the X-City area. This is a position of responsibility for a high-energy, assertive individual with a mature understanding of people. Responsibilities include scheduling of medical personnel, interviewing applicants, computer, and general office duties. If you are comfortable making decisions independently, are able to maintain detailed scheduling charts despite frequent telephone interruptions, and are interested in working for a company whose reputation for excellence is a direct result of team work, then call . . .

Discussion: This is another advertisement with some excellent language and some questionable language. The best part of this description is the inclusion of the mental requirements. The statement "independent decision making and the ability to conduct detailed work with frequent interruption" is a perfect example of including mental capabilities as part of the essential functions of a job.

On the other hand, there are some criteria in this advertisement that have the potential to discriminate and/or be nonessential to the job. The first is the requirement that applicants live in a certain area of the city. This employer needs to validate why residence is pertinent to job performance. Unless the employee has to be able to report to work within a minute's notice, this residency requirement could be discriminatory in several EEO areas. The other terminology to avoid is *high-energy*. This term implies wellness, and could be substituted with something job-specific rather than person-specific, such as "ability to work at a fast pace or under pressure."

Example 5

Ticket Sales

You can be one of 50 commissioned phone sales executives if you . . .
   • Have a college degree or some college education with product sales experience
   • Have clear legible handwriting
   • Have a pleasant, professional telephone voice
   • Are a good listener
   • Will make a commitment to work one of three shifts for the entire seasonal campaign: 9:00 A.M. to 1:00 P.M.; 1:00 P.M. to 5:00 P.M.; or 5:00 P.M. to 9:00 P.M.

   Please call our employment line at XXX-XXXX. Leave a message indicating your interest in the position along with your name, phone number, and shift preference. In addition, please send a handwritten cover letter with your resume or stop by to complete an application. EOE

Discussion: This employer puts a lot of emphasis on a single job requirement: clear, legible handwriting. It is being used as a primary element to screen out otherwise qualified applicants for this position. If challenged on this issue, the employer will claim that writing and recording sales calls are essential functions of the job. However, if an applicant with limited dexterity, resulting in poor writing ability, applies for this sales position, this requirement actually provides a perfect opportunity for a job accommodation. There are alternative methods for recording conversations if legibility is a problem. This employer may need to place more emphasis on the essential function of sales ability and telephone skills as screening standards. Emphasizing the writing may discriminate against people with disabilities who have the other job skills.

Example 6

Clerical Assistant

We have an entry-level opening in our Group Sales Department. The position is responsible primarily for answering telephone calls, typing documents, filing, photocopying, assembling reports, and general office support. Qualified applicants must have a pleasant telephone personality, a positive can-do attitude, strong work ethic, and accurate typing skills of 40–45 wpm (a typing test will be given to all interviewees). You must be able to work in a fast-paced, customer-focused environment. Strong mathematical abilities, ten-key skills, and office experience or education preferred.

Discussion: This is an exceptionally clear classified advertisement. It lists all the essential job functions without describing how the incumbent must perform them. The detailed job requirements even include a statement regarding testing of applicants and acceptable scoring level. An employee who may need an accommodation on the typing test can prepare to make that request because the employer clearly states the test requirements. This ad also includes specific abilities (math and ten-key). While the list of duties does not sound quantitative in nature, the job description should list several tasks requiring these skills.

A Proactive Approach to Job Advertising

One key component of effective employment advertising is where and how to place the ads. You need to determine what newspapers, magazines, schools, colleges, associations, or placement firms are best to reach a qualified pool of applicants. Also develop systems to make your listings more available to the public. If you have a telephone system for job listings, make sure to include it in job advertisements. Consider adding a telephone device for the deaf (TDD) so that applicants with hearing impairments can call in for job listings.

If your company is proactively seeking applicants with disabilities, there are resources in every community that can help you find qualified job candidates. These agencies may be publicly or privately funded; either way, they try to match your job description and requirements to people who can perform the essential functions of the job with or without accommodation. In some instances, these organizations help train the new employee in how your company operates, how machines work, and the like. The important thing is that these agencies will not supply you with nonqualified applicants. They work with you to ensure that their applicants meet the standards your company has set.

As for internal applicants, you need to evaluate your job-posting procedures to determine how effective they are. Does your company actively recruit internal candidates for every opening or is the effort inconsistent? If the company truly supports hiring from within, then verify the effectiveness of the program. What percentage of openings are filled by employees? If the figure is lower than it should be, review the system more closely. Ask yourself, "How many people are actively aware of each job posting? What methods do you use to inform qualified people of openings? Where are the jobs posted? Are they accessible to all employees?"

Brainstorm ways to make these postings accessible to all employees. If you use bulletin boards to post openings, place them in areas of heavy employee traffic. Put the descriptions at eye level for employees in wheelchairs or of short stature. If you lock job descriptions or other postings in glass cases, have extra copies available for employees to read at their convenience. If you use electronic mail or computer access for job postings, make sure that everyone has regular access to a computer. If you have visually impaired employees, make sure they have a mechanism to access visual postings.

ADA-Compliant Job Advertisements

Chapter 4 presented three job descriptions: External Custodian, Records Clerk, and Sales Associate. Let's develop ADA-compliant employment advertising that targets the essential functions and required qualifications of those three positions.

Maintenance
External Custodian

Come join the team at our large, modern office park facility. Qualified applicants must have experience with outdoor landscaping and snow removal equipment, mowers, tractors, plows, and snowblowers. Must be able to work outdoors in all weather conditions and work nights, weekends, and holidays as needed. Must be able to lift 25–50 pounds, shovel snow, and work independently. Driver's license required. We offer excellent benefits and pleasant work environment. Send resume or apply at Park Place Management, 500 Monopoly Road, Gamesville, MA 02111. EOE.

Records Clerk

If you're looking for a fast-paced opportunity, this is it. Busy records department needs an organized, detail-oriented clerk to maintain central file system. Primary responsibilities include sorting and filing documents; pulling, delivering, and tracking files throughout company; and processing telephone requests for documents.

Position requires a high school diploma or equivalent, at least one year filing experience, good interpersonal and communication skills, and experience using microfiche equipment. Must be able to file in a standing position for at least half the work day. Hours: 8:30 A.M.–5:00 P.M. M–F.

Lotsa Data, Inc., offers a competitive salary and benefit package and a comfortable, professional working environment. Please submit resume, including salary history, to Human Resources, 55 Applicant Way, Paper, GA 30333.

Retail
Sales Associates

One More, a high-quality department store chain with over 65 locations nationally, has immediate openings for customer and fashion-oriented sales associates in our downtown store. We have full- and part-time positions open in our women's and junior clothing, children's wear, electronics, and domestic departments.

Qualified candidates will have a strong interest in selling, good interpersonal skills, and previous experience with POS systems. All sales positions include merchandising responsibilities. Product knowledge a plus. Excellent wages, paid holidays, personal discounts, and advancement opportunities. Apply in person only at Downtown Plaza, 2020 Main Street.

Remember, the most important part of advertising a job opening is ensuring that it produces a qualified pool of applicants without discriminating against people with disabilities. A well-written advertisement is effective only when placed in the appropriate location. Think about your target employees and where they are likely to look for a job. Consider advertising openings in locations where diverse applicants will apply.

What information should you include in the advertisement? Make sure you provide as much detail as space or budget allows. Focus on the essential job functions and the most important job responsibilities. Be sure to include an accurate representation of the skills required to perform them. An ADA-compliant ad does not include requirements intended to discriminate. State experience and education qualifications in terms of minimums to help screen out underqualified applicants. Emphasize those essential qualifications that you have to have, not the nonessential ones that would be nice to have.

Be as creative as your corporate culture allows. Help the reader know your company by the wording you select. Sell the company and the job opportunity. Have someone else read the ad or posting to make sure that it conveys your message and is attractive to candidates.

After applicants respond to the ad, evaluate the effectiveness of each advertising method and location. If you placed the ad with a company that places people with disabilities in jobs, evaluate the success or the match of the position with their applicant population. Get feedback from candidates regarding what attracted them to the job. Keep a file of all advertising, recording placement of ads as well as the associated costs. Use efficient recordkeeping to avoid reinventing the wheel each time you have a job opening.

Chapter 6

The Application And Screening Process

Every company wants to hire the most qualified person for its job openings. After updating the job description and advertising a vacant position, the next step is to collect resumés and applications from prospective employees. Then, the task is to read each document, screen out candidates who do not meet the position's requirements, and determine whom to interview.

The Job Application

Almost every company uses a job application form to collect basic employment information. One reason for using an employment application is that it allows you to review applicant information in a similar manner for every candidate. It is easier and more effective to study people's professional experiences and backgrounds in a consistent format, such as on a job application. The application also provides more information than you might get from a resume, such as the position applied for, salary history, and reasons for changing employment. It also allows the company the opportunity to include any legal information, and to explain employer rights to terminate employees who falsify application information.

One company will design its application in a slightly different way from the next; however, the overall information collected is very similar. A typical application may look like the one shown in Figure 6-1. If so, not only is this a coincidence, but you have included some questions that are *illegal* according to EEO law. Before you read further, go back and review the application. Write down all the errors you find. Once you complete this mini-exercise, read the following corrections.

(Text continues on page 82.)

Figure 6-1. XYZ Company employment application.

PERSONAL INFORMATION

Name _____

Present Address _____ How long there? _____

Previous Address _____ How long there? _____

Telephone Number _____ Social Security Number _____

GENERAL INFORMATION

Position(s) Desired _____ Expected Salary _____

Hours Available to Work:
    Full-Time _____ Part-Time _____ Nights _____ Days _____ Weekends _____
Date Available for Employment: _____
Are you over 18 years of age? Yes _____ No _____ If not, you must submit a work permit after employment.
Are you an American citizen? _____
Do you have any handicap, disability, or health problem that will affect your ability to safely perform the job for which you are applying? (Example: heart condition, allergies, back trouble, etc.)? Yes _____ No _____ If yes, please explain. _____
Have you ever filed a workers' compensation claim? Yes _____ No _____ If yes, have you ever been absent from work due to a workers' compensation claim? Yes _____ No _____ If yes, please explain. _____
In the last three years have you been absent from work for a period greater than five consecutive days?
Yes _____ No _____ If yes, please explain. _____
Have you ever worked at XYZ company before? Yes _____ No _____ If yes, what position did you hold and when were you employed? _____

EDUCATION/TRAINING

High School _____

Address _____

From _____ To _____ Graduated: Yes _____ No _____

Major Course of Study: _____

(continues)

Figure 6-1. Continued.

College _____

Address _____

From _____ To _____ Graduated: Yes ____ No ____

Major Course of Study: _____ Degree: _____

Other (Graduate School, Trade, Vocational, Military) _____

Address _____

From _____ To _____ Graduated: Yes ____ No ____

Degrees/Training/Skills _____

BUSINESS SKILLS (circle all applicable)

Typing WPM	CRT
Word Processor	Ten Key
Calculator	Cash Register
Data Entry Keystrokes	Accounting/Bookkeeping
Programming Languages	Dictaphone
Other	Personal Computer
Shorthand WPM	

EMPLOYMENT EXPERIENCE (begin with last or present employer)

Name of Employer _____ Type of Business _____

Address _____ Telephone _____

Starting Pay _____ Ending Pay _____

Start Date _____ Leaving Date _____

Reason for Leaving _____ Job Title _____

Supervisor's Name, Job Title, and Phone Number _____

Description of Work and Responsibilities _____

Name of Employer _____ Type of Business _____

Address _____ Telephone _____

Starting Pay _____ Ending Pay _____

Start Date _____ Leaving Date _____

Reason for Leaving _____ Job Title _____

Supervisor's Name, Job Title, and Phone Number _____

Description of Work and Responsibilities _____

Name of Employer _____ Type of Business _____

Address _____ Telephone _____

Starting Pay _____ Ending Pay _____

Start Date _____ Leaving Date _____

Reason for Leaving _____ Job Title _____

Supervisor's Name, Job Title, and Phone Number _____

Description of Work and Responsibilities _____

BUSINESS AND PROFESSIONAL REFERENCES (Do not list relatives)

1. Name _____

   Address _____

   Type of Reference (Business, Professional, Other) _____

2. Name _____

   Address _____

   Type of Reference (Business, Professional, Other) _____

3. Name _____

   Address _____

   Type of Reference (Business, Professional, Other) _____

NOTICE TO ALL APPLICANTS (Please read before signing.)

I certify that the information I provided on this application is true and correct to the best of my knowledge. I understand that any misstatement or omission of fact is grounds for refusal to hire, or release if I am employed.

XYZ is an equal opportunity employer. No question on this application is asked for the purpose of limiting or excluding any applicant's consideration for employment because of his or her race, color, religion, sex, age, national origin, or handicap.

I authorize XYZ to make any investigation of my background deemed necessary. I authorize the companies, schools, or persons listed in this application to give any information regarding my previous employment and education.

(continues)

Figure 6-1. Continued.

XYZ may request, either prior to employment and/or after employment, that I take a medical examination. I agree to a medical examination, if required, now or in the future.

In consideration of my employment, I agree to conform to the rules and regulations of XYZ Company. I understand that I am an employee at will and either myself or XYZ can terminate my employment at any time.

I understand what I have read. I understand and agree that continued employment depends on satisfactory references, completion of training requirements, and satisfactory work performance.

Applicant's Signature _____ Date _____

What Is Now Forbidden

The ADA tells us we cannot make any preliminary inquiry regarding an applicant's disabilities. Before the ADA, employers regularly inquired as to an applicant's health. Employers wanted to know whether the employee was a health risk, would incur excessive medical claims, or would be absent from the job more than average. These inquiries are now illegal, irrelevant to the hiring decision, and grounds for a discrimination suit.

Eliminate from your job application anything related or similar to:

Do you have any handicap, disability, or health problem that will affect your ability to safely perform the job for which you are applying? (Example: heart condition, allergies, back trouble, etc.)? Yes___ No___ If yes, please explain.

Have you ever filed a workers' compensation claim? Yes___ No___ If yes, have you ever been absent from work due to a workers' compensation claim? Yes___ No___ If yes, please explain.

In the last three years have you been absent from work for a period greater than five consecutive days? Yes___ No___ If yes, please explain.

Employers cannot make pre-employment inquiries regarding current disability, previous disability, or the disability of a family member or associate. Eliminate all similar clauses from your employment application.

Workers' compensation history falls into the same category. Eliminate all reference to workers' compensation. Employers included this type of language to spot workers' compensation patterns, fraud, or when seeking information for state second-injury funds. Employers assumed that if you had a work-related injury, filed a claim, or missed work because of an on-the-job injury, you are suspect for further claims. This assumption is highly discriminatory.

Inquiries regarding a history of absence from work are also discriminatory. These place applicants on the defensive for having been ill. The questions force women to disclose maternity leave and the possible existence of minor dependents. The inquiry implies that a person out of work owing to illness will be an attendance problem in the future.

From a disability perspective, this type of questioning maintains the stereotype that people with disabilities, workers' compensation injuries, or major illnesses are not good employees. It reinforces the perception that people with disabilities have absenteeism problems, lower levels of output, and are problem employees. Employers need information that relates to an applicant's ability to do the job. Previous illness is not an employer's business.

Another area that is questionable from an EEO perspective is inclusion of graduation dates from educational institutions. Requesting graduation dates allows the employer to estimate the age of the applicant, which can lead to age-discriminatory behavior. The employer's interests are in learning whether the applicant graduated, not when they graduated, so a yes or no question is more appropriate.

In the Notice to All Applicants section of our sample application there are several changes needed. The first has to do with the use of the word *handicap*. Although this word is in common usage, the term has a negative connotation. Remove the word *handicap* from company documents and everyday language. (See information on disability etiquette in Chapter 8.)

The next outdated part of the job application relates to medical examinations. According to the ADA, employers may give medical examinations only after offering the job to an applicant. Employers must conduct medical exams consistently within the company, requiring them of all individuals in a particular position or at a certain job level. Random examination of applicants is not allowed, and the purpose of the medical examination must relate to business necessity. An employer cannot screen out people with disabilities for non-work-related reasons. As such, medical examination language on the application should comply with the ADA; it can be given only after offering the individual the job; and it must be given consistently to people with and without disabilities.

What to Avoid on the Job Application

1. ADA requires employers to eliminate the following questions and statements from job applicant inquiries:
    *   Do you have a disability?
    *   Have you had a disability?
    *   Do any of your relatives have a disability?
    *   Please describe any disabling condition you have or may have had that affects the job for which you are applying.
    *   Do you have a physical or mental disabling condition needing accommodation?
    *   Are you a disabled veteran?
    *   Have you been absent from work for a prolonged or continual period?
    *   Have you incurred any workers' compensation injuries?
    *   Have you ever filed a workers' compensation claim?
    *   Have you ever collected workers' compensation pay?
    *   Describe the workers' compensation accident or injury.
    *   You must take a medical examination before we will offer employment.
2. As a general EEO refresher, job applications and interview inquiries should also avoid asking questions regarding the following areas directly or indirectly:
    *   Age, date of birth, or employment history further back than the previous five years
    *   Marital status, number of dependents
    *   Sex, race, creed, color, religion, or national origin
    *   Date and type of military discharge

Job applications are one of the most visible documents a business provides to nonemployees and prospective employees. Anyone can come into a company's offices and request an application to determine whether the application complies with the ADA. Review your company's document thoroughly for compliance. If you are not sure whether one of the application questions complies with EEO regulations, ask yourself, "Will this information help me select the best qualified candidate for the job?" If yes, ask why. If no, leave it out. If in doubt, leave it out. The objective of the application audit is to be sure that you do not screen out qualified applicants with disabilities.

Screening the Applications

Imagine that there's a fifteen-inch-high pile of applications and re-sumés on the corner of your desk. These are the responses to your advertisement for a Sales Associate. What is your first step? How do you go about selecting the candidates to interview?

First, determine who is actually responsible for screening the applications. If it's you, then you need to establish screening crite-ria. If you are not going to screen the applications, select a person to screen them for you. Then decide whether this person under-stands the qualifications and details of the job. Be sure the employee has the expertise or knowledge to perform this important screening task.

If the advertised position will report to you, you have consid-erable investment in the outcome of the selection process. It is your responsibility to ensure that whoever screens the applications does not miss the best of the bunch. If you are selecting the candidates for interviewing, be sure you have all your selection criteria estab-lished. The key is to keep all application screening efforts on target.

So, whether this is a do-it-yourself or a delegate-it effort, first establish the screening criteria. This is the time to refer to the essen-tial functions of the job, the key component of the selection process. Remember,

- Base the hiring decision on the applicant's ability to perform the essential functions of the job.
- The ability to perform the essential functions of a position is what helps classify the individual as a qualified applicant.
- If the individual cannot perform the fundamental duties of the job, he does not qualify for the position.

Review the position description and the essential functions, and highlight the key qualifications. Consider the overall objective of the job and how this job fits in with the rest of the operation. Then map out what the work history of a qualified applicant might be. Make a brief list of the typical positions a qualified person might have held before applying for this job.

Next, explore the job description from the perspective of skill level. Make note of the most important skills needed to perform the job. Determine which skills an employee develops on the job and whether the candidate needs to have these skills as a prerequisite for hiring. Then sketch out a sample applicant resumé to show what jobs, skills, and qualifications an applicant may have.

These steps will help you understand the job. To be more effective in selecting the best candidates, you must also know some of the buzzwords that will appear on resumés. These may include job titles, technical language, certifications, and accomplishment words.

As a final step, prioritize the necessary skills and work experience for the screening process. You need to be able to search for the most important criterion first, then fill in with remaining skills and requirements. Note directly on the job description or the training outline the primary and secondary buzzwords, then translate them into real concepts. For example, must the secretary have five years' experience using WordPerfect or will five years of word processing experience be sufficient?

The actual screening task begins once your preparations are completed. Never forget that the screening phase is based on the job's essential functions and their related requirements. Review each application and resumé to see whether the applicants meet all, some, or none of the selection criteria.

Most people who screen applications do not have a formal method for sorting and rejecting. Typically, the person separates applications into several piles consisting of no's, maybe's, and yes's. Instead, try the following approach. For the first round of screening, sort the applications into three piles: one for applicants who do not meet the minimum job requirements; a second for those who exceed job requirements; the third for those who need further consideration. Study the third-pile applications in greater depth and determine whether to move them to pile one or two—as candidate possibilities or not.

The ADA does not require that you develop a screening system. However, documenting how you screen the applications can be useful from an organizational perspective as well as provide evidence that discrimination did not take place.

Keeping Records

If a person with a disability claims that he is qualified for a particular position but was never called in for an interview, how do you go about proving otherwise? How did you file the rejected applications? How do you know what position each individual applied for? What documentation do you have as evidence to prove you screened the applications fairly and equitably?

There are several options for organizing rejected applications;

select the one that best fits your company and operation. Some companies have computerized applicant-tracking systems whereby all applicant information is entered and maintained on a computer system. Other companies file and track applications manually, storing the original applications and resumés. Still others file their applications in a central corporate location, while some file them at a department or branch location. Whatever method you use, the objective is consistency throughout the company. The more standardization in the selection process, the less chance for someone to discriminate. And this includes routine tasks such as filing rejected applications and resumés.

The application form is not the only useful piece of information to retain. Companies should also track the circumstances surrounding the application. For example, it may be important at a later date to reference or reconsider the application. If you don't know the position that was applied for, whether the person was interviewed, and why she didn't get the job, you will have a hard time re-creating the applicant's history.

Whether using a manual filing system or a computerized applicant-tracking system, include the following information along with the rejected application:

1. Position(s) applied for
2. Receipt date of the application
3. Application review date
4. Name of employee who screened the application
5. Interview date, if applicable
6. Name of employee(s) who interviewed the candidate
7. Reason for rejection of the applicant—i.e., did not meet skill requirement, employment history requirement, education requirement
8. Identify the person hired for the position

If the company uses a computerized tracking system, you need to develop a file that includes this information. For a manual filing system, attach this form to each application or to groups of applications. This will show you considered each applicant. It is impossible to remember every application or every interview, let alone the reasons why you rejected each person. So complete the documentation at the time of screening, and be prepared with written evidence that you considered the individual and include the reason for the rejection. If you are clustering applications—for example, all those who did not have the necessary employment experience—it may be helpful to include a copy of the current job description along with the screening sheet. If at a later time you need to reference this decision, you can compare the specific job characteristics with the applicant's background and identify the gaps in qualifications.

Consider creating a separate filing method for candidates who interviewed for the job, and document why these candidates were rejected. You will have more information on these individuals, so document appropriately. Also, determine whether to file the information on interviewed candidates separately or group them with other interviewed applicants. One documentation method is to staple the interview evaluation to the job application; however, this is discussed further in Chapter 7.

Chapter 7

General Interviewing Techniques

Interviewing is one topic where there has been considerable information published. Each publication presents its perspective on the most effective way to interview prospective employees, yet the techniques have similar components. Much of the information is common sense to the experienced interviewer.

Despite the volume of information on interviewing, and despite the similar approaches, interviewers do not consistently apply effective interviewing skills or behaviors. All interviewers—experienced and inexperienced—should review their techniques and commit to developing stronger interviewing skills. The failure to interview effectively results in expensive hiring errors paid for by the company, its employees, and its customers.

The typical interviewer has attended at least one training session on interviewing, and probably applied those techniques religiously for a while. But then he became secure in his efforts and began interviewing more casually. Over time, the interviewer used fewer and fewer of those techniques until, eventually, he went back to his old interview habits. Typically, an interviewer's skills do not improve with time; in fact, the skills diminish.

In this chapter, we walk through the general interview process and outline the stages of an interview. I present interview methods that focus on getting the right information from each candidate, so that the company can make the right hiring decision. In Chapter 8, we then focus on interviewing people with disabilities. Then Chapter 9 considers the particular needs of the ADA-compliant interview.

Preparing to Interview an Applicant

You've reviewed the applications and resumés. You've selected six potential candidates for the job. Each of the six candidates meets the job's basic requirements, however each has different work experiences that led him or her to the qualifications you seek so those unique experiences need further exploration. How do you begin to differentiate between the candidates?

The first step is to review each candidate's resumé to determine what particular questions to ask of each person. The candidate's distinct experience and background raise a few questions in your mind. These points might include gaps in employment, unique responsibilities, special projects, or experience in similar industries. Use a separate sheet of paper for each candidate and write down the questions that come to mind during this preliminary resumé review. These questions are important to include in your interview. You can use the candidate's responses to fill in the information gaps in the resumé.

The second interview preparation step accomplishes two objectives: You organize the hiring criteria for the position and you use the criteria to compare your six candidates on their job-performance abilities. Keep in mind the objective of acquiring job-relevant information from each candidate. That's why it is so important to develop this criteria list before any interviews take place.

A simple way to compare and evaluate candidates is by developing an evaluation chart. Draw a column down the left margin of a sheet of paper. In this section, list the key qualifications required of a new employee, using the position description to identify those essential functions and key qualifications. (When listing these on the evaluation form, shorten them to phrases.) On the right side of the paper, draw a separate column for each candidate. Use these columns to record the candidate's abilities (see Figure 7-1).

Use this simplified evaluation form both before and after the interview. Do not use it for note taking during the interview; this is a summarizing tool. If, after listing the criteria, you discover that the evaluation list is too extensive, rank the items in order of importance. This helps you prioritize the particular skills when identifying the candidates' strengths and weaknesses.

Before beginning the interviews, review each applicant's resumé. Write the basic applicant information on the Candidate Evaluation Form. Extract information such as education, years of experience, and basic items such as typing, PC, and ten-key skills. This will establish the basic background of each candidate before the interview.

You have identified the selection and interview criteria and developed a simple evaluation tool. Now it is time to set the interview stage. To prepare for each interview, do the following:

Figure 7-1. Candidate evaluation form.

Key Qualifications	Candidate 1	Candidate 2	Candidate 3	Candidate 4
1.				
2.				
3.				
4.				
5.				
6.				

1. *Allot sufficient time for each interview.* The length of the interview depends on many factors. To determine the interview length, consider the level of the job, how many interviews are scheduled for each candidate, and whether this is the candidate's first interview or it is part of a series of interviews. As a rule, interviews should never take less than twenty minutes; thirty- to sixty-minute interviews are most common. However, for positions where skill levels are high, interviews can exceed an hour.

2. *Hold the interview in a private area.* Your candidates are likely to speak more frankly when you eliminate their fear of being overheard.

3. *Eliminate any opportunity for interruptions.* Interruptions distract the interviewer's concentration from effective listening; they can also affect a candidate's performance. Create an environment in which the total focus is on the interview. Hold all telephone calls. Inform your staff not to disturb you. Place a "do not disturb" note on the door, then close the interview room door. Try not to interview in a room with an inside window or one located near excessive noise or heavy traffic.

4. *Clear yourself of other distractions.* If you are interviewing at or by your desk, clear away obvious paperwork. Don't leave memos and other business matters around to distract you and impede your listening.

5. *Consider the interview setting.* Try to make the physical setting as comfortable as possible. If space permits, sit alongside your desk instead of behind it; this is less intimidating and can make candidates feel more comfortable. If a work or conference table is available, use it as the interview location. Provide the candidates with a comfortable chair, a beverage, or whatever fits the setting. Your objective is to get the most job-related information from each candidate. By providing a comfortable interview setting, you improve this possibility.

Why Prepare Interview Questions?

Prepare all your questions well before the interview. The structure and consistency evident in the preparation is your key to interviewing success.

Don't make up excuses as to why you can't prepare a list of questions in advance. Yes, it takes time and effort. No, it doesn't mean that you can't add related or exploring questions later on. Yes, it means that all your interviews will be similar in content. No, your interviews won't be totally spontaneous, but who really wants a spontaneous interview? You want to control the information you collect from each candidate so as to make an effective hiring decision. Structured questioning focused on the essential hiring criteria will help you achieve your objective.

One reason people dislike interviewing is because they find themselves scrambling to make up the next question for a candidate. This (lack of) style results in a highly disorganized interview. You are so busy thinking up the next question that you haven't really listened to the candidate's answer. What are the results of this ad hoc interview style? First, you receive a poor flow of information because there is little pattern to the questioning. Second, you don't ask the same questions of each candidate, and therefore don't have a valid base for comparing candidates. This list can go on.

The key point is that if you prepare a list of ordered, job-related questions, you can focus on:

- What candidates are saying during the interview
- How they are saying it
- How their answers relate to the skills and qualifications you need on the job

Since a primary objective of this structured effort is to elicit the same information from each candidate, develop a list of core questions you will ask of each candidate. Follow this list of questions and you will acquire all the information you need from the applicants. You will have job-related information on all your candidates, with a complete applicant picture for comparing the applicants. The list of interview questions also ensures that you don't forget to ask each candidate a pertinent "decision-making" question.

Preparing the Interview Questions

There is one important consideration remaining before you begin designing your interview questions: Ascertain how many people are interviewing each candidate. If more than one interview is scheduled for each candidate, coordinate these interviews. How boring it must be for candidates to have several similar interviews at the same company. And how counterproductive it is for each interviewer to collect the same information from the candidate.

Have each interviewer select a particular job area, skills grouping, or qualifications set. Each should focus her interview questions on this area. The interviewer's introductory questions may be similar; however, if each interviewer covers different job-skills objectives, the total interview process is more productive—more variety and better quality information will be collected. The interviewers will be able to explore the candidate's experience and knowledge more deeply if they don't have to cover every qualification area.

Each interviewer should develop a formal set of questions to meet the information objectives for his focus area. Review each set of questions with the group. This will double-check for overlaps and missing components. Be sure every job area is discussed by someone on the team; don't assume another interviewer will discuss something you are responsible for. Cover all your bases.

The following tips will help you prepare your interview questions.

1. *Start off with easy questions.* This helps the candidate relax and gets you into your most comfortable interview mode.
2. *Don't ask questions obviously included in the application or resumé.* It isn't the best use of your time to merely confirm facts stated in the resumé. Build on and explore the information in the resumé.
3. *Avoid asking closed-ended questions.* These are questions beginning with *is, can, will, are, could, should, did, have, were,* and they produce only yes and no answers. These questions do not give you the depth of information you need for hiring decisions. Closed-ended questions merely confirm or repeat facts. An effective interviewer makes answering questions a challenge.
4. *Ask open-ended questions.* These questions begin with *why, what, how, when, tell me, describe, explain,* or *give me an example.* These questions avoid a defensive response from the candidate and focus on the candidate's past behavior. Open-ended questions help you explore the motivation behind the candidate's experience.
5. *Follow open-ended questions with requests for elaboration.* Ask *how, why, who, when, where, which.* This exploration helps validate the first answer. They get you to another level, deeper into the candidate's experience and motivation.
6. *Ask questions that probe.* Get the candidate's facts, opinions, ideas, feelings, values, attitudes, and self-concept. Ask questions aimed at helping you understand the candidate, her ability to perform the job, to fit into the organization and her work ethic.

7. *Develop questions using superlative adjectives.* Ask about past experience in terms of the *most, least, best, worst, hardest, simplest.* This gives you a perspective on how each candidate views the extremes within his professional experience.

8. *Ask about difficult situations.* Have the candidate describe situations she has faced and how she handled them. This gives you an idea how she might respond to circumstances in your company and whether her response would be appropriate.

9. *Determine the candidate's reasoning ability.* Ask questions to evaluate how the candidate thinks.

10. *Create hypothetical cases.* Base these on a situation the candidate might encounter in the company. Ask how he would handle it. What steps would he take? What outcome would he expect?

11. *Probe for specifics.* When a candidate doesn't volunteer an example of how she acquired a skill, ask a question that elicits more detail.

12. *Question the candidate's range of expertise.* Don't merely accept the candidate's statement that she knows how to perform a task. Have her describe the administrative task, explain the technical concept, or illustrate the improvements made to the process.

13. *State questions broadly, then use more specific probing questions.*
    Q1. "Tell me about a time when you saved the company money."
    Q2. "How did you notify management of the circumstances?"
    Q3. "How did you implement the change?"
    Q4. "How did the employees respond?"

14. *Require more complete responses.* If a candidate provides short answers to questions, ask her to elaborate. Control the effectiveness of the interview by directing the candidate to give you the quality and quantity of information you need. Superficial answers don't help you evaluate candidates.

15. *Ask for clarification when you don't understand.* Double-check statements that don't make sense. Point out possible contradictions in a candidate's response. Don't leave the interview with unanswered questions or doubts. There may be a simple explanation for a contradiction. You might have misunderstood something the candidate said. Get closure on your concerns during the interview.

16. *Talk about what the candidate has accomplished.* Discuss how he

got to his current level of responsibility. Give the candidate room to sell himself.

17. *Don't put words in the candidate's mouth.* Don't imply the desired answer to your questions. Frequently we give away the answer we seek, such as, "We work long hours at XYZ company. Is that a problem for you?" Create a question that gets the same response without giving away the "long hours" answer: "Tell me about the work schedules you have had in the past" may provide more information and the truth about the candidate's willingness to work longer hours as needed.

18. *Don't ask the standard questions.* Candidates have ready-made answers for these questions. Develop and ask questions that make a candidate think on her feet.

19. *Ask questions that show the differences between one candidate and another.* There are certain typical questions that candidates answer similarly. Make sure that your questions explore the candidate's unique job-related experience and skills. This will help you determine who best meets your requirements.

20. *Avoid long questions.* Don't string questions together. It is better to connect a candidate's response by asking additional probing questions after he has answered the first part of the question. Don't have an important question lost in a line of questions.

The following guidelines relate to questioning and the interview process:

1. *Be consistent.* Ask the same questions of each candidate. Interject exploratory questions that relate to an individual's specific experiences, but be sure to ask the same skill, experience, and ability questions of every candidate. Interviewers who are inconsistent will have no true basis for making comparisons.

2. *Only pursue areas relevant to the job.* Keep the interviewing tight and efficient, so you obtain the decision-making information you need. Additionally, this keeps your inquiries within the legal boundaries established by the EEOC. The more personal you get, the more chance you'll step beyond legal questions.

3. *If the candidate volunteers personal information, don't explore it.* Just because a person initiates a personal discussion, it does not mean you must follow her lead. Move away from this line of discussion and bring it back to the job opening.

4. *Don't assume that long job tenure is synonymous with high performance or job knowledge.* Ask for proof of the candidate's skills and traits.

5. *Don't assume that lateral or promotional job changes mean that the candidate has acquired multiple skills.* Some companies move people around for reasons other than good performance. Explore these issues with the candidate and with his professional references.

6. *Watch what emotions the candidate presents with each answer.* Is she enthusiastic about an opportunity? Angry at a previous circumstance? Comfortable with her presentation of certain material? Read between the lines. Note inconsistencies between verbal and nonverbal communication.

7. *Don't merely consider the details offered in an answer.* Study the skills the candidate used in presenting the answer. Consider how well the candidate organized the answer, how well he phrased the response, how much thought he gave to the question before answering, and how consistent the answer is to other information given.

8. *Use effective nonverbal skills.* Pay attention to your nonverbal expression, such as eye contact, facial animation, nods, and tone of voice. Show interest in the candidate's responses and descriptions. Additionally, do not pass judgment (verbally or nonverbally) on the candidate's comments; no matter what the candidate shares, you must be the acceptant interviewer.

9. *Rephrase the applicant's statements as a method for obtaining more information.* This technique is especially useful to continue a discussion if the topic is sensitive, if the message is unclear, or if you are at a loss as to how to continue the discussion.

10. *Listen to the candidate without interrupting him.* A good interviewer is a listener and a director. Although it is important to use the interview to sell the company to the candidate, it is more important that you collect the information necessary to hire the most qualified candidate for the job. The interviewer who speaks more than she listens does not get maximum benefit from the interview.

Organizing and Sequencing the Interview

There is so much information to collect during the limited time of an interview that you must make this time work to your benefit. Sequence your list of interview questions, both the standard questions and the candidate-specific questions. Determine how you can most effectively learn about a person's knowledge, experience, abilities, work habits, personality strengths and limitations, motivational characteristics, and environmental fit. Look at your questions and cluster them by topic or objective. Then consider how you can make each question flow into the next in a logical or conversational sequence. Determine if there are any important areas not included in the list, and fill in these gaps.

The following is a suggested sequence of components in a job interview. Arrange your questions in this sequence or develop another order more suited to your style. Be sure not to omit any important categories.

1. Introductory conversation, small talk, warm-up
2. Brief introduction of company and position
3. Review of candidate's education
4. Overview of work history (explore commonalities to position opening)
5. Technical abilities and job knowledge
6. Personality traits (work-related)
7. Interpersonal skills
8. Managerial abilities
9. Motivational characteristics and work objectives
10. More complete review of company and position
11. Open discussion for candidate's questions
12. Interview closure

After you have sequenced your questions, look at the total time you allocated for each interview. How are you going to ask all those questions in that small amount of time? You plan ahead and determine how much time to spend on each item. Let's say you scheduled one-hour interviews. For the twelve topics listed above, you could divide the hour by twelve and spend five minutes on each area. But is each area of equal importance? I doubt it.

You could complete your warm-up conversation in the two minutes it takes to settle into chairs. The company and position overview can take three minutes. You will provide more information later, and may anticipate that the applicant did some company research. The resumé includes education information in detail, so unless the education relates closely to job requirements, you may wish to only briefly explore the benefits of the education to the job or the person's expertise.

The candidate's work history and technical skills will probably take the bulk of the interview time, but phrase your exploration of these experiences in terms of the job being applied for. Don't ask the candidate merely to describe her responsibilities. Instead, tie the vacant position's responsibilities into her past experience to get the most information possible. Spend perhaps thirty to forty minutes detailing this important area.

Information on the candidate's personality or interpersonal, managerial, and motivational traits will appear throughout the interview. However, getting a self-assessment of these skills and exploring examples of these abilities is exceptionally useful information. An interviewer may spend ten to fifteen minutes in this area. Relate these questions to the work environment, and emphasize areas that provide you with the most information on potential job performance.

Spend another three to five minutes describing more of the work environment, company culture, company operations, and employee benefits. Then allow the candidate five minutes to ask questions about the job and the company. Wrap up the interview and exit with the candidate.

You can modify this example to the position level and responsibilities. Assess the amount of time scheduled for an interview, and consider how many interviewers are participating. There is no rule for effective use of interview time, so prioritize your questions based on the information you need to make your decision and allocate your interviewing time accordingly.

Meeting and Greeting the Candidate

The first few minutes of the interview set the stage for the remainder of the meeting. As interviewer, it is your responsibility to ensure that the candidate feels welcome, is comfortable, and becomes ready to share information. A poor introduction by the interviewer can deter a potentially good employee from joining the organization.

Think about the poor interviews you have experienced. List all the incorrect interviewer behaviors you observed and the negative impressions you acquired regarding the company. Keep this list at your side, and remind yourself of the professional responsibility interviewers have for representing the company and how fragile that representation can be.

The most important message to give to an applicant is how important he is to you. One of the best nonverbal ways to share this message is to be on time for the interview. If an interview is scheduled for 1:30 P.M., the interviewer should greet the candidate at 1:30. Frequently, candidates arrive at an employment interview earlier than scheduled; this shows their interest in the position and their respect for the interview time allotted. Interviewers should show the same respect for the candidate. A candidate's time is as valuable as the interviewer's.

Start the interview with a friendly opening. Typically, people are uncomfortable having to sell themselves and their skills to match a job. The interviewer needs to relax the candidate in order to have a constructive, effective meeting. Put the candidate at ease with some social—not personal—conversation. Help the candidate speak freely and share her professional experience with you.

One of the first things interviewers do is "check out" the candidate. This entails looking for a professional appearance, assessing the handshake, and generally making a snap judgment about the person. In our society, we get first impressions whenever we are introduced to someone. However, in the job setting, the impact of a first impression can make or break an interview. An effective interviewer should not make a snap decision to hire someone based on the introduction. There is so much more to a candidate than first impressions. It is grossly unfair to bias an interview by overemphasizing a first impression.

A better approach is to use that initial impression as you would any other information collected during the interview. Assess the individual's initial image; determine its relevance to the job. Record this information in your notes. For example, if the person is applying for a sales position or a customer service position, the way she presents herself at an introduction can be important. Include these criteria on your evaluation form along with other factors and weight them relative to the job.

Initiate the interview by introducing yourself and describing your role in the interview process. If you are the sole interviewer, let the candidate know. If there will be a series of interviews, share the schedule with the individual; this helps the candidate mentally prepare. Next, present an overview of how you plan to conduct the interview. Let the candidate know the sequence of events; this helps eliminate his fear of what may take place during the interview. The interviewer's warm introduction, small talk, and presentation of the interview format should eliminate much of the tension and apprehension that candidates feel.

Then the interviewer should provide a brief description of the job. This may be repetitive of earlier conversations or of the employment advertisement, but it helps clarify the job for the candidate.

Describe the job realistically. Both the applicant and the interviewer hope for a good job fit between the candidate and the company. Being overly enthusiastic, promising too much, or exaggerating the benefits of the job can result in unrealistic and unattainable job expectations. Employees who receive a clear, accurate picture of the job generally are more satisfied with their position and stay on the job longer.

Conducting the Interview

You have prepared for the interview. You understand the vacant position and have completed and sequenced your interview questions. You welcomed the candidate to your office. Now the candidate is sitting before you. Remember the following important requirements for an effective interview:

1. *Put your maximum effort into the interview.* Interviewing is just as important as your other job responsibilities. Don't miss out on the opportunity to hire the right person. Give the interviews your all.
2. *Concentrate on being a good listener.* Pay attention to the candidate's verbal and nonverbal responses. Don't daydream and assume you know what the person's going to say next. Don't miss out on important information or messages.
3. *Don't monopolize the conversation.* Be in control of the interview by leading the candidate to share the information you need for your hiring decision. Don't take over the interview with company tales, lengthy descriptions, or long questions. Direct the candidate to present you with her qualifications for the job.
4. *Keep the interview on track.* If the candidate gets off the track, gently nudge him back. Don't relinquish control of the interview. Don't waste time on areas not related to the job and on areas not on your agenda.
5. *Follow your interview plan.* Stick to the questions you listed, adding exploratory questions as needed. Keep track of interview time. Don't spend too much time on a particular subject unless it is pivotal to your decision.
6. *Interview internal candidates as carefully as external candidates.* Give all candidates a fair opportunity and equal consideration for the position. The experience, knowledge, and skills of current employees may surprise you. Be thorough and

conduct the same interview for employees as you do for other candidates.

7. *Don't extend the length of the interview beyond what it needs to be.* After initial application screening, the remaining candidates should meet minimum qualifications; therefore, no candidate should be extremely out of line with the other interviewees. However, should you discover otherwise, continue with the basic interview and make notes to document lacking job qualifications, but don't feel obligated to spend sixty minutes with the candidate when after twenty minutes you realize her skill level is inadequate.

8. *Give each candidate the opportunity to ask questions.* Not only will questions fill the candidate's need for information, they also will give you information on the person. What is the candidate's primary concern? Has he come prepared with questions? Are the questions repetitive of something you said earlier? You can learn much from these questions.

9. *Don't mislead applicants regarding their candidacy.* Don't tell applicants that they are top candidates if you are not going to consider them further. Inform each candidate when the final decision is anticipated, then be sure to follow up. Maintain goodwill between your company and the public by communicating the results of the job search with every interviewee and, if possible, in writing to all applicants.

Taking Notes during the Interview

It would be interesting to know what percentage of interviewers take notes. Whether you have never taken notes or you are an avid note taker, it is time to analyze the effectiveness of your methods. Ask yourself the following questions:

1. Is there organization to my note taking?
2. Can I read my notes?
3. Do my notes repeat information found elsewhere, such as on the application or resume?
4. Do I write in full sentences or do I write down key words?
5. Do my notes correspond directly to my interview questions?
6. Do I write down positive and negative observances equally or just negative reminders?
7. Does my note taking distract the candidate?

8. Do I take notes consistently throughout the interview or are there gaps in my note taking?
9. Do I or can I use my notes after the interview to help me make my hiring decision?

This list could go on. The primary point is to consider the over-all effectiveness of your note taking. When applied properly, note taking can help you make your hiring decision. It can remind you of each candidate's characteristics, behaviors, examples, and abilities. It can fill in those gaps when you can't put your finger on exactly why you favor or disfavor a particular candidate.

People typically remember the information shared at the beginning and end of an interview, but tend to forget the middle. Consider the volume of information shared during a sixty-minute interview. By relying strictly on our memory, might you lose the middle twenty, thirty, or forty minutes of the interview? Note takers have the documentation to recall and retain more information than non–note takers. Think about how you can improve your interviewing technique and selection decision with effective note taking.

But, you say, taking notes is a threat to the candidates being interviewed. Candidates find the scribbling distracting. They want to see what we are writing. They know we're writing down only the bad stuff. Besides, note taking gets in the way of really listening to what the candidate has to say.

There must be a solution. Every interviewer needs a way to take notes during an interview that is not distracting to herself or the candidate. Since the objective is to provide information that helps make selection easier, the notes should not repeat facts found on the resumé and should not include irrelevant data. The notes should correspond to the essential functions of the job and to the corresponding job requirements. The notes should not include any information that would prove discriminatory. (Notes, even "doodles," are discoverable evidence in discrimination litigation.)

The following note-taking tips should get interviewers started:

1. Determine the best way to write while sitting at a desk, table, or in opposing chairs. Select the most comfortable note-taking posture. Remember, you could be sitting in that position for an hour or more.
2. Choose the best tool for recording notes. Use a clipboard, notebook, interview questionnaire, or whatever else you find comfortable.
3. Keep the note pad angled on your lap. This eliminates some

of the distracting qualities of note taking, and it stops the candidate from peering over the desk to see what you're writing. It makes the act of writing less visible to the candidate.

4. Take notes consistently. Many people forget to take notes halfway through the interview. Don't stop your note taking until the interview is over. Break the habit of recording only negative information or answers to certain questions. Be thorough.

5. Don't write down everything the candidate says. That's too exhausting and counters effective listening. Jot down key words; abbreviate where possible. Try to write down only one or two words at a time. Don't write down comments and analysis—just write words or phrases to remind you of comments, stories, experiences, and abilities. Do not write anything even arguably related to age, sex, race, or marital status.

6. If you need more structure, take short notes directly on your interview questionnaire. This will help you compare candidate responses. Consider developing an interview note-taking form where you can record facts, examples, behaviors, observations, and comments.

7. If note taking doesn't come naturally, practice in other circumstances. Take notes at staff meetings, during telephone conversations, or in seminars. Develop your own style of note taking that captures the key data, uses the least words or letters, and generates a broad picture of the information.

8. Rely on your notes as you complete your evaluation form and narrow down your list of qualified candidates. The more you use these notes, the better your note-taking skills will become.

9. Save your notes; do not discard them. They can serve as evidence that you did not discriminate in your selection practice. If the same position should open again in the future, you can use your notes to remind you of previously interviewed candidates.

After the Interview

Fairness in interviewing also applies to an interviewer's actions directly following the interview. Take time to recap each interview as soon as possible. Complete your sheet of notes by adding comments that you were unable to include during the interview. Don't rely on your memory to think of those facts an hour or day later. Whereas memories fail us, notes do not. If interviews are in close succession, take the time to refresh yourself before jumping into the next meeting. Both candidates fare better with an interviewer who takes time to reflect on the prior interview, record some reflections, finish a written interview summary, and then clear her head before interviewing again.

Some Actions for after the Interview

1. *Read all the notes you took during the interview.* Review the candidate's performance and begin to assess her knowledge, skills, and abilities.
2. *Try to avoid making a snap judgment.* Some interviewers make a quick evaluative decision immediately after an interview. These judgments tend to bias the interviewer for or against other candidates, and the bias can make it difficult for other candidates to get a fair interview. Don't mentally dismiss or categorize the candidates. It makes the final hiring decision more difficult if other information or opinions prove contrary to your snap judgment. Also, second interviews may bring more information to light.
3. *Don't rely solely on your gut reactions.* Consider why you may have a positive or negative reaction to the person. Determine whether your personal biases are getting in the way of fairly considering this candidate. Read and review your notes to see whether this negative reaction is due to a lack of job-related skills or to something else. Consider whether the positive reaction stems from some commonalities between you and the candidate. Make note of your gut reaction and include it in your considerations, but don't let it overpower your decision.
4. *Study the candidate's answers.* Determine how the responses you've just heard relate to the knowledge and skills needed to perform well on the job.
5. *Determine whether any performance patterns took place during the interview.* For example, did the candidate become tense each time you discussed previous supervisors? Was the candidate enthusiastic each time you mentioned new project development? Patterns in the candidate's work history can serve as predictors for future work behavior. Make note of any pat-

terns you observed in the resumé or from interview performance.

6. *Try to control your prejudices and stereotypes.* Each of us has
   some prejudice, even if it is in areas that we don't recognize
   as such. Don't let your preference for tall people or your dis-
   dain for people with large ears get in the way of your decision.

7. *Don't let the pressure to fill the job opening affect your judgment.*
   Frequently, the urgency of filling a vacancy puts pressure on
   peers and supervisors. It is not uncommon to hear a manager say, "I can't live without an accounting assistant for another day. Just get me a warm body!" Don't bend to this
   pressure, even if it is self-induced. If you hire the wrong person for the job, you will find yourself filling the job again—
   too soon. If you take time to make the right decision,
   chances are you won't have to make that decision again for a
   long time.

Chapter 8

Interviewing People With Disabilities

Have you ever interviewed a person with a disability? If your answer to this question is no, chances are you are mistaken. If you answered yes to this question, chances are you've interviewed a lot more disabled people than you realize. Don't make any assumptions when it comes to determining who has a disability and whom the ADA protects as disabled.

There are people whose disabilities are highly visible to the public, such as those who use wheelchairs or who have a total loss of vision. There are also people who have disabilities that are invisible, including people who have diabetes, a back ailment, or partial loss of hearing. The Americans with Disabilities Act also protects certain groups of individuals we would not otherwise consider as disabled, such as recovering alcoholics or people who associate with people with disabilities.

As a result of the broad definition of who is disabled or who is protected under the ADA, interviewers and others involved in the hiring process have to remember one important message: Treat all applicants and candidates fairly. Complying with the ADA will be easy if you treat all applicants with the same high level of "customer" service before, during, and after the interview.

With that in mind, let's discuss why treating someone who is different means treating him the same. The ADA states that it is the employer's responsibility to ensure that "an employee with a disability enjoys *equal* benefits and privileges of employment as are enjoyed by other similarly situated employees without disabilities." In fact, this new wording was a deliberate change from the original draft of the ADA. Employers are responsible for making accommodations or adjustments to give applicants and employees with disabilities equal opportunity to participate in company offerings.

This EEO requirement includes the selection process as well as every other term and condition of employment. So how do we make selection equal? The first step is to understand the job qualifications and the skills and abilities required for job performance. The next step is to judge candidates on the basis of these criteria in screening and interviewing. You need to focus the job interview on these essential qualifications, and give each candidate the opportunity to explain and/or show how she meets these job requirements. The hiring decision must be based on selecting the person who best meets these requirements.

But how can you interview a person with a disability and ensure that the interview is equal to those of candidates without disabilities? The ADA message and the answer to this question is to treat people with disabilities the same way as you would treat people who do not have disabilities. Common courtesy and common sense are the key components for interviewing all job applicants.

It is common, however, for interviewers to feel some discomfort when interviewing someone with a disability. Most of us have learned in our school systems, from the media, and from those around us that people with disabilities are different. People with disabilities have been distanced from many areas of public life. They have had separate school systems. They have been shut out of inaccessible public buildings. Because of this separateness, and because of the erroneous impression that a disability makes a person different from others, many people are uncomfortable.

This discomfort stems from myths and stereotypes we all have acquired about disabilities. But as an effective interviewer and coworker, you will eliminate any misconceptions you may have had. You must consider each applicant an individual with individual strengths and weaknesses. Whether the applicant is disabled or not, the objective is the same: Determine the person's ability to perform the essential functions of the job, with or without accommodation.

Consider these statistics. Fifteen million—approximately 35 percent—of people with disabilities are of working age. A great majority of these individuals have the skills or ability for effective employment. Until recently, restricted opportunities for employment have limited their ability to contribute through employment. The ADA and nondiscriminating employers will change this.

Respectful Terminology

We have all heard a variety of terms used to describe people with disabilities. The interviewer (or anyone else, for that matter) should not use words that refer negatively to people with disabilities. Some of the words we used to use for certain groups are no longer appropriate. Many other terms are degrading and discriminatory. Since the language we use tends to describe how we feel about others, when we use outdated language we perpetuate stereotypes, misconceptions, and prejudice against these individuals. Changing our language will help change our attitudes.

You will notice that this text does not use the word *handicap*. The word derives from disabled individuals begging for money, holding their caps outstretched in their hands; "cap in hand" evolved into *handicap*. This word conveys a negative image, which people with disabilities do not want to continue. The preferred term is *disability*. You should even replace the common phrasing of "accessible to handicapped" with the term *accessible*—for example, use "accessible parking."

Other words and phrases to eliminate are those that generalize rather than respect the individual. Rather than say, "He is disabled," say "He has a disability." The first statement ignores the person, replacing the image of an individual with the image of a disability. It ignores the wholeness, the personality, and the abilities. The second statement sees the person first and the disability second.

Your language should eliminate all negative-sounding words and phrases, such as *crippled, a victim of, suffers from, afflicted with,* and *stricken by*. These describe a person without a life beyond his disability. No one wants to hear a description of herself as "suffering" or "stricken by" something. Replace this negative terminology with the simple word *has*: "Jane has diabetes," not "She suffers from diabetes." Jane is probably not suffering at all. Such a term creates emotions such as pity and fear, and no one wants to have these emotions placed on him.

Frequently, people are described as "wheelchair bound" or "confined to a wheelchair." It is better to say "Mark uses a wheelchair." Many wheelchair users can stand or walk with assistance, but they prefer to conserve their energy or move more quickly using a wheelchair. It is better that we don't make assumptions as to someone's abilities and inabilities.

People also still use terms such as *the blind, the deaf, the disabled, epileptic, the retarded*. These terms also generalize and categorize a person's disability. They group people with disabilities into clusters and stereotypes. As more people with disabilities join the workforce, you will see that generalizations about disabilities are unreliable. Conditions vary with the person. Just as any two people have different personalities, two "blind" people may have different impairments. So replace "blind" with "visually impaired"; replace "deaf" with "hearing impaired"; replace "epileptic" with "has epilepsy"; replace "retarded" with "has a developmental disability" or "has mental retardation."

Other terms to eliminate from your vocabulary include *crazy, nuts, insane, maimed, invalid, lame, spastic, deaf and dumb, deaf mute, deformed, physically challenged,* and *special.* Even referring to people as "able-bodied" differentiates the population into separate groups. And certainly do not refer to people as "normal" versus disabled.

Think about the words and phrases you use—how they may have originated and how they may be offensive. Negative speech habits reinforce negative attitudes. When people stop using and hearing negative references, their attitudes and perspectives toward people with disabilities will also change.

Meeting and Greeting an Applicant with a Disability

As children, many of us were taught not to stare at people with disabilities, not to ask questions, and to ignore people different from us. This blatant disability avoidance created a circumstance in which children and adults never learned what to do or how to talk to people with disabilities. Through the ADA's efforts to increase the accessibility of public places, meeting people with disabilities will be less the exception and more the common situation. We all will become more courteous and comfortable. We will eliminate the fear that we acquired during childhood of having direct contact with people with disabilities.

For any interview to be successful, the interviewer must be courteous and must make an applicant feel comfortable. The interviewer who meets an applicant with a disability must make sure he handles the introduction well. Interviewers cannot panic, ignore, or offend a candidate with a disability. Not only is it unlawful according to the ADA, but it also is detrimental to the company to disqualify a qualified candidate because of interviewer bias. It is the interviewer's responsibility to welcome, greet, and make every candidate comfortable at the start of the interview. Companies must teach managers how to work with people with differing disabilities. Interviewer comfort will increase, making the interview more successful for both the candidate and the interviewer.

The interviewer-candidate introduction requires several basic techniques: greeting the person verbally, making eye contact then physical contact, leading the candidate into the interview room, and seating the candidate. This is routine for the interviewer. If the candidate has a disability, you should maintain the same routine. Do not change these common actions unless an accommodation is required. The candidate will sense an unnecessary change made owing to interviewer discomfort. And the objective is to increase comfort, not eliminate it.

The verbal welcome must be genuine. Extend pleasant greetings to all candidates. Don't assume that because the person has a disability, she doesn't need the same respectful and warm welcome. If the person is hearing or vision impaired, he may not know you are speaking to him unless you touch him lightly on the arm or shoulder to get his attention.

Make eye contact with each candidate. Direct eye contact means that you focus your attention on the individual and not on the disability. It is a sign of respect for all people. If the candidate has a visual impairment, the interviewer should make eye contact and direct her voice to the person. If the interviewer veers away and speaks away from the candidate, he knows that the interviewer is not offering the respect of a face-to-face introduction. If the candidate uses a wheelchair, also maintain eye contact but don't stand over the person's wheelchair for an extended period. Move to an area where you can sit. The two of you need to speak at eye level to avoid neck discomfort for the candidate—try talking to someone for several minutes with your head arched back. Of course, a prolonged standing conversation with any candidate is unnecessary.

Physical contact with candidates includes shaking the person's hand in greeting. The interviewer should always outstretch a hand for the candidate to grasp. If the candidate has a visual impairment, you may need to take his hand or he may have already extended his hand in anticipation of your handshake. If the candidate has a disability that involves her arms or hands, still extend your hand in greeting. If she doesn't respond, take your hand back and don't worry about it. If the candidate's right arm or hand is unable to move, he may shake with the left hand. If the individual uses a prosthesis and extends that for shaking, then shake it. The important action here is to extend your arm naturally, and to handle this step with common courtesy and common sense. Many times the candidate will make the first move regarding a handshake and put the interviewer at ease.

Typically, the interviewer leads the candidate to his office. All interviewing areas should be accessible. If there is an accessibility problem that may affect the candidate, tell her—for example, if the candidate is using crutches and the interview room is quite a distance away. Describe the walk and ask her whether she needs any assistance, or whether this will create a problem for her. Make any accommodations as possible. If the person uses a wheelchair, do not take the chair and steer it to the interview room; he will be able to move it himself. If the person has a visual impairment, don't grab her arm and take her to the location. Ask if she needs assistance and what type of assistance she is comfortable with.

Once in the office, the interviewer directs the candidate to a seat or allows the candidate to select a seat. If the candidate uses a wheelchair, the interviewer may need to make space in the room by moving a chair. The selection of seating for partial visual impairments and hearing impairments may also improve the conversation level. Once seated, you may choose to ask the candidate whether the seating arrangement is okay. If the person uses crutches or a walker, do not remove them. She will want direct access to them.

Remember the objectives of the greeting period: It sets the stage for the remainder of the interview. If that stage is comfortable and positive, the interview should follow suit.

Common Courtesy

If you make a slight mistake when meeting or interviewing a person with a disability, let it pass by. The more you react, the more uncomfortable you will make the candidate. Also, it draws attention to the fact that you are treating this candidate differently from a candidate without a disability. Relax and enjoy the interview as you would with any other candidate.

Don't jump to any conclusions regarding the person's disability and the assistance that person may require, either during the interview or on the job. We have acquired so many stereotypes and received so much misinformation on disabilities that it is important not to fall back on what you *think* is knowledge. Let the candidate take the lead if he requires something different during the interview or on the job.

For example, just because someone you knew who had the same disability (or so you think) needed a certain accommodation, it doesn't mean that this particular candidate needs the same effort. If you want to offer assistance, do so as you would assist anyone. If the person refuses assistance, let it go. Don't force your help on anyone. It only adds to the problem. Step back from the circumstance and ask yourself: Would you behave this way if the person did not have a disability? If not, don't do it.

Don't assume that a person cannot perform a task or do a job just because she has an apparent disability. A person who appears totally blind may have partial vision and may be able to read independently using magnifying equipment. An interviewer would be doing the candidate a gross disservice by assuming that she could not perform reading duties.

Don't assume that a person with one disability has other disabilities. It is common for people to talk louder to a blind person. Why would you assume that person has a hearing impairment? Some people assume that people with disabilities also have a mental impairment. Don't judge a person's mental capacity or other abilities based on a stereotype. Let each individual be himself. Let each person show what he can do rather than focusing on what he cannot do.

Don't be afraid of people with disabilities. Don't assume they are more fragile than others. Don't judge them differently during the candidate evaluation process. The person with a disability must meet the same qualifications as a candidate without disabilities. And don't feel sorry for the person with the disability. No one wants your pity. This especially applies to someone whose background and qualifications have gotten her this far in the interview.

Don't treat people with disabilities like children unless they are children. People know when they are being talked down to, and they dislike it. Just because a person has a disability it does not mean you should speak differently to him than to anyone else; it shows a lack of respect for the person. When interviewing someone who has mental retardation, you may use smaller words and ask more direct questions, but do not talk down to or for the person.

If you think you misunderstood someone or she misunderstood you, *don't* ignore it. Ask her to repeat what she said so that you can understand her. Confirm whether she heard what you said. It will not upset a candidate if you ask her to repeat something or for clarification—it shows your interest in what she has to say. Effective communication and trust are keys to a successful interview. If the candidate's answer is unimportant, then you shouldn't be interviewing. Show respect by getting all the information you need to make a hiring decision. Also, make sure the candidate has all the information she needs to determine whether she wants to work for your company.

If a person has difficulty speaking, whether owing to a speech disorder or nervousness, never speak for him. Do not complete a person's sentence. Do not finish his words or his thoughts. Be patient. Let him set the pace for his own speaking. If it is easier to ask more yes and no questions than you originally planned, do so. But don't limit the quality of the interview and avoid probing questions because of your impatience with a person who may not speak as quickly as yourself.

Disability Etiquette

Wheelchair Etiquette

When considering how to handle a person's wheelchair, the best response is not to handle it at all. Think of the person's wheelchair as an extension of his body. Do not rest on it. Do not push it without asking whether the person needs your assistance. Don't force your assistance on anyone. He knows how to control his wheelchair and his own movement. Do not move the wheelchair out of reach of the person using the chair.

As regards the person using the wheelchair, do not assume she has any other disabilities besides the need for a wheelchair. Don't talk down to the person as though she also has a mental impairment. Don't try to guess the reason for the person's use of the wheelchair, either. People use wheelchairs for a variety of reasons. Do not pat the person in the wheelchair on the shoulder or head. This is extremely demeaning.

When speaking to a person in a wheelchair for any length of time, sit down and communicate at eye level. If someone is pushing the person's wheelchair, talk directly to the person in the chair and not through the person pushing. Don't be afraid of saying things like, "Let's walk this way to my office." Using everyday language does not bring attention to the person's disability. In fact, it shows that you are comfortable with the person.

Etiquette for a Person with a Hearing Impairment

There are many levels and types of hearing impairments, so don't make any assumptions regarding a person's abilities. Chances are you have interviewed many people with hearing impairments and weren't aware of it. If a person does not respond or turn around when you call him, he may not be ignoring you—he may not hear you. Try to get the person's attention visually by waving a hand or tapping the person gently on the shoulder.

Different people with hearing impairments have learned different methods for communicating with hearing people. They use sign language, read lips, or use written language to communicate. If the hearing loss is obvious, you may politely ask the individual how she would like to have the interview conducted. If the individual prefers to use an interpreter, most likely she will have asked the company to provide an interpreter prior to the interview or she will have brought one along. If you use an interpreter, remember to direct all eye contact and conversation to the candidate and not to the interpreter.

If the person will be lipreading or speech reading, there are many considerations. First, it is important to recognize that only three out of ten spoken words are clearly visible. Therefore, it is your responsibility to make sure the candidate gets your message and can answer your interview questions. Speak only when you are in a position where the person can see you. Position yourself about three to six feet in front of the person. Don't sit or stand with your back to a light, window, or mirror; the glare makes it difficult for lipreaders. Look directly at the person when speaking. Speak at a calm, regular rate without raising your voice. Avoid extremes that exaggerate your lip movements. Don't eat, drink, chew, smoke, or cover your mouth when speaking. Also, don't pace or walk around the room. It is difficult to read the lips of a moving target.

Because not all of your words are visible, the speech reader must guess at some of your words. Additionally, he cannot hear how you change your tone of voice or how you accentuate certain words. This communication gap must be overcome for an effective interview to take place. It is the interviewer's responsibility to ensure that the person with a hearing impairment understands every interview question. Do not rush through the questions. Use natural hand gestures and facial expressions as part of your communication. Watch the person's facial expression to see whether he understands what you have said. If repeating the sentence or phrase doesn't work, select different wording or shorter sentences. Don't keep repeating the same unreadable words—it only adds to the frustration. Have paper and pencil available in case written communication is needed.

If you have difficulty understanding a deaf person's speech, ask the person to repeat what she's saying. If you still have difficulty understanding, ask her to write down the word or phrase. The important point is that you want to be sure to get equal information from each candidate you interview. You are showing your respect and interest in the candidate by asking her to repeat her statement.

Never pretend to understand. This is not only profoundly rude but defeats the purpose of the interview. During the interview you will get more accustomed to the individual's speech patterns. Don't get impatient or try to speed up the interview.

Etiquette for People Who Are Vision Impaired

As with other disabilities, vision impairment can take many forms and levels. Some people have partial vision while others have no vision at all. You will not be able to tell what level of vision a candidate has, so don't try to guess or make assumptions. When greeting a person with a visual impairment, it is best to initiate some physical contact to let the person know you are addressing him. If you just start talking, the person may not respond, not knowing whether you are directing the conversation to him.

If you are calling out someone's name in a reception area or human resources waiting room, the person will respond. Introduce yourself and mention your title so that the candidate knows whom she is speaking with. You will then need to direct her to the interview room. Ask the candidate whether she needs any assistance. If she does not, don't force it on her. She knows her abilities. If she would like your assistance leading her to the interview room, ask her how she would best like you to assist. Never grab the arm of a visually impaired person, push her, or pull her to a location. This is dangerous and rude.

Generally, the candidate will request that you walk half a step ahead of her with your arm bent. She will hold on to the back of your elbow and follow your movements. Help the person who is moving through new territory by describing changes in the terrain and slowing down at intersections, turns, or steps. For example, your conversation may go as follows: "We are leaving the waiting room and entering the corridor to go to the human resources offices. I am pausing because there are three steps up to reach the next level. We're at the top of the stairs and will turn right. The flooring is changing to carpeting. We are turning left into my office. There is a chair alongside my desk on your right."

Then you would place your arm on the back of the chair, allowing the person to feel the chair and determine the height of the back and seat. If the person uses a cane, do not remove the cane or place the cane out of reach of the candidate. You can offer a suggestion for a convenient location for the cane so that it is not in the way of someone else walking by. The rest of your conversation becomes common sense and common courtesy. Your job is to make the person comfortable for the interview.

If the person uses a guide dog, there are several rules. Never touch a guide dog wearing its harness because the dog is "on duty." Do not distract the dog in any fashion from its job of providing sight to the person. Do not question a guide dog's presence in your office building. Guide dogs are allowed in all public places including restaurants. Don't ask the dog's name before you ask the candidate's name. Don't welcome the dog before you welcome the candidate. Show courtesy to the candidate.

Remember that the visually impaired person may not be able to see your facial expressions or your hand movements. Be specific in the descriptions you give. Don't say, "The secretary's desk is ahead and to the left." Quantify wherever possible, such as, "The secretary's desk is five feet in front of you and two steps to the left." When describing something on a desk or a plate, it is often useful to use clock terms such as, "The keyboard is at 3:00 and the telephone is at 10:00."

As you speak, listen to your tone of voice. Try to put expression in it to help the person visualize what you are describing. Put a smile in your voice when greeting the person. If you are meeting this same candidate at a later time, reintroduce yourself, providing your name and title once again. Don't assume that after one meeting the person will remember you from your voice. If the greeting is in another setting, your meeting will be out of context. This makes it even more important that you don't embarrass the person by not introducing yourself.

If you plan to distribute a job description, company benefits booklet, or other written material during or at the completion of the interview, you may need to plan how to accommodate the applicant with a visual impairment. If you know about the disability in advance of the interview, when you set up the interview ask the candidate how he would like the information shared. Offer different options such as a version in Braille or on tape, or provide someone to read it. Perhaps he would like the information in advance of the interview, if that is possible. If during the interview you read the job description item by item, make sure you read it clearly. Number items for easier comprehension and ask whether he would like you to repeat the information for better retention.

Etiquette Regarding Speech Impairments

There are a variety of disabilities that may affect speech clarity. Some of these may accompany other disabilities or may be totally independent. Speech disabilities could include stuttering, slurring, or slowness of speech. Do not hurry along someone with a speech disability. Do not finish her words, thoughts, or sentences. Be patient, listen, and confirm that you understand what she is saying. If you do not understand certain words or phrases, politely ask her to repeat those words you did not catch. Repeat the words if understood. If still not understood, either ask the person to repeat it again or, if appropriate, to write the words down.

If you are aware that the candidate has a speech impairment prior to the interview, schedule additional interview time if you believe it will be necessary. This will lessen the pressure of an otherwise tight time frame. The extra time will give you the opportunity to listen rather than watch the clock.

Etiquette for People with Manual Impairments

People with carpal tunnel syndrome, missing digits or limbs, multiple sclerosis, cerebral palsy, or paralysis may have impairments that prohibit or limit manual dexterity. Earlier in this chapter I discussed greeting these individuals and extending your hand in welcome. If the person returns his hand, do not squeeze the hand excessively. Provide a gentle, firm handshake. If the person does not return the handshake, do not presume this to be rude. Just continue with your introduction.

Manual dexterity may become an issue when considering the performance of essential functions of the job and when conducting pre-screening tests, such as typing tests. As you discuss job tasks or screening tests, provide an opening in the discussion to allow the candidate to ask for an accommodation or to describe or show you how he would perform the task.

Etiquette for Candidates with Mental Retardation

As with other people, do not make assumptions about the capabilities of those with mental retardation. Introduce yourself and explain the format and content of the interview. Cluster the interview into sequenced groups for the candidate to follow. For example, "To start off the interview we will talk about what jobs you have had. First, we will talk about what you did in the jobs. Next, we will talk about what you liked about those jobs."

Provide the candidate with the opportunity to show or explain whether he is able to learn or perform the tasks required of a job. When explaining job functions, speak as you normally would to other candidates but use clear, concrete, specific language. Showing the candidate pictures or touring the work site may help the person with mental retardation to better understand the tasks.

Do not talk down to candidates with mental retardation or treat them like children. Do not finish their sentences for them. Give positive reinforcement during the interview. This doesn't mean telling the person she has the job. But you can reinforce good answers and good experience. Pay attention to your voice tone and articulation. Avoid unnecessary distractions during the interview.

Don't describe job responsibilities abstractly. Break down concepts and tasks into components and singular steps. Repeat the steps as necessary. Repetition may help the person with mental retardation retain the information.

Etiquette for People with Learning Disabilities

Three primary learning disabilities are dyslexia (a reading disorder), discalculia (a mathematical disorder), and aphasia (a language disorder). People with learning disabilities generally are of average intelligence or above, however they don't learn by the teaching methods typically applied in schools and businesses.

If you are aware of a person's learning disability, you may be able to assist by providing job information in writing, drawings of tasks, or modeling tasks. Showing the candidate the work site could be beneficial to help the person with a learning disability better understand the job tasks.

Try to avoid extraneous interruptions and other concentration breakers. Repeat the information you gave to see whether he understood you. Repeat the candidate's response if you think it needs clarification.

*   *   *   *

When interviewing and working with people with disabilities, remember that it is not your responsibility to understand the disability. You don't need to know the specifics of the impairment, how it occurred, and what it affects. What you do need to know is how to respond to the disability, how to interview and assess the person fairly, and how to make sure that you are evaluating him fairly.

Many public and private resources are available in every community to assist employers in the employment of people with disabilities. Use these resources to assist you in understanding how to effectively communicate both in the interview and on the job.

A Simple Discrimination Test

There are so many myths about minority groups that need to be dispelled. The same applies to people with disabilities. We need to examine the myths and replace them with truth.

There's a simple test to help you determine whether you are discriminating against a person with a disability. Write down the thought, sentence, or stereotype on a piece of paper. For example,

"I hired a *deaf* person once, but it didn't work out."

We know this statement reflects a general assumption. There are people who feel that since they had a negative experience with one member of a minority group, then a similar experience with anyone else in that group will produce the same result.

Now, remove the word *deaf* and replace it with another type of group, such as bald people.

"I hired a *bald* person once, but it didn't work out."

Does this make sense? Try using other adjectives to determine whether you generalize in other areas. How about tall? Short? Blue-eyed? If you get stuck on a fear or mired in a generalization, use this discrimination test to see if your concern is valid. Then go back and reconsider the candidate.

Chapter 9

The ADA-Compliant Interview

Why is an ADA-compliant interview so important? One reason is that the interview is a point of discrimination vulnerability. During the interview process, a company's management style, interview style, organizational structure, and selection methods are exposed to the public. The business is especially visible to the people applying for employment. Applicants get a firsthand view of how a company operates its selection process. If a rejected applicant from a protected minority group perceives that a company is unfair in its interview methods, the company is in trouble: The applicant can file a discrimination charge.

Avoiding a Lawsuit

Managers are concerned about discrimination charges because of the organizational and financial ramifications of being sued for discrimination, whether or not the company is found guilty of discrimination. A company notified of a discrimination charge has considerable work ahead to defend itself against the charge. That work includes research into the circumstances of the case, interviews of the employees involved and possible observers, a search of records for examples of nondiscrimination, reviews of policies and adherence to policies, and consultations with legal experts. The company pays for the legal expertise and the lost work hours spent on the case. And this is just the beginning. If the case goes to trial, related time and financial expenses to the company can be even more extensive.

If the courts find an employer guilty of discrimination in its hiring process, they will also determine the compensatory damages the employer must pay. First, the court can require the company to hire the person for the original position. This reinstatement or new hire can severely impact the company's morale. The financial penalties may include retroactive wages, retroactive seniority status, and re-imbursement for the person's legal fees and expenses.

Prior to the Civil Rights Act of 1991, this was the extent of a company's obligations. However, with the introduction of the Civil Rights Act of 1991, a claimant can also sue an employer for punitive damages related to the discrimination. The maximum amount an individual can receive for both punitive and compensatory damage awards is $300,000.

So when we ask ourselves, Why should we consider compliance with the ADA in the interviewing process? we should be asking, What manager wants to be responsible for costing his company $300,000 because he failed to interview properly?

Actually, opening yourself and your company up to a potential discrimination suit is pretty easy. Just follow these *not*-recom-mended selection tips:

Don'ts of Interviewing

- Make snap judgments about a candidate.
- Be overtly uncomfortable and unprofessional when meeting or interviewing a person with a disability (or someone from any other protected group).
- Ask questions that are irrelevant to the specifics of the job in question.
- Show candidates a lack of respect.
- Start the interview late.
- Appear to not be listening.
- Shortchange the candidate's interview time.
- Hire the person you like the best, the one most like you, rather than the most qualified person for the job.

On the other hand, you will have few concerns regarding dis-crimination charges if in your interviews you follow these recom-mended tips:

Do's of Interviewing

- Outline the essential job functions and identify the job's cor-responding skills, required knowledge, and abilities.
- Prepare a list of interview questions based on the essential functions and qualifications for the job.
- Establish good rapport with the candidate during the inter-view.

- Respond positively and comfortably to any requests for interview or potential on-the-job accommodations.
- Explore each individual's skills and abilities thoroughly.
- Listen well to the candidate's presentation of her work experience.
- Interview each candidate as identically as possible, asking the same questions, focusing on the same key qualifications.
- Take useful notes throughout the interview.
- Thoroughly complete candidate evaluation forms on each interviewed candidate.
- Select the candidate who best satisfies the qualifications.
- Call or correspond with all interviewed candidates regarding the hiring decision.

Another way to avoid discrimination charges is to take the initiative in ensuring that all company interviewers handle their selection efforts responsibly. It takes only one person asking about day care, marital status, religious holidays, ethnic origin, or "by the way, how did you become disabled?" to ruin a company's record of good employment practices. If you supervise interviewers, make sure your employees are interviewing properly. To do this:

- Periodically sit in and observe interviews run by others.
- Schedule refresher sessions for your employees that offer interviewing skills. Include a section on legal and effective note-taking techniques.
- Read their list of interview questions before the interviews begin.
- If two of you are interviewing candidates, plan your interview strategies together. Coordinate the questions. Avoid overlapping questions to save time. However, repeat questions in key areas as an information double-check.
- Remind interviewers to complete the interview evaluation form thoroughly.
- Read each evaluation form after the interview.
- Discuss each candidate's strengths and weaknesses based on the information collected.
- Hold your employees accountable for meeting your interview standards.
- Include your employees in the hiring decision. Show them where you found their input valuable and explain any gaps in candidate information gathering.

- Create a selection file to reference the next time the position becomes vacant.
- Follow all the same interview procedures yourself. Critique yourself periodically and remind yourself that you must adhere to the same high-quality standards of interviewing.
- Be an interviewing role model.

One of the fundamentals of the ADA is that employers hire the best qualified person for the job. While this has been employers' intention all along, they could legally exclude and ignore certain groups of qualified individuals. Now, for the first time, they must consider qualified applicants who have a disability. This opens a previously untapped applicant pool. It also requires that companies consider qualified people who may not have been considered before because of bias or fear. The ADA introduces a new group of people into our offices—a group of people who were slowly joining companies, but not at a pace fast enough to keep them from being the poorest minority group in the United States.

The best way to effectively welcome this new group of qualified candidates is to view them as you would any other candidate. Offer people with disabilities the same interview that everyone else gets. Don't treat people with disabilities as special or different. Just greet, meet, and seat them, then fulfill the objectives of the interview. Ask the best questions to get the pertinent job-related information. Then use this information to determine whether these candidates have the skills and abilities to perform the jobs to the company's standards.

Guaranteeing a Fair Interview

The successful ADA-compliant interview will follow a structured format consisting of a formal list of questions to ask every candidate for the position. The structure also requires you to prepare in advance a list of questions specific to each candidate's background. The structure has you allocating specific time for each discussion area. It also provides for responsible note taking and recording of facts that relate to each candidate's ability to perform the job. This structure reinforces the thoroughness of the interview. It provides assurance that you have collected all the information you need to make an effective hiring decision.

That sounds tough. People's first response to interview structure relates to its connotation of rigidity. However, you need to see the interview structure as a benefit and an advantage to your efforts. The structure frees you to relax and enjoy the interview. You can listen better to the candidate. You can identify key points to record in your notes. You can focus on what the candidate is saying and how he says it. By developing structure, you create a greater informational flow that benefits both the candidate and the interviewer. The candidate knows he has had a fair opportunity to present himself and why he is best for the job. You will know that the information you received from the candidate is complete.

To comply with the ADA, you need to focus the interview questions on the essential functions of the job and on the skills and qualifications tied to those functions. While you may ask the candidate questions related to nonessential functions, remember that a decision to hire one person over another cannot be based on the ability to perform nonessential functions. It's nice to determine who can perform everything on the job description and more; however, when it comes to deciding who is the most qualified, you can consider only essential functions.

How Do You Know Who Has a Disability?

There is no circumstance before, during, or after the interview where it is legal to ask, "Do you have a disability?" Now, if that's the case, how do you know who has a disability?

The simple answer is that you don't. Some disabilities are more visible than others. If someone is in a wheelchair, the only thing you know about the person is that at this time he isn't walking. You don't know why he is using a wheelchair. You don't know whether the person can stand or walk with assistance. You don't know if his disability is permanent or temporary. You don't know whether the current immobility is due to a spinal problem or to recent foot surgery. You don't know whether he is protected under the ADA. So don't rely on what you see or jump to any conclusions regarding what you think you know.

What is more common are the many disabilities that are invisible. There is no way to know whether someone has diabetes, a heart condition, a back ailment, carpal tunnel syndrome, head trauma, a respiratory condition, or epilepsy. Yet each of these could be a disability under the ADA if the illness affects an individual's major life function. In fact, it is highly likely that several employees at your company have disabilities that are invisible to the observer. If they have not brought that disability to your attention or not requested an accommodation, the ADA still protects them. There is no legal requirement for the disabled person to notify you of a disability. So your concern should be the same as for any employee: ensuring that the individual performs the responsibilities of the job.

Which Candidates Do You Ask the Detailed Ability Questions?

Now what do you do about interviewing people with disabilities? You figure that if you identify an applicant with a disability, then you will ask all the right, detailed questions. Otherwise, you'll use the usual ad lib questions for candidates without a disability. Wrong! Lawsuit time. You must ask detailed questions of *every* candidate you interview.

It makes no difference who has a disability, whether you know about a disability, or if you must provide a job accommodation. This information is irrelevant to the interview and hiring decision. Just because an interviewer conducts an interview, she does not have the right to acquire privileged, private information about a candidate's disability. The interviewer does have the right and obligation to learn about each candidate's ability.

Since the need to know who has a disability is irrelevant, you need to conduct all interviews for a particular position alike. If you have selected five final candidates, the five interviews should be almost identical regarding questions asked. These mirror-image, structured interviews eliminate the chance of discrimination because your questions focus on candidate experience and knowledge. Your behavior, your questions, and the depth of information you collect should not fluctuate between candidates.

Consider how you may discriminate when you alter interviews based on assumptions about a disability. For example, suppose you conduct an in-depth one-hour interview with Candidate V who has a visible disability. You have a thirty-minute interview with Candidate W who has no obvious disabilities. Both candidates have similar professional background and skills that qualified them to interview. These interviews will be the deciding factor in determining whom to hire.

Scenario 1: You determine that Candidate V with the disability has the best qualifications for the job. You hire this person. Do you have a discrimination problem? Since you did not conduct as thorough an interview with Candidate W, you have not given the second candidate an equal chance to show you all of his qualifications. However, this is not illegal unless the second candidate is a member of another protected minority group.

Scenario 2: You decide to hire Candidate W, the person with no visible disability. Is there cause for alarm? Possibly. The rejected Candidate V may perceive the long interview as your attempt to discover performance weaknesses and to set up a situation whereby you don't have to hire her. You took the time to explore her experience and dig into her strengths, weaknesses, abilities, and inabilities. Since you know about the person's disability, she believes you intentionally let her hang herself. Now Candidate V claims discrimination and wants you to prove that you interviewed the two candidates fairly. You clearly didn't get as much information from the second candidate. How are you going to prove that the person you hired was better qualified when the level and quantity of documentation for the two candidates are not equal?

Consistency is the solution. Conduct a consistent interview with every qualified candidate. Ask the same questions. Explore the same issues. Take the same quality of notes. This will help eliminate any concern over whether you discriminated in the interview process. Whether a person's disability is visible or invisible is irrelevant to nondiscriminatory interviewing and employee selection. By being thorough and consistent you will always have enough interview information to make an effective hiring decision. Also, you will have thorough interview documentation on each candidate as evidence to support your hiring decision.

Who May Need Accommodation on the Job?

You can't say to a candidate, "Since you have an obvious disability, what accommodations do you need?" However, the ADA does permit you to ask, "Can you describe or show me how you would perform this task with or without accommodation?" This is a legal interview question. At first glance, the question seems to target people with disabilities. Remember, in the structured interview you should ask the same questions of each candidate. So this question may force someone with a disability to explain a limitation or an accommodation need. It also allows her to explain how she doesn't need an accommodation. She may describe how she circumvents the limitation and can perform the duty unassisted.

It is irrelevant whether a person's disability is obvious, invisible, or nonexistent. If you have concerns about the candidate's job performance, his answers provide you with the details necessary for making the hiring decision. Either a person knows how to perform the task or he doesn't. If a person does not have a disability and you ask this question, you still benefit. The result of asking this question to a nondisabled individual is that you acquire a graphic description of how he performs the task. If the person cannot explain how to perform the task, then you have also received important information.

Think back to previous interviews. How many times have you asked a candidate whether she can perform a particular function and gotten a positive answer? When it came time for her to perform, you discover she understood the concept but couldn't really put it into action. If you had asked, "Can you describe for me how you would perform this task with or without accommodation?" you would have had your answer during the interview and not after she was hired.

The key ADA-compliant question to ask is *"Can you describe or show me how you would perform this task with or without accommodation?"* When you prepare the interview questions, be sure each essential job task described to the candidate includes this question. It is legal and gives you valuable information on the person's understanding of the job.

Don't forget to include the phrase "with or without accommodation." This phrase frees the person needing an accommodation to discuss the accommodation. The candidate might otherwise be hesitant to share this need with you. Your phrasing can be a relief to the candidate who does not want to just come out and say, "Oh, by the way, I need an amplifier on my phone so that I am sure to hear every caller clearly." You help the candidate feel safer about disclosing an accommodation need; the effort also corresponds with the interviewer's objective of making the candidate comfortable enough in the interview to portray a full picture of her job-related capabilities.

The Right Questions to Ask

The best guarantee for interviewing consistently is to review the detailed job description and jot down the primary objectives of the interview based on that job description. Then establish a template for what you want to accomplish in the interview and what information you want to elicit from each candidate. Start off by using the outline of interview components found in Chapter 7. Establish a flow that is comfortable for your interviewing style.

With the template and the ADA-compliant job description side by side, start brainstorming your interview questions and write them down as they come to mind. Create questions that probe and prompt the candidate to offer details about experience and knowledge. (Refer to Chapter 7 for tips on developing interview questions.) Merge this list with the candidate-specific questions you created based on the candidate's resumé.

Once you complete your first draft of questions, review it and discard those that are repetitive or shallow. Organize the questions into a logical sequence. Be comfortable with all the questions. Rewrite any uncomfortably worded questions. Practice saying them out loud until they flow naturally.

Determine how long to interview each candidate. Also estimate the time each interview segment will take. Make sure the length of each segment reflects the importance of the corresponding performance item for the job. Don't forget to include time in each segment for exploratory questions. The more you interview, the easier it will be to estimate the length of time it takes to answer each question.

Stick to your prepared questions and your structured format, and you won't go wrong. Remember, the questions are your interview base, but there will be times when you need to explore a particular point with the candidate. Be very careful! You can go off track by adding questions that are irrelevant to the job. Once you lose control of the interview and veer from your plan, you can get into discrimination trouble. You also lose valuable time for gathering job-related information. The more "personal" or "individual" you get in your questioning, the less professional will be your answers. Keep the questions focused on how the candidate's experience relates to the job opening. While some of the extraneous information is interesting and can provide insights into the person, your planned questions should do the same *and* be job-relevant.

Avoid slanting any questions differently for some applicants. When you change the wording of your questions, you change the answers you'll receive. And it is difficult, then, to make valid comparisons. If your interview becomes more personal with one candidate, that candidate may be at a disadvantage because he lost the opportunity to provide pertinent job information; those side questions may have provided irrelevant and possibly illegal personal information. For example, if the conversation moves toward family life, you may discover details that are irrelevant to the job but that bias you. The further you stay away from this information, the safer and better the interview. No one can say you are biased against Candidate X if you didn't know he had *x* disability.

What NOT to Ask

From an ADA perspective, there are many areas to avoid. The key is to avoid any questions related to:

- A current disability
- A previous disability
- Changes in a disability
- How the disability occurred
- The nature of the disability
- The prognosis of a disability
- The severity of a disability
- The disability of a relative
- Disability-related volunteer work
- Absences due to illness
- Previous illnesses or hospitalization
- Workers' compensation accidents or illnesses
- Absences owing to workers' compensation
- Disabled veteran status (affirmative action employers may inquire on a sheet separate from the job application)
- Why a person cannot perform a job function
- Why the candidate needs an accommodation
- Anticipated absences for medical treatment
- Friends or relatives with disabilities
- Drug or alcohol problems

If you have any doubt whether a question is legal, don't ask it. If the question relates directly to a job skill or qualification, phrase it in terms of the job rather than the disability. For example, suppose a candidate mentions a recent car accident and physical therapy treatment. Do not comment on the accident or its possible impact on performing the duties of the job. When you get to the segment of your structured interview describing the physical requirements of the job, then you can discuss ability to perform the specific task.

For example, you may say, "Mail room clerks lift several bags of mail weighing thirty-five to fifty pounds. They pick up and drop off mail from the loading dock twice a day. Can you perform this function with or without accommodation? If so, describe for me how you would do it." The candidate might ask for more information about the task, such as how far to move the mail or whether hand trucks are available. The candidate might describe how she performed this task in the past and what accommodation she used following her accident. She may add that she can lift and carry seventy-five pounds for a distance of fifty feet without difficulty. For any longer distances, she would prefer to use a hand cart or dolly to speed the delivery time. You did not inquire as to the disability and she can respond without having to detail a disability if one exists. The important thing is that you have the answer you need without exploring the sensitive and potentially dangerous issue of an actual disability. You controlled the interview and explored job requirements. (Refer to Appendix A for other questions to avoid in accordance with Equal Employment Opportunity law.)

Proper Documentation

Note taking is critical. Since our memories frequently fail to provide us with the details of a one-hour interview and a person's complete work history, we must rely on tools. As discussed in Chapter 7, be sure that your interview questions and note taking complement the resumé rather than repeat it. If your notes are more effective written on a form or on your list of questions, use the system that works best for you. It is vital that between your memory and your notes you recap as much information as possible about each candidate. After the interview, record this information on an interview evaluation form. Both documents along with the job description can serve as evidence of a fair hiring decision, should a discrimination suit ever occur.

Focus your notes on the person's abilities and experience related to the job. People are accustomed to taking notes in classes or seminars. Out of habit, you may just start writing and taking notes for the sake of note taking. The interview is not the time to take expansive notes. Interview notes should be abbreviations, phrases, and concise mini-sentences. The less you write, the more you can listen, and the less distracting your writing will be to the candidate. The objective is to write key words that will later jog your memory and help you complete the interview evaluation form.

Be sure to take notes throughout the interview. Don't listen so hard that you forget the importance of your notes. Write consistently. Be careful what you write. Make sure you don't use anything that even slightly resembles a coding system regarding candidate traits. Years ago people coded applications for race, gender, and appearance. This is highly discriminatory and should not occur. Do not take notes on the person's resumé or application. Write all notes on a separate piece of paper.

Another important note-taking point concerns documenting the existence of a disability or need for accommodation. Do not make any assumptions regarding the disability or why the person may need an accommodation. For example, don't try to label the person's disability if the candidate has not specified the disability. Record the person's exact description or words, but don't write a diagnosis of the disability. If during the interview you discuss accommodations for a person using a wheelchair, note the facts of the discussion. Write: "wheelchair—requires desk raised to height of 33 inches." Do not be creative. Do not guess the disability. Do not expound on what the person told you. Be brief and to the point. It raises fewer questions and avoids any appearance that you are judging or interpreting.

Watch Your Assumptions!

Be careful not to get caught up trying to assess the why's and what's behind a person's nonverbal behavior. Our society places high value on such things as posture, eye contact, clear speech, and a firm handshake. However, some of these nonverbal criteria are not valid when interviewing and hiring people with disabilities. For example, someone with a back problem may not be able to carry himself or sit with the posture you expect. A candidate with mental retardation may not be comfortable with sustained eye contact. Open yourself to the possibility that the reason a person doesn't fit your nonverbal stereotype may be unrelated to poor job performance. Be open-minded and aware.

*   *   *   *

In conclusion, remember that the more frequently you interview, the simpler the structuring of your interviews becomes. Once you have practiced identifying the objectives of each interview segment and directing questions to that objective, you will see the benefits of consistently applying an organized interview technique. The method will become increasingly effective. The more practice you have taking notes specific to job functions and qualifications, the easier it will be to recap the interview and describe the candidate to those not present during the interview. The interview is your primary information-gathering source. The more structured the interview, the more detailed your information, the better prepared you are for making a hiring decision. Note, to put theory into practice, read the typical interviews in Chapter 10 and decide how well they meet ADA requirements.

Chapter 10

Sample Interviews

There are many ways to conduct an interview, some more effective than others. Also, some methods are more ADA-compliant than others. Your objective is to make sure your interview methods and those of your peers and employees are both effective and ADA-compliant. An error in either of these circumstances will affect you directly. An ineffective interview can lead to selecting an ineffective employee. And a non–ADA-compliant interview can result in considerable financial expense for your company.

This chapter presents three interviews. Classique's Department Store has a position open for a Sales Associate. The job description developed in Chapter 4 forms the basis for the interview questions. As you go through each interview, make note of questions and conversations that are appropriate and inappropriate. Make special note of those that comply with the ADA and those that present potential discrimination problems.

When reading the three interviews, assume that the same candidate is interviewed in each scenario.

Interview 1: Sales Associate

Interviewer:	Welcome to Classique's Department Store. My name is Herman Rhesus and I am the Personnel Manager at this location of Classique's.
Sue:	Hello, I'm Sue Ewe.
Herman:	Is this your first visit to our store?
Sue:	No, this isn't my first visit. I've shopped here many times. I found your sales staff to be so friendly, I decided to see what employment opportunities may be available.
Herman:	That sounds great. We have 120 Sales Associates at our store. Each one works hard to ensure that our customers keep coming back. Let me take a look at your application

form and see what kind of experience you are bringing to us.

Hmmm. I see you graduated from Imperial High School several years ago. That isn't one of the regular local high schools. Isn't that a special school for kids who can't hear?

Sue: Well, yes. It's a high school serving students with a variety of hearing impairments. I graduated with honors. It's a great school offering traditional academic classes as well as some basic career-focused courses in secretarial, accounting, and retail sales. I took the sales classes.

Herman: I guess I don't understand how you can hear me if you went to this school for the deaf.

Sue: I wear hearing devices in each ear and can lip-read very well. Most people don't realize I have a hearing impairment. In fact—

Herman: Okay, let's move on with the interview. I see here that you worked as a sales clerk at two other stores before you applied for this job. Did your deafness cause a problem in serving customers?

Sue: I provide excellent service to every customer. Frequently, my customers sent in recognition letters remarking on the quality of my service skills. I also received Employee of the Month twice at each company. I think that because my hearing improves when I face each customer, this attentiveness helps me work closely with the client and meet her shopping needs.

Herman: Oh. Well, how did you become deaf?

Sue: I was born with a partial hearing impairment. When I was an infant, my parents noticed that I wasn't responding to different noises. Our family doctor identified the impairment.

Herman: Do you need to be absent from work frequently for medical treatment?

Sue: No. Not at all. I am very healthy. I have had nearly perfect attendance both at school and at my jobs.

Herman: Well, that's good. Returning to the Sales Associate job, what do you like about selling?

Sue: I have always sold casual clothing to women. I enjoy meeting people's shopping needs by suggesting items and helping fit them correctly. I have an eye for what

	looks good on people. I think they appreciate that when they're making clothing purchases.
Herman:	This job requires that you communicate effectively, use the POS terminal, hang and arrange merchandise, and operate a telephone. I think the communication and telephone requirements are going to be a problem for you. What do you think?
Sue:	Since I've worked in a large department store before, I have learned how to stay aware and notice customers approaching me from out of my range of hearing. I do have some hearing and have always been around hearing people, so my communication skills are excellent. I can also use a telephone if the receiver has an amplifier on it. So neither should be a problem.
Herman:	I just don't know. I'm not sure how the supervisor will react. Let me think about this some more. We have other candidates to interview for this position. Once we complete those interviews, I'll get back to you. Is that okay?

How do you think this interview went? Let us hope that no one would be so blatantly uncomfortable with a person's disability and unaware of the extent of illegal questions being asked. However, think about whether there's someone at your company who may ask one or two of these questions. Would that person ask the same type of questions but indirectly? Both direct and indirect questions about a person's disability are illegal.

The first interviewing issue arises when Herman begins to read Sue's application form during the interview as if he had never seen it before. He must have only skimmed the application ahead of the interview. Otherwise, based on Herman's perspective, he would have seen the school's name and immediately discarded the application. He never would have interviewed someone who attended a school for the hearing impaired. Of course, screening out applications that denote or imply a disability is illegal according to the ADA.

Herman's behavior also tells us that he does not understand or is totally unaware of the Americans with Disabilities Act requirements for fair interviewing. He asked questions specifically aimed at exploring the candidate's disability. Some of these questions he tried to relate to the job, but they were still discriminatory. He aimed each question toward exposing Sue's inability to perform the job owing to her hearing impairment.

Herman should never have said that he identified the school as one serving people with hearing impairments. Would an interviewer make a similar statement about a school in an ethnic area or a wealthy side of town? "Oh, I see you graduated from Imperial High School several years ago. That isn't one of the regular local high schools. Isn't that school in the neighborhood where all the rich kids live?" The comment is unprofessional and displays the interviewer's prejudgment and bias.

This line of questioning also places the candidate in a very uncomfortable position. She is put on the defensive. In this case, Sue tries to return the interview to its original purpose—discussing her qualifications for the job. However, that is the interviewer's responsibility, not the candidate's.

The candidate may or may not know that this type of questioning is illegal. At minimum, the candidate can see the extreme bias in the interviewer. However, most candidates will not respond angrily or even request that the disability-based line of questioning be stopped. Most candidates trying to secure employment try to stay on the good side of the interviewer.

How many ADA errors did Herman make? He brought up the disability. He asked questions trying to determine the extent of the disability and its effect on the job. He asked personal questions regarding the disability. This led him to jump to the assumption that people with disabilities are going to need medical treatment and will be absent from work.

Herman did not explore the essential functions of the job. He became so side-tracked when he realized that the candidate had a hearing impairment that he barely asked any job-related questions. The question he asked about the candidate's qualifications only addressed those behaviors possibly related to the disability: communicating and using the telephone. Herman prejudged the candidate's abilities and created problem areas where none existed. He even assumed that the supervisor would share his concerns and rudely mentioned them during the interview.

This example is somewhat extreme. However, the bottom line is the same whether these questions take place during a forty-five-minute interview or are thrown at a candidate in ten minutes. The disability is irrelevant to the interview. This interview should focus on determining whether the candidate can perform the essential functions of the Sales Associate position. Herman did not collect any information to help him select the best candidate for the job. In fact, Herman would not even consider this candidate's qualifications because of the depth of his bias. Does Sue have a good EEO case? No question she does.

Interview 2: Sales Associate

Al: Welcome to Classique's Department Store. My name is Al Most and I am the Human Resources Manager at this location of Classique's.

Applicant: Hello, I'm Sue Ewe.

Al: Is this your first visit to our store?

Sue: No, this isn't my first visit. I've shopped here many times. I found your sales staff to be so friendly that I decided to see what employment opportunities may be available.

Al: That sounds great. We have 120 Sales Associates at our store. Each associate works hard to ensure that our customers keep coming back. Let me review your application form to refresh myself on the experience you are bringing to us.

Hmmm. I see you graduated from Imperial High School several years ago. Tell me about your education and how it might help you in this Sales Associate position.

Sue: I really enjoyed high school. I took the traditional high school academic classes. I did best in English and math. The school also offered some basic career-skills courses in secretarial, accounting, and retail sales. I found the sales classes attractive and took as many classes as they offered.

Al: That's interesting. What attracted you to the sales classes?

Sue: I enjoy working closely with people and like to help them. I knew I didn't want to work a desk job as a secretary or accounting clerk. I saw retail sales as a way to meet people and help them solve their purchasing problems.

Al: After you graduated from high school, you started working as a sales clerk at Brandy's Stores. What would you say was your best learning experience while you worked there?

Sue: Since that was my first sales experience, I really learned about how to handle the customers. I learned how to listen to what they were looking for in a product. Along with that, I learned the importance of knowing the merchandise throughout the store so that I could help customers find just the right thing.

Al: Why did you leave Brandy's and why did you choose Kendall's as your next place to work?

Sue: I left Brandy's because I wanted a change from working in a specialty store. I wanted experience in a department store. I figured there would be more opportunity for growth and I would learn more working with a broader line of women's clothing.

Al: Let me tell you about our Sales Associate job here at Classique's Department Store. The Sales Associate helps customers select merchandise, uses the point-of-sale terminal for processing transactions, and merchandises the department. Are these activities you've performed before?

Sue: Yes. I am familiar with POS terminals and have organized and hung merchandise for customer displaying.

Al: Terrific. The Sales Associate also processes telephone orders and does basic housekeeping functions. Will you have any problem doing these?

Sue: No, not really. At both locations, I picked up litter from the floors and straightened merchandise on the racks and counters. It's important to keep the store attractive for customers. At Kendall's, we also had basic security responsibilities. We would need to keep an eye on customers for loss-prevention purposes.

Al: Well, it seems you understand the scope of the sales job. What would your current supervisor say about your performance on the job?

Sue: My department manager would say that I come to work on time. My attendance is nearly perfect. I always complete the tasks assigned, and serve customers well. Several times, my customers sent in letters to my department manager complimenting my customer service skills. I also received the Employee of the Month award twice at each company.

Al: I'm very impressed. You have included your supervisor's name on the application. Do you have any problem with my contacting her?

Sue: No. She will be an excellent reference. We have become friends as well as co-workers. She knows I have an interview here and will be glad to help me advance my retail career.

Al: To wrap up our meeting, we have several more candidates that we'll be interviewing this week. Then I will recommend the top three candidates to our area manager for further interviewing. She will be responsible for the final selection of a Sales Associate. I will call you next week to let you know whether you will be considered further. Thank you for coming in.

How do you think this interview went? It certainly is an improvement over the first interview. This interviewer avoided the pitfalls that the other interviewer experienced and the results are more successful. Al collected basic candidate information to help him make a hiring decision. What did Al do correctly?

- He did not explore the candidate's hearing disability. We don't even know whether he recognized that Sue had a disability. It was not a component of the interview.
- Al's interview had a formula to it. He began with the candidate's school and work history. He explored the aspects of school and work to acquire information related to Sue's performance as a sales associate at Classique's. He described the responsibilities of the job. He had Sue tell him whether she could perform these duties. He got some information on her relationship with her supervisor and informed her that he would be checking references. Lastly, he explained where he was in the hiring process and what the next step would be.

It appears that Al covered his interviewing bases. This type of interview is probably very common in style and content. Many people will look at this interview and say that Al conducted a good interview. But did he truly get enough information during the interview? If the interviewer does not select Sue for the Sales Associate job, does she have grounds to sue for discrimination under the ADA? Did Al get enough information from Sue to defend a discrimination suit?

Al did not get into the detail required of an ADA-compliant job interview. He presented an overview of the responsibilities and requirements of the job, but did not address each essential function of the job. Not only did he fail to mention each job component, he did not ask Sue how she would perform each task with or without accommodation. If he noticed her hearing devices, he did not leave the interview with an idea of how or whether they would impact her performance of the job.

He did not go through each qualification and determine whether she could meet each requirement. He mentioned the need for telephone skills, but did not provide her the opening to ask for an accommodation. Al took a safer tactic by ignoring the disability, but lost out on the opportunity to gain vital accommodation information for Sue's possible first day on the job.

Al also is relying heavily on Sue's self-evaluation. She states that she can perform the job and he responds "terrific." He doesn't offer a method to test her skills, either formally or informally. Al needs to create a test or challenge in the interview to allow the candidate to describe or show some skill level. For the Sales Associate position, the test could involve math skills (returning change to a customer or taking a simple math test) or sales skills (role playing a sales transaction). Al could create several scenarios between a Sales Associate and a customer, and ask Sue how she would handle the situation.

If Al has to prove that he did not discriminate against Sue based on this interview, how would he proceed? Sue could claim that he did not explore the details of the job with her because of her disability. Perhaps he spent more time and got more information from other candidates, thereby helping him select someone without a disability. This relatively superficial interview did not give Sue the opportunity to show how successfully she can perform the job. She didn't have the opportunity to become the best qualified candidate.

The possibility of discrimination did not jump out at us in this interview as it did in Interview 1. However, it is important to remember that only consistent, *thorough,* documented interviews will provide interviewers with the best decision-making information and the best defense for these decisions.

Interview 3: Sales Associate

May: Welcome to Classique's Department Store. My name is May B. Wright and I am the Human Resources Manager at this location of Classique's.

Sally: Hello, I'm Sally S. Pearson. Nice to meet you.

May: Is this your first visit to our store?

Sally: No, this isn't my first visit. I've shopped here many times. I've found your sales staff to be friendly and I like the quality of your merchandise. So I decided to see what sales opportunities might be available.

May: That sounds great. We have 120 Sales Associates at this store.

Each associate works hard to ensure that our customers keep coming back. I'm glad that you're one of them.

Let me tell you a little about us. Classique's is a chain of sixty-five high-quality department stores located in the Midwest, Northeast, and southeastern United States. The company has been in business for thirty years. Our corporate offices reside in this city. This gives us considerable contact with our buyers and senior management. Frequently, corporate headquarters selects us as a test market for new merchandise because of our close proximity to their offices.

We have one full-time and two part-time Sales Associate positions open. You stated on your application your interest in the full-time position.

Sally: Yes. That is correct. I can work flexible hours, and would like to work approximately forty hours each week.

May: That should be no problem. I've read your application and resumé. Your retail background is impressive. First, let's talk about your education. I see you graduated from Imperial High School several years ago. Tell me about your high school experience and how it might help you perform the sales associate position.

Sally: I really enjoyed my high school. I graduated with honors. The school offered a variety of classes. In the traditional academic classes, I did best in English and math. In elective classes, I had the choice between secretarial, accounting, and sales. The sales classes always sounded good, so I took as many classes as they offered.

May: That's interesting. What attracted you to the sales classes?

Sally: I enjoy working closely with people and like to help them. I also enjoy fashion. I knew I didn't want to work in an office setting as a secretary or accounting clerk. I wanted a more active job. Retail sales seemed to be a perfect way to meet people and help them select their wardrobes.

May: During school, was there someone at the school or elsewhere who helped you focus your career in retail sales?

Sally: Funny that you ask that question. Yes, the teacher of the retail class actually worked full time as a clothing buyer. She taught this class on the side to help prepare high school kids for retail jobs. She and I spent a lot of time talking about what it was really like in the stores. I couldn't help getting excited about the work.

May: After you graduated from high school, you worked as a sales clerk at Brandy's Stores. What knowledge and skills did you acquire by working there?

Sally: Since that was my first sales experience, I primarily learned about how to handle the customers. I learned when and how to approach the customers. Some people don't want any help from sales clerks. Others want a constant shopping companion. I figured out how to read some of the customers before approaching them. My introduction is a little different depending on what I can sense about the shopper.

I also learned how to listen to what they were looking for in a product. I won't show customers just anything. I discovered the importance of knowing all the merchandise in the store so that I could help them find just the right thing. I evaluate what they're wearing when they come in the store and what they say they're looking for. Then, I offer them the selection of what we have.

May: It sounds as if you work hard to know your customers and meet their needs. That is something we try to do here as well. Tell me, why did you leave Brandy's and why did you choose Kendall's as your next place to work?

Sally: I left Brandy's because I wanted a change from working in a specialty store. I wanted to experience working in a department store. I figured there would be more opportunity for growth. I also wanted more exposure to a full line of women's, ladies, and junior fashions. At Brandy's everything targeted one type of female dresser.

May: And why did you leave Kendall's?

Sally: I want to join the top of the line department store in the area. Although I was getting prepared for a promotion at Kendall's, I thought that the promotion could wait until I got experience working with higher quality merchandise.

May: I'm glad you think that way about our stores. We are very pleased with the quality and variety of our merchandise. Let me tell you about our Sales Associate job here at Classique's Department Store. First, I will describe for you the general sales function. Then we will discuss each responsibility one by one.

The primary function of the Sales Associate is to assist customers in merchandise selection, to process their sales transactions, and to help maintain an organized department.

The Sales Associate's first responsibility is to acknowledge and approach customers courteously and in a timely manner.

Please give me an example of how you would approach a new customer.

Sally: I learned at Kendall's that you shouldn't merely walk up to a shopper and say "Can I help you?" It's too easy for the customer to answer "No," and walk away. So, I try to ask an open-ended question or begin some light conversation. I try to make the conversation or comments relate to the person, like "Good afternoon. I see you're trying to match that red sweater. There are more pants and skirts over in that area as well. What type of outfit are you trying to create?" You just can't answer that one with a "No, thank-you."

May: You're right. It's harder to walk away from a conversation with someone interested in helping. That leads us right to the next job responsibility. The Sales Associate must be able to assist the customer in locating merchandise and describing the item's features, benefits, trend information, and availability. Can you describe for me how you have performed this task in other jobs?

Sally: One of my favorite parts of the job is attending product information training. Customers appreciate it when a salesperson can quickly answer how to wash a piece of clothing, whether it needs frequent ironing, or what these new synthetic fabric names really mean.

Product information becomes even more important when a customer is trying to decide between two items. Although you want them to take both blouses, for example, their budget probably only allows for one. I'll walk up to the customer and say something like, "It's not easy trying to decide between those two. Perhaps I can help." I might describe the benefits of both blouses, saying, "The silk is dressier but the polyester blouse is machine washable." I'd ask if she was planning to wear the blouse for a specific occasion. Then I could provide additional information to help her decide. I might also be aware of another blouse that she missed that would be the perfect compromise between the two. In that case, I would show her the third blouse.

May: Now, I'd like to know about your experience with point-of-sale registers. Can you tell me about the registers you worked on previously and walk me through a transaction?

Sally: That's easy. First, I would take all of the customer's merchandise, fold each piece, and line all of them up on the counter displaying the price tag of each item. At Kendall's we had an ABC POS system that is similar to your XYZ POS system. I initiated the transaction type, entered quantities, and used a portable bar-code scanner to read the price tags. If there was a special sales event, I would also enter the appropriate discount coding. Then I processed the cash, check, or credit card and returned the change and/or receipt to the customer.

May: Did you have any repeat customers at either location? If so, how did you develop long-term relationships with them?

Sally: I developed longer relationships with people in the specialty store than I did at the department store. I think that was owing to the clientele of each store and the higher quality of the specialty store's merchandise.

I kept my own file of repeat customers. I had regulars provide me with their phone numbers, a list of the type of clothing they generally purchased, their size, and their primary wardrobe colors. If something in their taste went on sale or a new line of clothing came in, I would contact them and let them know. I would also try to hold merchandise in their size if they were coming in for an item. It would be a serious mistake if they came to our store at my suggestion and I didn't have anything in their size. That would certainly not help develop repeat business.

When I left Brandy's and went to Kendall's, several clients requested that I continue to call them about merchandise at my new location. I imagine that they will also start shopping at Classique's.

May: We would certainly like you to bring your customers with you to our store. Now, let's discuss one of the Sales Associate responsibilities that most people don't realize is part of the job description. Our associates are also responsible for merchandising their department and maintaining Classique's visual presentation standards.

This is the most physical part of the job. It requires moving merchandise on rolling racks from the stockroom onto the sales floor. It includes participating in department reorganization, moving fixtures, setting up or taking down fixtures, signing, and other related items for sales events. Can you describe to me what similar merchandising responsibilities you've had and how you've performed them?

Sally: I've always performed merchandising on a routine basis. Stores always have additional merchandise in back to ticket and stock. There are always fixtures to relocate and merchandise to rotate into better selling positions.

As Sales Associate I also regularly checked the dressing rooms for merchandise that needed rehanging and restocking. Whenever sales slowed down, I would walk through my area of responsibility and reorganize clothing neatly on their hangers, replace like items together, and group sizes in chronological order. During busier periods it's harder to keep the department well ordered, but I would always try.

As seasons change, there are considerably more merchandising efforts. Sometimes we would work in jeans before or after store hours. We knew we would get dirty, opening and lifting boxes of merchandise and moving them around the store. Hanging a season's worth of merchandise on fixtures and folding and arranging merchandise on tables was time-consuming and physically exhausting. We figured we could accomplish this faster and easier without customer interruptions.

There were regular merchandise shipments during the week that I was also responsible for merchandising. I tried to take these in small batches so that I could keep my area clean while I worked. I didn't want to clutter the aisles when I was servicing a customer.

May: The last essential area of the job includes paperwork processing. On a regular basis each department receives a list of items to mark down. The Sales Associates must go through and identify these items and mark the tickets accordingly. Also, Sales Associates must learn our procedure for handling holds, layaways, transfers, counts, defective merchandise re-ticketing, etc. What has been your experience with store paperwork?

Sally: Each of my sales responsibilities included paperwork. At one of my jobs my supervisor disliked the time-consuming effort of markdowns. At Brandy's, I ended up in charge of this effort. I trained and coordinated the other Sales Associates in how to read the computer printouts of markdowns, identify the sales merchandise, and note on the tickets the new prices. Then we would regroup and consolidate these items onto clearance or discount racks to better attract the customers. I enjoyed going through this effort because then I could notify my regular customers which of their favorite items had price reductions. They really appreciated that extra discount.

I also performed the other paperwork duties you listed. It was important to check actual counts against the computer lists of our merchandise. That helped us identify unaccountable shortages in certain items before major sales. We couldn't have an advertised sale on merchandise that already sold out at our location. So these efforts helped us coordinate merchandise levels with the buyers and the other stores.

May: There are a few functions that are not regular requirements of the job, but which your supervisor may request. The first is processing telephone orders and sends. Can you describe to me how you performed this task in other jobs with or without accommodation?

Sally: I'm glad you asked me that question. As you may have noticed, I have a hearing impairment. Although my hearing aids correct much of the problem, it is difficult for me to use a regular telephone. If the other party speaks very loudly, I may pick up some of the conversation. But as a rule, I am better off if the telephone has an amplifier device on it. Once the new device is installed, I can adjust the volume of the amplifier to conduct a conversation with anyone. Other associates can decrease the volume to its regular level and use the same phone.

        I frequently used the phone to check other stores for merchandise that we did not have in stock. Customers appreciate your checking other stores for an item they like in other colors or sizes. We rarely had any telephone orders in either of the stores I worked in. But I am sure that I would be able to handle customers' purchases over the phone.

May: I appreciate your telling me about the telephone accommodation. If we hire you as Sales Associate, I don't think that installing an amplifier would be a problem. We would need to identify how many phones would be in your area of use and proceed from there.

        Other duties-as-assigned tasks include housekeeping activities in the department and stockroom. These could include cleaning and dusting as well as arranging and sizing merchandise. Can you describe to me how or whether you performed this task in other jobs with or without accommodation?

Sally: Cleaning and dusting are routine department maintenance I performed at each of my jobs. While I can't say that these are my favorite tasks, I recognize the importance of keeping everything in order for our own activities and, of course, for our customers. In other jobs, we rotated housekeeping activities so that everyone performed her share of the fun.

        Arranging and sizing merchandise is a constant effort in every store. As I walk from customer to customer, I always check what racks need straightening and what sizes are out of sequence. When I organize the merchandise throughout the day, closing is a lot easier. At Kendall's we can't close out our registers until we prepare our areas for the next day.

May: It sounds as if you are well organized on the job.

Sally: I like to think so. I don't like to be idle during the slow periods on the sales floor, so I make sure that I always pick up my area.

May: Along with the job responsibilities, we want to make sure that you have the qualifications that accompany the duties. The primary skills we seek are professional communication with customers, store management, employees, and coworkers and good reading, writing, and mathematical skills.

From our conversation, I can see that you are an effective communicator. What we want to do is evaluate everyone's skills in the same way. After this interview, you will meet with Ann Quire, our Personnel Assistant. She will give you a brief test that will include basic math problems, customer service questions, and examples of store problems to be solved. Is there any reason you can't take this test today?

Sally: No. I don't foresee any problems taking the test. How much does it weigh in selecting candidates?

May: We use the results as one criterion for selecting the best qualified person. Certainly, if we discover that a candidate cannot add or subtract, he or she would not be able to perform the sales job because of the requirement to handle money. However, you don't have to score 100 percent on the test to qualify for the job. The test looks for a candidate to have basic math skills.

Sally: Thank you. Taking the test should be no problem for me.

May: I have a few more questions for you before you go to Ann. Think of a time where you came across a problem in the company. Describe for me how you identified the problem, brought it to management's attention, and solved it.

Sally: Let me think for a minute. Oh, yes. One time at Brandy's I was stocking merchandise that had just come in. I was placing it on the floor and decided to check the pricing. I realized that the tickets weren't consistent. Some of the prices and stock numbers were different on tickets for the same merchandise. So I pulled the merchandise off the floor and back into the store room. My store manager was not working during my shift, so I called the regional manager's office to request instructions. They contacted corporate, who overnighted us the right tickets.

That was one of the times I was awarded Employee of the

Month. I saved the company hundreds of dollars in potentially lost sales. Other stores also had the wrong tickets but no one noticed. They had to pull their merchandise and reticket as well.

May: It really pays to be thorough like that. I'm sure you were proud of catching that problem.

Sally: I sure was. It's so easy to just go through the motions without checking all the steps. We lose too much quality that way. So I try to take a little more time to be a little more thorough.

May: Terrific. That's what we like to hear. One last question. What are your professional objectives? What do you hope to learn here at Classique's?

Sally: I would like to be a department manager. I know that I have more to learn in selling, merchandising, and supervising. But eventually I would like to move up in your store to Assistant Department Manager and Department Manager.

I think I have strong retail skills and would like to apply them as a manager. I know what a reputable operation Classique's is, and would like to experience my career growth here. I would like to participate in as many training programs as possible to make sure that I can meet the standards you set in managing. I'm willing to work hard to meet these goals.

May: I believe you will work hard. I will be interviewing several more candidates this week. We will call the final candidates in for a second interview with the department manager, who will make the final Sales Associate decision. We will notify everyone within two weeks regarding candidacy for the position.

Before I take you to Ann, do you have any questions for me regarding the position?

Sally: If you do not select me for this opening, how do I remain active for future openings?

May: That's a good question. The top candidates' applications and interview files will remain active for sixty days. If you want to remain an active applicant after that time, call Ann Quire and she'll take care of keeping you on active status.

Sally: Good. Because I am really interested in joining Classique's. I appreciate your interviewing me. I know I can do a good job for you if given the opportunity.

May: Thank you. Let's go over to Ann so she can administer the test. Good luck.

How do you think this interview went? This is an example of an ADA-compliant interview. Although it is not a perfect interview, it basically follows the formula given in Chapter 7. It included a warm-up, a brief introduction to the company and position, and a review of the candidate's education. May stayed close to the job description, walking through the essential functions of the job to determine the candidate's professional experience and abilities. The open-ended questions allowed the candidate to share her interpersonal skills, customer service skills, product knowledge, job skills, and personality traits. Sally was able to share her professional goals and objectives. The interviewer allowed the candidate time to ask questions. The interviewer also introduced the job-related testing required of every candidate for the position. She explained that the skills were requirements of the job and the test was only part of the selection process. She closed the interview explaining the timetable for making a hiring decision, which is most helpful to job candidates.

What did the interviewer do wrong? May omitted a few of the job skills and abilities. She should have included the physical requirements of lifting, reaching, and standing for x hours. She also compounded questions. She could have stated some of the questions more simply, breaking up a longer question into multiple short questions. This would have enabled her to truly explore the details of each essential function. May could have included more information on scheduling requirements, length of the workday, and so on. This information is vital for a person needing to determine whether she can meet the basic requirements of the job.

You will probably identify additional omissions in the interview. The objective here is to provide you with an idea of the in-depth questions to include in an ADA-compliant interview.

Chapter 11

Making the Hiring Decision

This chapter brings us to the culmination of the employment process: the selection decision. In earlier chapters we developed an ADA-compliant job description and identified the job's essential functions and qualifications. We developed a job advertisement to reflect the essential job requirements and the company. We highlighted and applied the selection criteria to screen employment applications. On the basis of these job requirements, we selected qualified applicants to interview. Then we developed a set of structured interview questions to ask of each candidate. During the interview we took concise but complete notes to recall and evaluate each candidate's responses fairly. The next objective is to select the best qualified candidate for the job.

The Interview Evaluation Form

To begin the process of making a decision, you need to compare each candidate's qualifications and abilities to the job's key components. You construct this information from the application, resumé, and interview. Most companies compare candidate qualifications using informal discussion and evaluation. However, it is more effective to use a formal evaluation tool to evaluate candidates' individual and comparative abilities.

The Interview Evaluation Form is important documentation. It guides you through and supports your selection decision. Each company can develop its own form consistent with its job descriptions and other job documentation. To implement this method correctly, companies should require all interviewers to complete these forms. They should consistently transfer their interview notes and individual assessments onto the company's Interview Evaluation Form immediately following each interview. This documentation will provide evidence for ADA-compliant hiring decisions. Additionally, the form enables interviewers and managers to visualize each candidate's qualifications, greatly enhancing the decision-making process.

The design of an Interview Evaluation Form should be given serious consideration. Think about your objectives. What should the form include to assist interviewers in the hiring decision? What design best provides specific candidate information that correlates directly to the vacant position? Who will be using the form? How can the form be designed to guarantee that interviewers use it?

The Interview Evaluation Form should be a nonthreatening, easy-to-use tool. Also, interviewers must understand and buy into the requirement to document every interview. Since the hiring decision is based on the candidate's ability to perform the essential functions of the job, the form should correspond with the job description. Since the structured interview is based on the job description, the Interview Evaluation Form becomes an extension of the job interview. If the interview and the evaluation correlate closely, comparing the candidates will be easier.

The Interview Evaluation Form should report the following for each candidate:

- Education and experience level
- Experience related to essential job functions
- Job-related qualifications
- Overall assessment
- Recommended hiring

Figure 11-1 is a template for developing a company's Interview Evaluation Form. The form serves a dual purpose in that the interviewer fills in hiring critria as well as comment sections and rating scales to assess candidates. One key benefit is that it offers flexibility and specificity for each job. It is flexible because it doesn't provide fixed evaluative criteria. It also doesn't list blanket qualifications assumed to fit every job—for example, communication, interpersonal, and mathematical skills. Each evaluation criterion (job duty and qualification) is entered onto the form by the interviewer. This makes the interviewer responsible for identifying the essential qualifications for the job in question.

In the criteria section, the interviewer writes a phrase or brief summary representing each essential job function. This all-inclusive list ensures that interviewers compare each candidate to all job requirements. It decreases the possibility of subjectivity in selecting

(Text continues on page 154.)

Figure 11-1. Interview Evaluation Form template.

Applicant's Name: _____ Date and Time of Interview: _____

Position Title: _____ Department: _____

Interviewer's Name and Title: _____

Interviewer's Signature: _____ Date: _____

Instructions: Complete the essential function and job qualification section of this form *before* interviewing the candidate. Complete the education and experience section using the candidate's application and resumé. After the interview, write your comments and analysis of how the candidate's experience and abilities relate to each job criterion. Then circle the number that best rates the candidate in each area, with 5 being most favorable and 1 being unfavorable. Add comments and additional evaluative information in the assessment and recommendation sections.

EDUCATION

List schools, majors, degrees, and training in candidate's experience:

_____

_____

_____

EXPERIENCE

List categories of relevant work, professional, or volunteer experience and length of service (i.e., sales management 5 years, store management 3 years):

_____

_____

_____

CRITERIA	COMMENTS	RATING	Weight	Score
Essential Functions				
1.		5 4 3 2 1	× _____	= _____
2.		5 4 3 2 1	× _____	= _____

CRITERIA	COMMENTS	RATING	Weight	Score
3.		5 4 3 2 1	× _____	= _____
4.		5 4 3 2 1	× _____	= _____
5.		5 4 3 2 1	× _____	= _____

TOTAL ESSENTIAL FUNCTION SCORE   Rating: _____ Weighted: _____

Job Qualifications

1.		5 4 3 2 1	× _____	= _____
2.		5 4 3 2 1	× _____	= _____
3.		5 4 3 2 1	× _____	= _____
4.		5 4 3 2 1	× _____	= _____
5.		5 4 3 2 1	× _____	= _____

TOTAL JOB QUALIFICATION SCORE   Rating: _____ Weighted: _____

Overall Candidate Assessment

_____

_____

_____

Hiring Recommendation

_____

_____

_____

Interviewer Signature _____ Date _____

evaluative criteria for each candidate. The less subjectivity, the less chance for discrimination. This list also requires interviewers to evaluate candidates in more detail with respect to job tasks and requirements. As a result, the decision maker has more complete information for evaluating candidates.

This form also helps interviewers conduct and document the interviews consistently. They are required to evaluate candidates based on certain criteria, so they are sure to collect information on those criteria. Also, should a discrimination suit arise months after the interview, the Interview Evaluation Form is documented evidence of a fair, ADA-compliant interview.

There is space on the Interview Evaluation Form for comments on the candidate's qualifications relative to each item. The interviewer must write an evaluation of the candidate's abilities regarding each essential function. He must also assign a numerical rating for the candidate on each job component. This quantifying of the task helps overall assessment of the individual and comparative assessment of candidates.

Review the template, considering a particular job in your company. Think about how you would list the hiring criteria in this format. Figure 11-2 then puts information for the Sales Associate position on the template. Consider how much easier it would be to complete an evaluation with this level of specificity. Consider also the ease of comparing several candidates' backgrounds and skills when information is aligned and consolidated on the evaluation forms.

Figure 11-2 demonstrates how specific interviewers can get in providing details of the person's skills and abilities. This offers interviewers and hiring managers sufficient information to identify the best qualified individual. The effort completes the application of the job description throughout the selection process. The only task remaining is the actual selection decision.

The Candidate Comparison Sheet

Once each candidate has interviewed, you should begin the process of determining which person best meets the essential requirements. You'll need to look at each task individually to determine which candidate:

1. Has the education and experience required for the job. Include information on whether the candidates exceed the

Figure 11-2. Interview Evaluation Form for Sales Associate.

Applicant's Name: _____ Date and Time of Interview: _____

Position Title: Sales Associate   Department: _____

Interviewer's Name and Title: _____

Interviewer's Signature: _____ Date: _____

Instructions: Complete the essential function and job qualification section of this form *before* interviewing the candidate. Complete the education and experience section using the candidate's application and resumé. After the interview, write your comments and analysis of how the candidate's experience and abilities relate to each job criterion. Then circle the number that best rates the candidate in each area, with 5 being most favorable and 1 being unfavorable. Add comments and additional evaluative information in the assessment and recommendation sections.

EDUCATION

List schools, majors, degrees, and training in candidate's experience:

_____

_____

_____

EXPERIENCE

List categories of relevant work, professional, or volunteer experience and length of service (i.e., sales management 5 years, store management 3 years):

_____

_____

_____

CRITERIA	COMMENTS	RATING	Weight	Score

Essential Functions

1. Offers effective customer   5 4 3 2 1 × _____ = _____
   service

2. Processes POS transactions   5 4 3 2 1 × _____ = _____

(continues)

Figure 11-2. Continued.

CRITERIA	COMMENTS	RATING	Weight	Score

3. Fills in stock and moves merchandise   5 4 3 2 1 × _____ = _____

4. Processes paperwork   5 4 3 2 1 × _____ = _____

5. Develops client relationships   5 4 3 2 1 × _____ = _____

TOTAL ESSENTIAL FUNCTION SCORE   Rating: _____ Weighted: _____

Job Qualifications

1. Communication skills   5 4 3 2 1 × _____ = _____

2. Reading, writing, math   5 4 3 2 1 × _____ = _____

3. Problem solving   5 4 3 2 1 × _____ = _____

4. POS operation experience   5 4 3 2 1 × _____ = _____

5. Telephone operation   5 4 3 2 1 × _____ = _____

6. Lifting and hanging   5 4 3 2 1 × _____ = _____

7. Moving merchandise   5 4 3 2 1 × _____ = _____

TOTAL JOB QUALIFICATION SCORE   Rating: _____ Weighted: _____

Overall Candidate Assessment

_____

_____

_____

Hiring Recommendation

_____

_____

_____

Interviewer Signature _____ Date _____

minimum requirements. However, remember that the selection process cannot discriminate against a person with a disability who fails to meet nonessential job factors.

2. Rates the highest on each essential function and job qualification item. If the ratings start to blend together or the candidates' backgrounds and experience are similar, weight each criterion according to importance or time spent. This can help differentiate between close-running candidates.

3. Rates highest regarding job experience and job knowledge. Include, in writing, any miscellaneous information that relates to the candidate's ability to perform the job effectively. These may include job-relevant criteria such as work attitude, professionalism, and motivation. These characteristics can be legitimate criteria for selecting the best qualified person.

Some people like to use a candidate-by-candidate evaluation form. This can be as simple as a matrix to chart candidate ratings. On the left-hand side of a sheet of paper, list the essential functions and qualifications included on the Interview Evaluation Form. Across the top of the page list the names of each candidate. Figure 11-3 shows such a form. Then complete the numerical rating of each candidate and compare either simple totals or weighted totals. The matrix will help guide you to the stronger candidates in each essential-function area. But you do not have to base your employee selection strictly on the candidates' scores. There are other factors involved in the decision, too. However, this quantification of skills can narrow the choices, help you identify strengths and weaknesses, and bring you close to your decision.

Again, remember that this matrix is merely a tool to help you identify the top candidates for the job. There is considerable subjectivity involved in a hiring decision, and subjective hiring criteria generally are nonmeasurable. This leaves considerable room for dis-

Figure 11-3. Candidate comparison sheet.

CRITERION	Joe	Joan	Jack	Jean	Jane
Essential Functions					
1. Offers effective customer service	——	——	——	——	——
2. Processes POS transactions	——	——	——	——	——
3. Fills in stock and moves merchandise	——	——	——	——	——
4. Processes paperwork	——	——	——	——	——
5. Develops client relationships	——	——	——	——	——
Total Scores on Essential Functions	——	——	——	——	——
Job Qualifications					
1. Communication skills	——	——	——	——	——
2. Reading, writing, math	——	——	——	——	——
3. Problem solving	——	——	——	——	——
4. POS operation experience	——	——	——	——	——
5. Telephone operation	——	——	——	——	——
6. Lifting and hanging	——	——	——	——	——
7. Moving merchandise	——	——	——	——	——
Total Scores on Job Qualifications	——	——	——	——	——
Ranking Total:	——	——	——	——	——
Weighted Total:	——	——	——	——	——
Candidate Scoring Sequence:	——	——	——	——	——

crimination in the final decision. The ADA message regarding the subjective criteria is to ensure that subjective elements do not eliminate people with disabilities based on their disability.

If the highest scoring candidate is someone with a disability, this individual must receive consideration equal to the other candidates. If there is a subjective reason for not hiring the candidate with the disability, be prepared to prove that the decision not to hire is discrimination-free. Note the reason on the Interview Evaluation Form, with an explanation for hiring the nondisabled candidate over the candidate with a disability. This final decision must be valid, related to business or operation needs.

Selection Responsibilities

Each organization determines who is responsible for making a particular hiring decision. In some companies, the hiring decision is the responsibility of one individual, often a reporting manager or someone in human resources. In other organizations, the responsibility is shared across jobs and functions. Perhaps several levels of management participate in the selection decision. The decision may include lateral input, whereby a peer group of employees makes the selection. Perhaps several managers at the same level make the decision.

However your organization makes its hiring decisions, every participant in the interview process should know who the decision maker is. This makes it easier for interviewers to report and share their discoveries about candidates.

If there are multiple interviewers, they should meet formally before and after the series of interviews. Don't take these discussions lightly. Don't conduct the meetings as you pass other interviewers in the hallway. Schedule a candidate review meeting and plan to include all interviewers. Don't ignore anyone's input, especially if contrary to general opinion. The reason for multiple interviewers is to gain varied perspectives on the candidates. So weigh all the input in a fair, open discussion of candidates.

If the senior manager is the actual decision maker, it is each interviewer's responsibility to provide a clear, complete presentation of findings on each candidate. Be honest. Don't hold back on positive or negative insights, even if it may be to the detriment of your favored candidate. Your insight may confirm something other interviewers sensed but couldn't verbalize. Give the decision maker as much job-related information as possible to help in making a good decision.

If you are the decision maker, go into the discussion with an open mind. Even if you have a favored candidate, be open to other interviewers' insights. Everyone can miss a key hire-or-don't-hire issue; don't be blinded by a hiring preference you brought into the meeting.

Focus the interview review on information that will help you determine who is the best qualified candidate. Don't let participants go off track, focus on the essential functions of the job and the qualifications related to those functions. Review each of these key determinants before exploring other possible hiring considerations.

If one of the final candidates has a known disability, keep the discussion focused on job knowledge, skills, and abilities. Avoid judgments, stereotypes, and assumptions regarding possible performance problems. If the candidate has portrayed himself to be the best qualified person for the job, any accommodations are secondary and irrelevant to the selection decision. If the candidate has performed the job elsewhere, it is likely that he will be able to perform the job at your company as well. Start viewing each candidate as a potential employee.

If you are using written evaluation tools, consider merging the forms of all the candidates to see what results they bring. A superior candidate or pair of candidates may emerge when you combine the numerical ratings of the candidates. Also, using individual tools as a group tool shows the value you place on these methods in your organization. Although the numbers may not be perfect assessments quantitatively, they begin to offer a ranking of candidates. Discussion can proceed from this vantage point.

If you choose the finalists based on group consensus, be sure it is a true group decision. If the decision is yours alone, explain this fact to the group at the outset. Provide participants with a timetable for your decision and commit to making a timely decision. Present your decision clearly and provide reasons why you selected one candidate over another. Associate the selection reasons with the essential functions and related qualifications of the job.

Make note of the primary reasons for the candidate's selection. If other candidates were close, provide specific reasons for their rejection. This documentation is an important task regardless of whether rejected candidates have visible disabilities. After a time, you can forget why you made a particular hiring decision. However, should a rejected candidate file suit claiming discrimination, your documentation should provide job-related evidence as to why the person selected was the most qualified.

Reference Checking

Once the top candidates are selected, the reference checks begin. Don't ignore this part of the process. You can fill in many pieces of the candidate puzzle if you ask the right questions about the right person. Handle the reference check with the same reverence and professionalism that you use when interviewing.

Over the years, reference checking has become more and more difficult. People have sued former employers for harming their chances of reemployment by providing negative information to potential employers. Many employers now refuse to share ex-employee information with reference checkers. Some companies confirm certain employee information, such as job title, hire and termination dates, and salary. Others do not allow managers to take reference calls; they refer all calls to the human resources department. Some companies provide only written reference information on employees who have signed a release for that information. As a result of this employer reluctance, you may have to work a little harder to get reliable information.

1. *Prepare in advance for the reference process by listing the information gaps you would like the reference person to fill.* This may include reasons for leaving a company, perceived strengths and weaknesses, or confirmation of job information. Remember, one of your objectives as a reference checker is to resolve issues. Prepare accordingly. Don't miss a key area—chances are you'll get only one chance to speak to each reference.

2. *Design questions that fill in these information gaps.* Write down each question ahead of time. Be sure the wording is nonthreatening and nonjudgmental, and that the questions do not discriminate. Assume that all or some of the conversation will get back to the candidate. Don't do or say anything that you do not want the candidate to hear.

3. *Acquire a list of references from the candidate.* Be sure that the candidate provides professional references, excluding immediate family and friends. You want information from reputable, work-related sources, concerning job performance and abilities. You don't want to hear what a great person your candidate is. If you didn't think she had strong points, you wouldn't be spending time on the reference now. You want information beneficial to your hiring decision.

4. *Respect your candidate's wishes regarding references.* If the candidate requests that you not contact a current employer, respect that wish. Do not jeopardize someone's current employment in your quest for reference information. Former employer information will serve you well.

5. *Add a few references not provided by the candidate.* Think who might be able to tell you more about this person. Consider how you may get in contact with former peers, direct supervisors, or professional associates. Perhaps the person volunteers for a professional organization. Perhaps you know someone at a previous company who can provide the name of someone in the candidate's department. Think about how you can learn more about the skills and abilities of your best candidates. The more information you have, the better your decision.

6. *Allocate your time well.* Use your human resources department to perform your reference checks. They will be able to com-

municate well with personnel departments to get general information on the candidates. Your efforts as manager may be more effective if you speak to other managers. If you develop a peer relationship with previous managers, you may acquire more information on the candidate.

7. *Determine how many references will benefit your decision making.* One reference is certainly insufficient. Two references may be okay, depending on the level of candidates and the information you are seeking. You can't have too much information on your candidates. These people have worked with or for your candidates. They have important practical knowledge you won't acquire until they work for you. Discover poor work habits or falsified skills before you place new employees on your payroll.

Target three or more references from different companies and different job levels. Don't rely on one manager's feedback. Peer and subordinate feedback is also important. If the candidates worked closely with external agencies or vendors, perhaps you can acquire information from these people as well.

8. *Develop a reference check form.* Design it to be flexible enough to fit each candidate. The more limited the form, the less information you collect. Leave a lot of room for note taking. Require that all reference-check conversations be documented as evidence of the hiring decision. Record reference information consistently. Retain the reference documentation with the candidate's Interview Evaluation Forms.

    a. Include the name of the reference person, his title, company, and telephone number on the form. Get this information first. It would be a shame if you saved this detail for the end of the conversation and the person had to get off the phone abruptly.

    b. Include a section to help the caller confirm the candidate's basic employment information with the reference. Include the candidate's job title, length of service, reasons for leaving, and salary (where appropriate).

    c. List reference questions related to the information collected during the interview. Ask about skills, knowledge, strengths and weaknesses, job responsibilities, and key job-related skills.

    d. Include a question for supervisors as to whether they would rehire the candidate and why.

    e. Provide a closing question such as, "Can you give me the names and telephone numbers of anyone else who may be able to help us make our hiring decision?"

    f. Offer your appreciation for their assistance and your willing-
ness to do the same for them.

To get the most complete information from the reference, develop some rapport with the person you are calling. People are hesitant to share information over the telephone. In essence, he is giving confidential information to a stranger. You must eliminate this
barrier.

Establish trust. Introduce yourself, give your title and your
company. Speak clearly and unhurriedly, so that he hears the information you're sharing. Relate the purpose of the call. Explain that
you have already interviewed the candidate and will be the person's
supervisor. Tell him the title of the vacant position and describe its
overall responsibilities. Let him know that you will hold his response in strict confidence.

Once these preliminaries are completed, then the reference has
some background on which to base his comments. Don't ask simple
yes or no questions. Ask open-ended questions based on the information you collected during the interview. Provide the opportunity
for conversational responses. For example, "The Sales Associate position requires that Sue have strong customer service skills. Sue
shared some examples of her abilities in this area. Could you give
me an example of her customer service abilities?" or "As you know,
Sales Associate work sometimes gets physical with the hanging of
merchandise and work in the stock rooms. I got the sense that Sue
wasn't enthusiastic about this work. Is this an accurate impression
of her attitude? Please tell me how she approached this work."

Since you are not meeting in person, you cannot see the reference's body language and facial expressions, so try to listen for both
the verbal and nonverbal messages. How one delivers a message
may influence the meaning of the message. Listen to whether the
person is delaying in making a response, trying to choose words
overly carefully, prefacing simple responses with "hmm, that's a
hard one," or avoiding an answer entirely. These may be nonverbal
messages of dissatisfaction with the candidate. The reference check
is similar to an interview. You can frequently obtain more information if you listen closely to how things are said in addition to what
things are said.

The Final Selection Decision

Once you have performed the reference checks and closed any gaps
in information about the candidates, you are ready to select the final

candidate. Inform the participants of your decision and prepare to make the job offer.

Some companies allow the manager to extend the hiring offer. Other companies wish to centralize job offers in the human resources department. However your organization conducts the offer, be sure to document this final step as well. Make a note in the candidate's file that you extended an offer on April 15 at 2:00 P.M. Include whether the candidate accepts at that time. Otherwise, agree on a response deadline.

Once the candidate has confirmed joining your company, contact all the other interviewed candidates. It is preferable that you make these calls. This enables the rejected candidates to inquire why they were not selected. Be prepared for these questions and answer honestly. Even though giving this direct feedback is uncomfortable for many people, it can benefit everyone.

There are a couple of reasons for explaining your decision. First, candidates will not jump to false assumptions if they understand how the other person's skills exceeded their own. If the person has a disability, the honesty can eliminate any perception that the decision was discriminatory. Second, if these candidates had good skills and abilities, you may have other openings in the future that fit their skills. By contacting these people directly, you leave the door open for a continued relationship and a possible business relationship.

Part Three

Related Compliance Issues and Exercises

Chapter 12

Medical Examinations And Other Screening Tools

The ADA provides specific guidelines regarding the use of medical examinations in the employment process. ADA's message regarding other screening tools, however, is less clear. This chapter examines ways to determine whether your current medical and other employment testing methods comply with the facts and intent of the law.

Medical Examinations

According to the ADA, an employer can require a medical examination of applicants only *after* an applicant has received an offer of employment. Companies that require applicants to submit to a medical exam before extending a job offer should *not* continue this practice. There are further specifications beyond this basic requirement. For example, employers can require medical examinations of all employees or applicants after extending a job offer. While examinations need not be job-related or consistent with business necessity, they must be administered consistently to all employees.

If the employer intends to use the medical examination as a screening tool to identify individuals who cannot perform job functions, the ADA presents different requirements. Under these circumstances, the criteria used in the medical exam to exclude a person must be job-related or consistent with business necessity. Furthermore, when an employer uses the medical examination as a screening tool, the testing must be consistent. All employees for that particular job or class of jobs must have the same requirement to take a medical examination. An employer cannot randomly test incumbents.

Consider this example. A warehouse position requires the routine lifting of boxes weighing seventy-five pounds apiece. There are two job openings for this position. The employer selects two candidates and offers them employment. One of the candidates has a slight limp. The other candidate has no visible impairment. Before the ADA was passed, the employer required the person with the limp to take a physical exam to determine whether he could perform the job, while the employer did not test the other candidate. Since the ADA, this discriminatory testing is illegal.

The employer must decide whether to create a policy requiring medical exams for all incumbents for this warehouse position and/or similar warehouse positions. If the employer decides to require medical exams, the policy must apply to any candidate who receives an offer for this position. Employers can no longer select certain candidates to examine—they must administer examinations consistently.

The following checklist offers a sequence for auditing and implementing medical examination efforts.

Medical Examination Checklist

1. Determine what position(s) or class(es) of jobs require medical examinations.

2. Decide whether (a) the medical examination will be used as a screening tool to identify incumbents who are unable to perform the job requirements or (b) medical examinations will be required of all incumbents but will not be used for screening.

3. Ensure that medical examinations are given only to those individuals who receive a job offer.

4. Prepare the medical examiner (doctor, nurse, physical therapist) before conducting any company examinations. Provide the medical examiner with a detailed job description. Have the medical examiner visit the work site and observe employees performing the job functions. Stipulate that the medical examination directly correlate with the physical requirements of performing the essential job functions. Explain the ADA's perspective that if an incumbent has a disability, the person with the disability should not pose a direct threat to himself or others on the job.

Base all screening considerations on medical fact, not on stereotypes or conjecture. If you require additional medical information to make a fair hiring decision, work with the medical examiner and the incumbent to collect information and written documentation from the incumbent's personal physician(s).

5. Develop a form with the examiner to record the results of

each examination. Use this form to document each incumbent's ability or inability to perform the essential tasks.

6. If, during the examination, the medical examiner discovers a disability that prevents the incumbent from performing a task, do not automatically reject the incumbent from the employment process. The employer must make every effort for accommodation or find another solution. Have the medical examiner consider accommodations to assist this person perform the task in question. Document this research on the medical examination results form.

7. Include the incumbent in any accommodation discussions. Perhaps the incumbent is already aware of a solution.

8. If an immediate solution is not apparent, conduct research on further job accommodation options. Document every alternative, the cost involved, and the source to purchase or develop the accommodation.

9. Create a separate filing system for all documents related to medical examinations, medical conditions or histories, descriptions of disabilities, or details of accommodations. Keep this information under strict confidence. The ADA limits personal access to these files to three groups of people: (a) supervisors and managers who need to understand work restrictions and accommodations; (b) safety and first aid personnel who need to know of a disabling condition that may require emergency medical treatment; and (c) government officials who request evidence of ADA compliance with relevant documentation.

Documenting accommodations efforts will yield many benefits. First, it provides evidence of the accommodation research. It shows that the employer considered a fair variety of accommodation options. Second, the documented options list is a convenient tool to visualize and select the most effective accommodation. Involve the incumbent when reviewing the accommodation alternatives—this improves the selection and is good employee relations. Remember, the employer has the right to make the final selection based on cost, convenience, and so on. If the incumbent refuses to accept a reasonable accommodation, she virtually eliminates herself from consideration for the job. Third, this documentation may be useful for later reference if you require a similar accommodation. As employers make more accommodations, they will develop a file of excellent accommodation resources. This will make the accommodation process easier in the future.

Drug Screening

The ADA considers drug and alcohol abuse separate issues. Current substance abusers are not protected by the ADA, as are individuals with disabilities. Employees who currently use illegal drugs or who are alcoholics must adhere to the same employment and performance standards as other employees. For ADA purposes, the employer is not required to change job performance, on-the-job behavior, or employment-qualifications requirements to accommodate current substance abusers.

Employers can prohibit the use of illegal drugs and alcohol in the workplace. They can also require that employees not be under the influence of alcohol or illegal drugs at the workplace. The ADA does not change a company's policies regarding the handling of substance abuse or any performance or discipline issues relating to that abuse.

There are two areas where the ADA is involved. First, the ADA protects as disabled people who have a history of drug or alcohol abuse but who are no longer using. If someone is undergoing treatment for substance abuse, she is also protected as disabled. Employers cannot discriminate against reformed substance abusers in any aspect of employment.

The second area of ADA involvement surrounds drug screening. According to the ADA, "a test to determine the illegal use of drugs is not considered a medical examination." Employers can conduct drug screening before a job offer is extended, after the offer is extended, or during employment. There are no ADA restrictions. However, if an employer conducts drug testing, it should be done in accordance with the company's written policy and procedures. All test results should remain confidential. Drug test results may be shared only on an as-needed basis with the three groups listed in the medical examination section.

Employment Testing

Many companies administer employment tests that are not medical examinations. These tests can include typing tests, personality tests, aptitude tests, and basic reading and mathematics tests. Employers also use work sample tests to show how an individual might perform a particular job function. Prior to the ADA, these tests could not discriminate against minority groups. Since the ADA, the protected applicants also include people with disabilities.

Some of the same issues discussed under medical examinations apply to employment tests. Selection criteria and standards resulting from employment exams cannot screen out people with disabilities, either intentionally or unintentionally. If the employment exam does screen out people with disabilities, the criteria must be (a) related to the position in question and (b) consistent with business necessity.

According to the ADA, selection criteria that are not job-related or consistent with business necessity violate the ADA only when they screen out an individual with a disability (or a class of individuals with disabilities) based on the disability. Selection criteria that screen out an individual with a disability for reasons not related to the disability do not violate the ADA.

For example, suppose an employer requires that all administrative assistants type 55 words per minute. After interviewing, each candidate takes a typing test. Candidate 1 with a hearing disability fails the typing test because she can only type 45 words per minute. The ADA allows you to eliminate this person as a candidate because her failure to perform the job is unrelated to the disability. Candidate 2 with a hearing disability fails the typing test; he types only 45 words per minute. However, this typing test was administered using a dictating machine that didn't have sufficient volume adjustment. Candidate 2 was screened out as a candidate because of his disability, not because of his typing skills. This can be a discriminatory test. The candidate should request an accommodation to amplify the machine and retake the test. If the candidate fails to request an accommodation and the employer does not realize that the person requires an accommodation, then the employer has not violated the ADA. Remember, it is the applicant's responsibility to request an accommodation.

The following is a checklist of points to consider when planning to administer employment tests.

Employment Testing Checklist

1. List all employment tests used in the company. This may entail contacting managers throughout the organization to determine how many design their own informal tests as part of their interview process.

2. Analyze each test to determine whether it is job-related or consistent with business necessity. Exams such as personality and aptitude tests provide interesting information; however, if the tests are used to screen out candidates, are not proven valid indicators of

job performance, and tend to target people with disabilities, they will not meet ADA requirements.

3. Determine whether the tests are administered consistently throughout the company. Are all secretaries required to pass a typing test? Are all filing clerks tested on their filing speed? Are all sales personnel tested on their cash register skills? Are the tests administered department by department or centrally? Are decentralized tests conducted consistently? Research how each test is conducted and who is responsible for administering and scoring the test. Observe the process for consistency and job-relatedness.

4. Ensure that all candidates are aware of the testing requirement and that you will accommodate when requested. Whether or not a person's disability is visible, the interviewer must give the candidate the opportunity to request a testing accommodation.

Ideally, any candidate scheduled for an interview should be forewarned that the interview includes a test. For example, when an interviewer calls to schedule an interview, she may say, "Our interview will last one to one and a half hours on Friday. Following the interview, candidates take a typing test using an ABC personal computer and XYZ software. Is there any reason you cannot take this test or any accommodation you might need?"

This gives the candidate the opportunity to describe a need or plan ahead for the test. Candidate 2 might ask whether the typing test requires reading a written document or using a dictating machine. Upon discovering that a machine is part of the test, Candidate 2 may request an amplifier or bring one from home. A candidate with arthritis may not need an accommodation, but may now take aspirin before the interview to reduce potential hand discomfort that would decrease the typing score. A third candidate with carpal tunnel syndrome may request or bring a keyboard pad. A fourth candidate with no disability would thank the interviewer for being so complete in presenting the requirements of the interview.

5. Be prepared for accommodation requests. This doesn't mean you need to purchase possible accommodations ahead of any requests. It does mean you must be open to requests and have a plan for making accommodations. Have an accommodation procedure and a person responsible for ensuring the accommodation works. Make sure all test administrators have sufficient ADA knowledge and interpersonal skills to handle accommodation requests as easily as they handle other parts of their job. Candidates requesting accommodations should believe that accommodations are a common

part of your company's interview process. Their request should not set them apart from other qualified candidates.

6. Develop an accommodation request form that does *not* describe the disability. This form should be simple for applicants and employees to use. Documentation and tracking of ADA efforts is important should compliance evidence ever be required. It also simplifies future accommodations because records offer a history of accommodations.

7. Even if you asked a candidate on the telephone whether he requires a testing accommodation, ask again before administering the test. Once a candidate sees the testing area, views the equipment, or determines the lighting level or seating arrangement, he may determine that an accommodation is necessary. Be open to a last-minute request or even a request in the middle of the test. Some people realize after completing the test that they should not have tried the test without their accommodation. Test administrators cannot say, "Too late!" You must accommodate and retest.

The ADA tells us that candidates should request accommodations before taking a test or as soon as they realize they need accommodation. However, some people may make the attempt to test without an accommodation, hoping that disclosing the accommodation need is not necessary. Employers cannot penalize candidates for this late disclosure. Have the individual complete the accommodation request form and test as soon as the accommodation is available.

You do not have to provide accommodations instantaneously. It may take several hours or several days to identify and provide an accommodation. The applicant should not lose the opportunity for employment owing to unavailability of an accommodation. On the other hand, the employer does not have to perceive the accommodation as an emergency action to be accomplished immediately. As long as you include the candidate in the current applicant pool, you will meet the accommodation requirement.

If the applicant requests an accommodation where the need is not obvious or is questionable, the employer may require medical documentation showing the need for accommodation. Include this on the accommodation request form and retain all requests in separate, confidential files.

8. Once the test is completed, score and handle the test as you would for someone who does not have a disability. The ADA will not challenge consistent selection criteria valid for business necessity. If all the secretaries must maintain typing standards of 55

words per minute, that is fine. However, if a company raises the standard to screen out people with disabilities and there is no valid job-related reason for this change, the ADA could challenge the discriminatory selection criteria.

There are several other selection testing circumstances to consider. Some companies use timed tests to determine an applicant's qualifications. If speed or certain levels of output are required on the job, then a timed test is appropriate. If you require reading and writing on the job, and conduct a test applying reading and writing skills, then a written test is appropriate. However, if the job does not require a quantified speed or the reading skills are not job-related, the company must consider whether the test is a valid representation of the skills required to perform the job. The test may discriminate unintentionally against people with certain disabilities. Regardless of whether the discrimination is intentional or unintentional, it is still illegal.

There are options available that are less dramatic than destroying all timed or written tests, however. There are accommodations available, such as providing a reader to a person with dyslexia or a typewriter for someone with a dexterity problem who cannot write the answers on the customary answer sheet. Timed tests might also be difficult for people with mental impairments, mental retardation, or learning disabilities. Determine whether there is another method of testing these candidates, perhaps using work samples whereby you can measure their aptitude and knowledge.

Psychological, aptitude, and personality tests do raise some questions and need to be reconsidered. Tests that don't truly measure job-related skills could be thought to screen out people with certain disabilities. Some of these tests screen out based on psychological history or perceptions of personality traits. If your company employs these tests, contact the creator of the test as well as legal or professional advisors. Some tests may still be valid indicators of performance in a particular position; others may open up the company for legal action.

Testing applicants' abilities by having them perform actual job tasks is a fair and compliant testing method. These tests offer a clear applicant portrayal of job question or skills. Of course, the same test must be given to all applicants and the scoring must be consistent. The test should measure essential job functions only.

Not all jobs are conducive to this work sample type of testing, however. Consider when these methods may be useful. For an administrative job, have the candidate role-play a telephone interaction. For a managerial job, have the candidate conduct a performance appraisal. For a technical job, have the candidate define and apply several key concepts.

In summary, be creative, open, and fair when considering testing. Remember the objective of selecting the best qualified person for the job. Sometimes you'll have to take a different approach to determine the most qualified candidate. As long as the end result is the quality candidate, the unique approach is worth the effort.

Chapter 13

Applicant Accessibility To the Workplace

Title III, Public Accommodation, of the Americans with Disabilities Act goes into extensive detail on how businesses should become accessible to people with disabilities. The implementation dates for Title III differ from those for Title I, the Employment Title. The overall intent is the same, however. In Title I, employers must make their jobs and employment sites accessible to people with disabilities. In Title III, businesses must make their services and products accessible to people with disabilities.

Title III has detailed information on new construction standards required to make a building accessible. Any business constructing new employee or public facilities should work closely with architects and contractors to meet the ADA's building codes. Companies in older buildings are not required to make their entire facilities immediately accessible. However, the ADA does state that businesses "shall remove architectural barriers in existing facilities that are structural in nature, where such removal is readily achievable, i.e., easily accomplishable and able to be carried out without much difficulty or expense."

The ADA suggests some steps to take to remove barriers, including installing ramps, marking curb cuts in sidewalks and entrances, repositioning telephones, adding raised markings on elevator control buttons, installing flashing alarm lights, widening doors, installing accessible door hardware, updating restrooms, creating designated accessible parking spaces, installing an accessible paper cup dispenser at an existing inaccessible water fountain, and removing high-pile carpeting.

Accessibility is an important point for employers operating in older facilities. The ADA suggests a sequence of priorities to approach readily achievable accessibility. First, businesses should consider external access to the building and update their sidewalks and parking. Second, companies can improve internal accessibility by improving signage, widening doors, adding visual alarms, and installing ramps. Third, businesses should try to make restroom facilities more accessible, by removing obstructions, widening doors and stalls, and installing grab bars. Fourth, companies need to consider any other inaccessible areas within the facility.

The ADA's definition of "readily achievable" is similar to its definition of "undue hardship." Readily achievable is determined on a case-by-case basis, so what is readily achievable for one company is not necessarily readily achievable for another. The ADA tells employers to consider the:

- Nature and cost of actions to improve accessibility
- Overall financial resources of the facility
- Effect on expenses and resources or impact of such improvements on the operation of the facility
- Overall financial resources of the covered entity, which can include the parent company
- Type of operation(s) of the covered entity

Reviewing Your Facility for Accessibility

Taking the ADA's suggestions to their fullest, employers need to begin a good-faith effort to open their doors to applicants with disabilities. You can accomplish this by formally conducting an accessibility audit of the workplace.

One important accessibility consideration is whether your company owns or leases the offices or building. If you own the building, the liability for accessibility rests with you. If you lease the building, you need to review your lease to determine who is responsible for making accessibility improvements. For example, the landlord may be responsible for all external and structural improvements. The lessee may be responsible for all internal changes.

Determine what the best method is for your company to audit its facility for accessibility. Decide whether the audit is the responsibility of one department or a joint effort. You'll need individuals who have the expertise to conduct a thorough and accurate audit. Invite "experts" to assist you; you'll find these experts among your employees as well as outside the organization.

First, consider who inside the company may be a resource. You may have a disabled employee or someone who has experience working with people with disabilities. If you have an employee who uses a wheelchair, crutches, or a walker, invite her to participate. Ask her to identify the physical barriers she encounters. Someone with a visual impairment may be able to provide suggestions for improving accessibility from a visual perspective. Without making the group so large as to be unmanageable, try to vary the expertise of participants.

If you use employees, provide them with accurate expectations of the task and outcomes of the audit. If your company intends to implement most of the suggestions, let them know. If the company has limited resources and plans to prioritize the suggested alterations, let participants know that too. They should understand that you want their input; however, you will implement only certain changes. The effectiveness of employee participation will correlate with their understanding of their role in the process.

Depending on the size of your company or the business your company conducts, there may be other internal resources, including a company nurse or doctor, or someone from the facilities, security, legal, or telecommunications departments. Each may contribute to your facilities audit.

Once you have determined your internal resources, consider external help. Locate nonprofit organizations and schools that service people with disabilities. Identify rehabilitation hospitals or residences. Call local support agencies for volunteers to join your audit team and make accessibility suggestions. If your business has a relationship with an architect or contractor, she may also volunteer to assist you. Lastly, many suppliers will do an on-site accessibility audit at no cost.

The next section will walk you through your company's parking lot and into your employment interview area to present what accessibility means according to the ADA. The measurements and standards listed are those provided by the ADA for new construction. It is up to your company to determine what is readily achievable from a difficulty or financial perspective.

An Accessibility Walk

Let's follow an applicant in his path to your offices. This candidate, who uses a wheelchair, drives to your office for the interview. He is looking for an accessible *parking space*. Accessible spaces should be convenient to a main building entrance. There should be an accessible route leading from the space to the entrance. The space should have a sign posted that includes the universal symbol of access (the wheelchair). It is insufficient to merely paint a parking space with the words or picture relating to accessibility. A sign must be posted.

The accessible parking space should be at least 96 inches wide and have a 60-inch access aisle to allow the person sufficient space to exit the vehicle and maneuver the chair. Two parking spaces may share the same access aisle. The parking spaces and the access aisles should be on level ground, without slope. For those individuals who do not drive, there should be a drop-off zone at the entrance of the building.

The candidate exits his car and goes to the entrance. Make sure all exterior *paths* or sidewalks leading from the accessible space to the door are at least 48 inches wide. This path should be made of a firm, nonslip material, safe in all weather conditions. Where the path turns, the path should allow enough space for the person to navigate a 90-degree turn. This path should not have any abrupt changes in level, such as steps. If it does, the path should also have a ramp, elevator, platform lift, or curb ramp. If the path slopes, angle it at less than 1:20. This means that for every 1 foot of rise, 20 feet of ramp is required. If the path meets a driveway, street, sidewalk, or parking lot, there must be a 36-inch-wide curb ramp.

The candidate approaches the main *door* to your office building. Evaluate what the door is made of, how heavy it is, what kind of operating hardware it uses, and whether the door opens easily. The door must be at least 32 inches wide. It should open using one hand without twisting or grasping. Levers, push mechanisms, and U-shaped handles are preferable. Opening the exterior door should require less than 8 pounds of pressure. If there are two sets of entry doors, there should be at least 48 inches between each set, plus the width of any door swinging into the space. Thresholds should be ½ inch high or less.

If a *ramp* leads to the door or replaces steps inside your office building, the slope of the ramp should be no steeper than 1:12. External ramps must be 48 inches wide. The landing of the ramp must be 60 inches long to provide enough space for the candidate to wheel back and open the door safely. For the length of the ramp, there should be a continuous, nonabrasive, securely attached handrail.

The candidate enters the building. He is trying to find the human resources department. Have you posted *signs* or directionals leading applicants to your office? Is the print large enough for someone with partial vision impairment? A sign's center point should be 60 inches in height. This allows persons in wheelchairs or of short stature to access the information on the sign. In some buildings a receptionist or security guard sits behind a desk or a counter in the entrance lobby. Make sure this area also is accessible. Frequently the entrance counters are too high for people using wheelchairs. These should be rebuilt to include a section 36 inches long with a maximum height of 36 inches.

The candidate must go to the third floor of your building for his interview. The *passenger elevators* are behind the receptionist. Make sure that the elevator is on an accessible path. The dimensions of the elevator floor should allow a turning area for wheelchairs of at least 51 inches. Elevator buttons may not exceed 48 to 54 inches from the floor, depending on elevator design. The emergency button and telephone should have their centerline no less than 35 inches from the floor. Buttons should light when depressed and should have tactile designations for the visually impaired. At each landing there should be a tactile floor number on the elevator's door jambs. There should be visual (for the hearing impaired) and audible (for the visually impaired) signals notifying the rider when the elevator has arrived. The door should remain open long enough to allow passengers to exit.

The candidate exits the elevator and begins down the *corridor* to the human resources department. Internal corridors and ramps must be 36 inches wide for a single wheelchair to pass. Minimum clearance for two wheelchairs is 60 inches. Directional signage should be easily visible. If signs are hung from the ceiling, there must be 80 inches of clearance from the floor. If the corridor is carpeted, the pile should be ½ inch thick or less. Wheelchairs, walkers, and crutches must be able to travel easily on the flooring. Fasten all area rugs or mats securely to the floor. If the floor is smooth, be sure that it is not slippery. These items are potentially dangerous for anyone walking, and more difficult for those who have difficulty walking.

The candidate notices several items obstructing the corridor. Remove or modify any *obstructions* such as potted plants or trees, fire extinguishers, water fountains, or public telephones. These items should not protrude more than 4 inches into the corridor. Check plants to determine whether they block the pathway, especially for outstretched branches.

The candidate passes a *drinking fountain* and becomes thirsty. The spout for drinking fountains should be 36 inches or less. The spout and controls should be at the front. A person should be able to manipulate the controls with one hand and minimum effort. There should be a clear space of 30 × 48 inches for access by a person using a wheelchair. If the public phone is in a telephone booth, consider removing the booth.

The candidate locates the human resources department and sees a *restroom* located across the hall. Make sure your company has at least one accessible restroom on accessible corridors. If redesigning both male and female restrooms is physically impossible or too costly, consider providing a single unisex bathroom with a locking door.

Doors to the toilet rooms should be at least 32 inches wide or larger, depending on the shape of the room. The door handles and locks should be easy to operate using one hand and without twisting or grasping. Grab bars should be placed on two sides of the toilet. Sinks should have at least a 30 × 48-inch space in front of it. The bottom of the sink should be at least 29 inches from the floor, enabling a wheelchair to slide under it. The top of the sink may not exceed 34 inches off the floor. Insulate the hot water pipes under the sink to avoid burning. Place faucets within easy reach and have easy-to-use handles, preferably lever style. Controls for towel holders, soap and other dispensers, blowers, and other tools should be no more than 40 inches from the floor. The bottom edge of mirrors should be no higher than 40 inches from the floor.

The candidate enters your offices. Depending on your company, this could be a small office or a large waiting room. To audit the room, first check how the entry door opens. The force for opening an interior door should not exceed 5 pounds. If the door has a knob handle, consider replacing it with a lever or easier style.

Study the room. Consider what the candidate first encounters as he enters the room. Many offices have a large plant or other decorative piece at the room's entrance. Although visually attractive, this may be an obstacle to a visually impaired person or someone using a wheelchair. Remove or relocate these items. Make sure the main pathway to the reception or application area is direct and accessible. Is the receptionist at a counter or desk? Are forms and other company materials within easy reach? Check the seating arrangement of the room. Is there sufficient space for a person in a wheelchair to wait until her interviewer is ready? Arrange the seating so that there is an open area of 30 × 48 inches next to other seating for a person in a wheelchair.

Next, audit the interviewer's office. If your company has a central human resources department responsible for all hiring, the offices should be accessible. They should be able to accommodate a wheelchair with at least 30 × 48 inches of space in reasonable proximity to the interviewer. If chairs need to be rearranged for this space to be available, that should not cause a problem. If the entire room needs rearranging, you may want to reconsider the room's use or its layout. If all the supervisors and managers in the company interview their own candidates, you do not have to make every office accessible. Be prepared to relocate an interview to a comfortable area in cases requiring such accommodation.

Other Accessibility Matters

Another area of accessibility relates to a company's *employees who serve the public*. These include a front-desk security guard, receptionist, and human resources administrators who greet applicants and interviewees. Train them in disability etiquette (see Chapter 8), and be sure they are comfortable handling applicants with disabilities. You do not want your front-line people to make errors when people with disabilities enter your building or are introduced to your company.

There are numerous other items with the potential to be serious barriers to people with disabilities. Consider, for example, the removal of unsturdy wall partitions or dividers, slippery floor coverings, rugs with fringe, wobbly book cases, and furniture that is low, soft, or without arms and difficult to get in and out of. Consider the alarm systems in place at your company. Are they both audible and visual, providing emergency notification for people with vision and hearing impairments? Replace older alarms with those that are audible and have flashing lights. Especially make these changes in areas where there are disabled employees, in public areas, and in human resources areas. Audit the emergency exit signage in your building. Consider replacing outdated exit signs with emergency signs notifying people of accessible exits.

The ADA does not require companies to perform all of these steps. These measurements and suggestions are meant to give some insight into the possibilities for creating an accessible environment. Your objective is to make people with disabilities comfortable in your business environment. This allows them the freedom to interview and perform well for you. If an applicant with a disability continually runs into accessibility barriers in your building, she is not going to feel that your company is interested in her or willing to accommodate her needs. The more physical barriers, the greater the chance a charge of discrimination may follow.

Chapter 14

An ADA-Compliance Exercise

This book has provided guidance transforming pre-ADA job descriptions into ADA-compliant descriptions, job advertisements, and interviews. Now, here's another opportunity to take a basic job description through each step to reach ADA compliance. Remember, the ADA does not provide a singular methodology for compliance. However, by applying the law's hints and tips practically, your employment practices will both improve and comply.

Administrative Secretary Position

Review the following job description for an Administrative Secretary and perform the following:

1. Bring the job description into ADA compliance. Identify essential and nonessential job functions, then add more detail to describe the tasks and job qualification requirements.
2. Develop a classified help-wanted ad for the position. Emphasize the job's essential functions.
3. Prepare to interview potential candidates. Compile a detailed list of questions to ask each candidate. Develop a list that is thorough enough to help you determine the best qualified candidates for the job.
4. Design an Interview Evaluation Form based on the criteria listed in the job description.

Enjoy this exercise. Be creative in developing the detailed task descriptions and qualifications. Enjoy representing your company when developing the job advertisement. Keep the ADA in the back of your mind as a basis for selection efforts rather than as a burden for compliance.

Job Description

Position title: Administrative Secretary

Accountable to: _____

Division: _____

Department: _____

Date: _____

Revised date: _____

Author: _____

Primary Objective of Position: To perform secretarial duties to support the activities of personnel in assigned area of accountability.

Major Areas of Accountability:

1. Perform secretarial duties including typing of reports, correspondence, memoranda, reports, and sorting and distributing mail for the department. Maintain, follow up, and draft routine correspondence.
2. Produce and distribute reports.
3. Receive, screen, and direct calls. Coordinate and control routing of correspondence.
4. Establish and maintain filing system.
5. Conduct administrative duties such as expense reports, schedule and coordinate meetings and travel reports.
6. Perform duties specific to assigned area and as requested.

Nature and Scope:

Applies specialized clerical skills to collect, prepare, or calculate data and/or compose written materials.
Good verbal and written skills.
Responsible for follow-up actions.
Willing to work overtime to meet deadlines.
Knowledge and use of standard office machines.
Typing 70 wpm.

Approvals:

Employee: _____ Date: _____

Immediate supervisor: _____ Date: _____

Next-level supervisor: _____ Date: _____

The ADA-Compliant Job Description

The changes made to the job description are noted in **bold.** This revision also includes discussion and comments relating to the changes. Remember, there are many ways to bring this job description into compliance. Compare your corrected version with this version to generate more ideas on means to achieve compliance.

Position title: Administrative Secretary

Accountable to: _____

Division: _____

Department: _____

Exempt/non-exempt: _____

Pay grade: _____

Job code number: _____

Date: _____

Revised date: _____

Author: _____

Primary Objective of Position: To perform secretarial duties to support the activities of personnel in assigned area of accountability. [*Note that this company chose to create a generic job description for multiple department use. This procedure will comply with the ADA as long as those job requirements that are unique to a particular position are documented. It is recommended that you attach these unique responsibilities directly to the job description.*]

Major Areas of Accountability:

40% 1. Perform secretarial duties including typing of reports, correspondence, and memoranda [*delete "reports and sorting and distributing mail for the department"*].
     1a. Take and transcribe machine dictation, shorthand and/or speed writing to generate documents.
     1b. Maintain, follow up, and draft routine correspondence.
     1c. Proofread all prepared documents for spelling and typographical errors.

[*Note the addition of percentage allocation for each area of accountability. The redundant listing of the word* reports *was eliminated. The mail function was moved out of this section that emphasizes working on correspondence. More detail of tasks is added.*]

10% 2. **Prepare and** produce [*delete "and distribute"*] **various routine and specialized** reports **as assigned, using some judgment for format layout.**
    2a. Gather input from various departments and sources and compile reports, charts, and graphs.
    2b. Use spreadsheet software, as applicable, to generate more elaborate reports, charts, and graphs.
    2c. Ensure that reports are received by all required individuals.

[*The original description for this task didn't offer enough information. More detail was provided.*]

10% 3. Receive, screen, and direct **telephone** calls **from employees, vendors, and customers.**
    3a. Take telephone messages.
    3b. Answer caller questions and/or refer caller to appropriate person.
    3c. Follow up with callers on information requests.

[*Again, more information is required to clarify the tasks and provide more foundation for determining job qualifications. Correspondence routing was moved to item 6 along with mail distribution.*]

10% 4. Establish and maintain filing system **for the department and supervisor.**
    4a. File all centralized documents routinely.
    4b. Create confidential file system for department manager.
    4c. Maintain correspondence file for all incoming and outgoing department correspondence.
    4d. Respond to customer file requests on a timely basis.

[*Describing this segment in more detail depends on the filing system's relationship to the incumbent's department. Are files maintained solely for the secretary and the supervisor(s), or are departmental files included in this responsibility? Determine the actual scope of the task, then describe more completely.*]

10% 5. Conduct administrative duties such as **completing** expense reports and travel reports **for supervisor, and** scheduling and coordinating **departmental, vendor, and client** meetings.
    5a. Be familiar with company-wide reporting methods to complete expense and travel reports accurately and in a timely manner.
    5b. Contact the facilities department to determine meeting and conference room vacancy.
    5c. Call all meeting participants to identify available meeting times and schedule accordingly.

[*More detail is provided describing the nature of the administrative duties.*]

10% 6. **Open, sort, and route all incoming mail and interdepartmental correspondence.** Sort and distribute* **outgoing** mail for the department.
    6a. Develop department mail routing system.

    6b. Be familiar with incoming and outgoing mail schedule to assist department in timely distribution or correspondence and reports.

    6c. Physical distribution of mail within company or to post office may be required.*

[*Be careful when using broad terms such as* coordinate *and* control. *Replace with more descriptive words if available. This task is asterisked (*) to note that distributing mail could be considered a nonessential function, depending on departmental staffing and the volume of mail to be distributed.*]

10% *7. Perform duties specific to assigned area and as requested.

[*This category is included in most job descriptions. Remember, if the duty is too minor to be listed, it is likely to have nonessential elements.*]

Nature and Scope:

[*Considerably more detail is provided here. Wording changed to capture specific requirements and eliminate generic hints at requirements.*]

High school graduate or equivalent and/or 1–2 years business or office training.

A minimum of two years' secretarial experience in a fast-paced office environment.

Mathematical skills to collect and calculate data and work with spreadsheet software.

Ability to compose written materials, edit, and proofread documents.

Good verbal, **interpersonal, and telephone/customer service** skills.

Ability to develop professional working relationships with other company employees.

Knowledge and use of standard office machines, **including telephone, adding/ calculating machine, copier, typewriter, PC, word processing software.**

Proficient in taking notes and dictation using speed writing, shorthand, or possibly a dictating machine.

Type **accurately at least** 70 wpm.

Ability to prioritize own workload, expedite, and organize flow of work through supervisor's office.

Responsible for *completing* follow-up actions.

Ability to work in large, fast-paced, office environment.

Willing to work overtime *periodically* to meet deadlines.

Approvals:

    Employee: _____ Date: _____

    Immediate supervisor: _____ Date: _____

    Next-level supervisor: _____ Date: _____

    Human resources: _____ Date: _____

The ADA-Compliant Employment Advertisement

Administrative Secretary

Join the team at Metropolitan Finance Services! We have an immediate opening for an Administrative Secretary with two or more years of administrative experience for our Marketing and Analysis Department.

We will rely on you to type and edit correspondence, answer phones, respond to vendor and customer inquiries, develop mathematical reporting, organize and maintain department filing system, and provide general secretarial assistance.

The outstanding candidate will accurately type 70 wpm, have PC word processing and spreadsheet experience, and 1–2 years of business/office school. You must be able to compose correspondence, work with a variety of people, prioritize work activities, organize, and support a busy department. We are seeking someone with strong interpersonal and interactive skills.

We provide excellent benefits, a 401(k) plan, and competitive compensation. Please send resumé or apply in person to:

Metropolitan Finance Services
10101 Main Street
Hiram, AL 10101

This advertisement attempts to highlight the essential functions and corresponding qualifications. Since this is a primary recruiting method, be sure your ad focuses on the experience, skills, and attributes that best suit your business needs without discriminating.

ADA-Compliant Interview Questions

Before reviewing this list of ADA-compliant interview questions, remember that your questions may be totally different. You may be equally correct and effective in determining the best qualified person for the job. There are no perfectly correct interview questions with respect to ADA compliance; however, there can be numerous incorrect questions. Be sure you avoid the discriminatory pitfalls. If you focus on the candidate's ability to perform the essential functions of the job, your questions should comply.

As a help, here are some job interview components. The asterisked items are those for which there are sample interview questions provided.

Introductory conversation
Company and position introduction
Review of candidate's education*
Overview of work history*
Technical abilities and job knowledge*
Work-related personality traits*
Interpersonal skills*
Managerial abilities*
Motivational characteristics and work objectives*
More complete review of company and position
Candidate questions
Interview closure

Review of Candidate's Education

1. "I see on your application that in high school you took several typing courses. What attracted you to these classes?"
2. "How did you decide what career or education to pursue following high school?"
3. "Following high school, you enrolled in Marshall Tech. Describe the classes you took there and how you apply them on the job."
4. "What would you say is the main result you got career-wise from attending Marshall Tech?"

Overview of Work History

1. "In your first clerical job, what were your most important responsibilities?"
2. "When your schedule got busy, how did you determine what tasks to perform first, second, third . . . ?"
3. "How important were your relationships to other people in this job?"
4. "Your second job is more similar to the position we have available. Describe to me a typical workday in this job."
5. "What special skills did you need to perform well at this job?"
6. "Give me an example of one special project you were primarily responsible for."
7. "What were the successes and failures in this project?"

8. "What types of tasks do you find easy to perform in your job?"
9. "What types of tasks do you find difficult to perform in your job?"
10. "Why are you seeking a new job at this time?"

Technical Abilities and Job Knowledge

1. "To get a sense of your potential to perform the Administrative Secretary position, I am going to walk through the job description so we can discuss each job component."
2. "The primary job responsibility is performing general secretarial duties, such as typing reports, correspondence, and memoranda. What percentage of time do you spend in your current job performing typing responsibilities?"
3. "Considerable time will be spent at the secretary's desk performing PC tasks. Can you describe for me your word processing skills and how you use the PC as a tool for increased efficiency?"
4. "List for me the types of documents you have prepared at your jobs."
5. "Give me an example of a larger document or report you had to prepare and how you went about completing the task."
6. "What steps do you take to prepare your documents for distribution?"
7. "One of the job's responsibilities is creating mathematical spreadsheet reports manually and on the computer. According to your resumé, you have used Lotus. What was the most elaborate spreadsheet you've created?"
8. "That sounds interesting. How did you figure out how to get the spreadsheet to perform that calculation?"
9. "Our spreadsheets typically need to include *xxx* and *yyy* as one of the calculations. How would you set that up in Lotus or in your spreadsheet?"
10. "Give me an example of a report you created where a graph or a chart was useful."
11. "Ten percent of the Administrative Secretary's time is spent on the telephone with customers, clients, and employees. Describe your strengths and weaknesses regarding your telephone skills."
12. "There's an angry client on the phone who wants to speak

to your boss. Your boss is unavailable. How would you handle this client?"

13. "In this department, you will need to acquire a lot of knowledge in our financial marketing area. How have you acquired department expertise in the past and how would you acquire it at Metropolitan Finance?"

14. "Another 10 percent of the position relates to maintaining a filing system for the department and for your supervisor. The filing cabinets are located behind the secretary's desk. Can you describe for me how you organize and complete your filing responsibilities, with or without accommodations?"

15. "Do other employees access your files? If so, how do you maintain the integrity of your filing system?"

16. "The administrative secretary is also responsible for completing expense and travel reports and scheduling meetings. How have you performed these duties in the past, with or without accommodation?"

17. "How have you resolved scheduling conflicts when trying to set up a meeting for six to ten people?"

18. "Handling the mail is another part of this position. The secretary opens, sorts, and routes all incoming and outgoing mail. The position may also be responsible for delivering the mail on an as-needed basis. Walk me through your methodology for performing this task for a department of fifteen employees."

19. "The secretary uses some or all of the following list of office equipment: PC, telephone, calculator, copier, fax machine, and typewriter. What are your skill levels on each tool and would you require accommodations to use these office tools?"

20. "To generate correspondence, the department supervisor uses a mix of dictated letters, letters on the PC for your 'clean-up,' and the dictating machine. Describe your comfort and ability with each of these methods. Include whether you would need an accommodation to perform these tasks."

Work-Related Personality Traits, Interpersonal Skills,
Managerial Abilities

1. "Tell me about a time when you were assigned a difficult letter to write. What steps did you take in your writing to produce this letter?"

2. "Relate to me a time when you were very well organized with a project or job duty and another time when you were not as well organized."

3. "If you were given the chance to redo the second scenario, how would you change your methods?"

4. "I want you to imagine the following circumstance. Your boss has just returned from a day away from the office. You have a pile of ten to fifteen telephone messages that you took during her absence, several letters to be signed, and a spreadsheet for her to review before you can distribute it. She has made ten minutes available to you to fill her in before her next meeting. How do you determine what is most important to cover in that hectic ten-minute opening?"

5. "How do you handle yourself under stressful circumstances?"

6. "If one of the people in your department is hard to get along with, how do you handle this relationship?"

7. "What is the most frustrating circumstance you ever encountered on the job?"

8. "Another responsibility of the Administrative Secretary is to follow up with people in the department, ensuring that assigned tasks have been completed. Sometimes this is not an easy responsibility. How will you accomplish this ongoing task?"

9. "Who was your best supervisor and why did you work well for this person?"

Motivational Characteristics and Work Objectives

1. "Of all your responsibilities, what is your greatest accomplishment?"

2. "How do you know that you have had a successful day at work?"

3. "What motivates you to do well on the job?"

4. "Some of our days are very hectic, requiring a fast work pace and overtime. How do you respond to and handle these types of days?"

5. "What are you looking for in this job that is missing from your current job?"

6. "Taking under consideration the position I described, what makes this the perfect job for you?"

THE INTERVIEW EVALUATION FORM

CRITERIA   COMMENTS   RATING   Weight   Score

Essential Functions

1. Performs secretarial duties,   5   4   3   2   1   × _____ = _____
typing reports/letters.

2. Prepares reports and   5   4   3   2   1   × _____ = _____
spreadsheets.

3. Handles telephone.   5   4   3   2   1   × _____ = _____

4. Establishes and maintains   5   4   3   2   1   × _____ = _____
filing system.

5. Handles administration,   5   4   3   2   1   × _____ = _____
paperwork, meetings.

6. Handles mail.   5   4   3   2   1   × _____ = _____

      TOTAL ESSENTIAL FUNCTION SCORE   Rating:_____ Weighted:_____

Job Qualifications

1. Mathematical and spread-   5   4   3   2   1   × _____ = _____
sheet skills.

2. Writing, editing, and proof-   5   4   3   2   1   × _____ = _____
reading skills.

3. Interpersonal and relation-   5   4   3   2   1   × _____ = _____
ship skills.

4. Telephone skills.   5   4   3   2   1   × _____ = _____

CRITERIA COMMENTS	RATING	Weight	Score
5. Skill with office machines, typing skills.	5 4 3 2 1 ×	_____ =	_____
6. Organizational ability— prioritizing and organizing workload.	5 4 3 2 1 ×	_____ =	_____
7. Handling of fast pace, overtime, deadlines.	5 4 3 2 1 ×	_____ =	_____

TOTAL JOB QUALIFICATION SCORE   Rating: _____ Weighted: _____

This exercise should be performed for every position you are filling. Retrieve the current job description. Update it for accuracy and ADA compliance. Identify the essential functions and corresponding qualifications to develop a cohesive set of interview questions. Then select key criteria to include on your Interview Evaluation Form. You will have completed the core documents as evidence of your selection standards. The only missing component is applying each of these tools in the hiring process.

Chapter 15

An ADA-Compliance Quiz

This chapter offers three quizzes that test the reader's knowledge of the ADA and the information contained in this book. There are fifty true-or-false questions, forty fill-in-the-blank questions, and forty-five multiple choice questions.

These quizzes provide a good refresher of the ADA and its implications regarding employee selection. Additionally, if you are using the book as a training tool, the quizzes are a good measure of the trainees' knowledge of this material.

Use all three quizzes as a complete package or select the individual quizzes or particular questions that relate to your company's needs. However you apply this chapter, it was designed to assist you in your learning/teaching process.

TRUE OR FALSE STATEMENTS

_____ 1. The ADA affects only employers with federal contracts.

_____ 2. Regardless of whether you follow the ADA guidelines perfectly, as long as your practices are consistent, you comply with the ADA.

_____ 3. A job description is not required for ADA compliance.

_____ 4. The essential functions of the job must be identified before you advertise a job opening.

_____ 5. If you updated a job description's essential functions six months ago and the position becomes available again, you do not have to check the accuracy of the essential functions again.

_____ 6. A company's job application can ask sensitive questions that cannot be asked in an interview.

_____ 7. Interviewers instinctively ask only legal questions of job applicants.

_____ 8. If the applicant mentions a disability, it's okay for the interviewer to discuss the details of the disability.

_____ 9. If you have not discriminated, you do not have to document your hiring decision.

_____10. If you hire only a few people each year, the ADA is not a concern in the employment process.

_____11. It costs the U.S. government over $300 billion each year to support people with disabilities.

_____12. There are six titles in the ADA.

_____13. Title III requires that employers not discriminate when providing services to customers.

_____14. A person with a broken arm is protected under the ADA.

_____15. A person with a disability who doesn't meet the job qualifications is not protected under the ADA.

_____16. The ADA determines the qualifications for each job.

_____17. An employer cannot refuse to hire a person because of her inability to perform a nonessential function of the job.

_____18. An employer cannot refuse to hire a person with a disability because of his inability to perform a nonessential function of the job.

_____19. A reasonable accommodation to the application process could include reading the application to a person who is visually impaired.

_____20. You are required to move an essential function to another employee if a person with a disability is qualified to perform all the job duties except one.

_____21. The employer must inform job applicants of their right to an accommodation.

_____22. If an employee or applicant does not inform the employer of an accommodation need, the employer can be sued for discrimination.

_____23. If you have made an accommodation for one person with a visual impairment, you can automatically make the same accommodation for a second person with a visual impairment.

_____24. Undue hardship gives most employers the opportunity to avoid accommodating people with disabilities.

_____25. According to the ADA, the terms and conditions of employment are a legal contract between the employee with a disability and the employer.

_____26. It is illegal to discriminate against employees with disabilities regarding company-sponsored parties.

_____27. The essential functions of the job are useful only to managers who have employee selection responsibilities.

_____28. Whether employees are actually performing a job function is critical to determining whether the function is essential.

_____29. If you don't spend the majority of your day performing a function, then it cannot be considered essential to the job.

_____30. There is only one correct method for documenting the essential functions of a job.

_____31. According to the ADA, you should lower your qualification standards so that people with disabilities qualify for your jobs.

_____32. Duties as assigned are typically essential functions of a job.

_____33. It is important to include the nonessential functions in a job advertisement.

_____34. ADA nondiscrimination requirements also affect what is asked on a job application.

_____35. Advance preparation for an interview is unimportant for effective selection.

_____36. To get right into an effective interview, start off with the hardest questions.

_____37. Don't use first impressions as a considerable part of the decision whether to hire a candidate.

_____38. It is unimportant if the interviewer is late for an interview.

_____39. Snap judgments and gut hiring decisions are generally the best way to select an employee.

_____40. Making eye contact is as important with visually impaired candidates as with seeing candidates.

_____41. It is your responsibility as interviewer to understand the person's disability.

_____42. If you don't know whether the person has a disability, ask.

_____43. The hiring decision must be made by comparing each candidate on the Interview Evaluation Form.

_____44. You must hire the most qualified disabled person.

_____45. Reference checking is an important part of the selection decision.

_____46. Medical exams can be given before an offer of employment.

_____47. A medical exam can be given before an offer of employment if it is not used to screen candidates.

_____48. Selection standards that screen people with disabilities must be job-related and consistent with business necessity.

_____49. If a manager uses an independent employment test, it does not have to comply with the ADA.

_____50. An applicant with a disability who requests a testing accommodation after completing the test is not protected by the ADA.

FILL-IN-THE-BLANK QUESTIONS

1. The ADA requires employers with _____ [number of] employees to comply by July 26, 1992.

2. By July 26, 1994, employers with _____ [number of] employees must comply with the ADA.

3. If you use job descriptions for selecting employees for certain positions, you should use job descriptions for selecting employees for _____ positions.

4. You _____ [can/cannot] discriminate during the application screening process since no one ever checks what applications are rejected.

5. The _____ Act of 1973 was the first legislation to end discrimination against people with disabilities.

6. There are approximately ＿＿ million people in the United States with disabilities.
7. The ADA protects people with disabilities who are ＿＿ to perform the ＿＿ ＿＿ of the job.
8. It is the ＿＿'s right to determine the qualifying standards for a vacant position.
9. If a person with a disability applies for a job, you must ＿＿ him or her.
10. An essential function is a ＿＿ duty of the job.
11. The most qualified person for a job is the one who can best perform the essential job functions ＿＿ or ＿＿ accommodation.
12. Accommodations can be made to either the ＿＿ or ＿＿ ＿＿ the functions of the job.
13. There are an ＿＿ number of accommodations available to assist people with disabilities.
14. An ＿＿ ＿＿ is an action that requires significant difficulty or expense to the employer.
15. A job's essential functions must be identified before any ＿＿ can take place.
16. A function may be essential if no one else is ＿＿ to perform the function.
17. A ＿＿ standard is the personal and professional attribute of the position, including the skill, education, physical, medical, safety, and other job requirements.
18. Each time a job description is analyzed and updated, have an authorized person ＿＿ and ＿＿ the description as documentation of the review.
19. All job advertising must focus on the ＿＿ ＿＿ ＿＿ .
20. Asking applicants about their medical history is ＿＿ according to the ADA.
21. The objective of an interview is to collect information from the applicant that is ＿＿ to the vacant position.
22. The interviewer should speak ＿＿ percent of the interview and listen ＿＿ percent of the interview.
23. Interview ＿＿ candidates as thoroughly as external candidates.
24. It is not helpful when interviewers ＿＿ taking notes in the middle of the interview.
25. Most disabilities are ＿＿ [visible/invisible] to the interviewer.
26. Common ＿＿ and common ＿＿ are the key components to interviewing all job applicants.
27. The largest group of people with disabilities are those with ＿＿ impairments.
28. When we use ＿＿ language we perpetuate stereotypes, misconceptions, and prejudice about people with disabilities.
29. [Do/Do not] ＿＿ finish the sentences for a person having difficulty speaking.
30. Ask "Can you perform this job with or without accommodation" to ＿＿ candidates.
31. The magic word to ensure that you do not discriminate between candidates is interviewing all candidates ＿＿.

32. The magic word to prove that you did not discriminate in the hiring process is _____ every step or action taken.
33. The selection decision [can/cannot] _____ include nondiscriminatory criteria separate from the job's essential functions.
34. _____ for the reference check just as you would prepare to interview a candidate.
35. An employer can test for _____ use at any time during employment.
36. Develop an _____ _____ form to ensure that a testing accommodation matches the needs of a person with a disability.
37. A company building a new office complex should work with _____ and _____ to ensure that ADA codes are met.
38. Readily achievable building changes are easily accomplishable and able to be carried out without much _____ or _____.
39. To conduct an effective audit use both _____ and _____ disability experts.
40. Conduct an employment accessibility walk from the _____ _____ to the _____ _____ to determine what changes should be made.

MULTIPLE-CHOICE QUESTIONS

1. Which of the following is *not* considered evidence of essential functions:
   a. Job description
   b. Organization chart
   c. New employee announcement
   d. None of the above
   e. All of the above
2. Job descriptions can be used for
   a. interviewer preparation.
   b. training new employees.
   c. performance criteria.
   d. none of the above.
   e. all of the above.
3. Screening job applicants and resumés should be
   a. an informal process.
   b. a formal process.
   c. delegated to lower level employees.
   d. none of the above.
   e. all of the above.
4. We don't want to learn that we conduct ineffective or illegal interviews from
   a. the interviewer.
   b. the candidate we hired.
   c. the candidate we rejected.
   d. none of the above.
   e. all of the above.

5. The benefits of effective nondiscriminatory interviews are
   a. comfortable interviewers.
   b. satisfied applicants.
   c. more qualified new employees.
   d. none of the above.
   e. all of the above.
6. People with disabilities are the _____ segment of our population.
   a. best protected
   b. most visible
   c. poorest
   d. none of the above
   e. all of the above
7. Providing people with disabilities with employment opportunities will help solve the
   a. unemployment problem.
   b. poverty problem.
   c. blatant discrimination in employment.
   d. none of the above.
   e. all of the above.
8. The two ADA titles that impact the majority of businesses are
   a. Title I and Title II.
   b. Title II and Title III.
   c. Title III and Title IV.
   d. Title III and Title I.
   e. Title I and Title IV.
9. The core provision of Title I is
   a. prohibiting discrimination in transportation services.
   b. opening business services to people with disabilities.
   c. guaranteeing equal employment opportunities for qualified individuals with disabilities.
   d. none of the above.
   e. all of the above.
10. According to the ADA, a person is disabled if he
   a. has an impairment that substantially limits a major life activity.
   b. has a record of such an impairment.
   c. is regarded as having an impairment.
   d. associates with someone with a disability.
   e. all of the above.
11. If a person with a disability applies for a job, you must
   a. hire the person.
   b. eliminate the essential parts of the job that the candidate cannot perform.
   c. determine whether the candidate is the most qualified for the job.
   d. none of the above.
   e. all of the above.

12. Accommodations for people with disabilities should be made for
    a. the job application process.
    b. interviews.
    c. the job functions.
    d. none of the above.
    e. all of the above.
13. The best way to accommodate a person with a disability is to
    a. select the accommodation without the person's input.
    b. ignore the disability.
    c. guess.
    d. none of the above.
    e. all of the above.
14. The employer has discovered three accommodation options for a person with a disability. The three options cost $20, $125, and $250. Which accommodation should the employer select?
    a. The one best suited to the employee's effectiveness on the job
    b. The least expensive one
    c. The most expensive one to avoid noncompliance
    d. Whichever one looks best to impress the other employees
    e. The one the employee wants
15. Undue hardship can be claimed
    a. when the employer has 25 employees.
    b. when the accommodation is expensive.
    c. when the person with a disability decides not to accept the accommodation.
    d. when the cost of the accommodation results in significant difficulty or expense regardless of available resources.
    e. when the accommodation severely impacts the company's ability to conduct business.
16. Employers can discriminate against individuals with disabilities
    a. in the recruitment process.
    b. by paying them less because of their accommodation.
    c. if they are not qualified for the job.
    d. by demoting them to a lesser position.
    e. if they are absent from the job due to illness.
17. Identifying essential job functions improves how we
    a. screen applications, interview candidates, and hire employees.
    b. orient and train new employees.
    c. supervise and evaluate employees.
    d. a and b above.
    e. a, b, and c above.
18. The selection decision should be made by matching applicant skills, abilities, and background to the
    a. job description.
    b. essential functions of the job.
    c. personality of the department.

    d. personality of the manager.

    e. all of the above.

19. If you use job descriptions in your company, the ADA requires that
    a. every job have a job description.
    b. there is a job description for every disabled incumbent.
    c. the job descriptions you use comply with ADA guidelines.
    d. you use the same format for all job descriptions.
    e. all of the above.

20. When determining job qualifications,
    a. focus on qualifications that match the essential functions.
    b. refer to previous job descriptions.
    c. emphasize preferred skills.
    d. a and c above.
    e. a and b above.

21. Which of the following should *not* be included in the job identification header of a job description?
    a. Employment status
    b. Job title
    c. Physical requirements
    d. Revision date
    e. Salary grade

22. The job qualifications section should not include
    a. years of experience.
    b. tools and equipment.
    c. emotional requirements.
    d. attendance requirements.
    e. none of the above.

23. Which of the following groups of information must be excluded from your employment application?
    a. Workers' compensation incidents, absenteeism, and skills tests
    b. Veteran status, disabling conditions, and workers' compensation absences
    c. Marital status, sex, and education
    d. Accommodation requirements, workers' compensation incidents, and pre-offer medical screening
    e. Medical screening, excessive absenteeism, work history

24. Interview preparation should include everything listed below, except
    a. thinking about interview questions.
    b. developing an evaluation form.
    c. meeting with other interviewers.
    d. overlapping candidates' interview schedules.
    e. eliminating possible interruptions.

25. Which one of the following excuses *not* to prepare interview questions in advance doesn't fit?
    a. too limiting
    b. consistent answers between candidates

    c. no spontaneity

    d. spend too much time listening to candidate answers

    e. too organized

26. Which of the following is *not* a good design for an effective interview question?

    a. Situational questions

    b. Questions beginning with *is, can, will, did,* or *were*

    c. Follow-up questions

    d. Questions beginning with *how, describe, show,* or *why*

    e. Short questions

27. A good reason to take notes during an interview is that

    a. the applicant is distracted.

    b. the interviewer listens less.

    c. the interviewer can remember more information.

    d. the interviewer's hand gets tired.

    e. no one can read them afterward.

28. Which of the following items should we use when referring to people with disabilities?

    a. Handi-capable

    b. Special

    c. Victim of

    d. Inflicted with

    e. None of the above

29. You encounter an applicant in a wheelchair who you think has difficulty moving her hands. When you greet the applicant you should _____.

    a. wave

    b. pat her on the shoulder

    c. extend your hand for shaking

    d. ask, "Would you like to shake hands?"

    e. ignore the greeting and start talking about the job

30. Which of the following is appropriate wheelchair etiquette?

    a. Pushing a person's chair without asking

    b. Sitting at eye level as soon as possible

    c. Saying, "Let's walk over to the break room."

    d. Talking louder

    e. b and c above

31. Which of the following is *not* appropriate for the candidate with a hearing impairment?

    a. Talking through the interpreter

    b. Sitting so your back faces a window

    c. Exaggerating your lip movements

    d. Chewing while you are talking

    e. All of the above

32. Which of the following is appropriate behavior for an applicant with a visual impairment?

    a. Greeting the guide dog

    b. Introducing yourself and your title to the applicant

    c. Quantifying and describing visual circumstances
    d. c and b above
    e. a and b above

33. Which of the following is *not* a common learning disability?
    a. Discombobulatia
    b. Dyslexia
    c. Aphasia
    d. Discalculia
    e. a and d above

34. Defending a charge of discrimination typically costs the company all of the following *except*
    a. $300,000.
    b. employee time to research the claim.
    c. attorney fees to research and file the case.
    d. employee morale.
    e. all of the above.

35. Avoid which of the following when determining whether your employees are interviewing legally?
    a. Observing an interview
    b. Retraining your interviewers
    c. Overlooking their list of interview questions
    d. Reading their evaluation forms
    e. Including them in the hiring decision

36. During an interview exclude which of the following from your note taking?
    a. Description of abilities
    b. Depth of experience
    c. Description of disability
    d. Examples of strengths and weaknesses
    e. c and d above

37. An Interview Evaluation Form should report the candidate's
    a. education.
    b. essential function experience.
    c. job-related qualifications.
    d. assessment and hiring recommendations.
    e. all of the above.

38. Do *not* include as potential employee references which of the following?
    a. Business references provided by the candidate
    b. Family references provided by the candidate
    c. Current employer not offered as reference
    d. Employee peers from previous employers
    e. b and c above

39. Employers who use a medical examination as a screening method must
    a. test all incumbents for a particular job or class of jobs.
    b. give the medical exam after a job offer.
    c. test for drug use.
    d. a and b above.
    e. a, b, and c above.

40. Medical and drug test results can be disclosed to the following *except*
    a. peer employees for emergency purposes.
    b. managers and supervisors.
    c. safety personnel.
    d. first aid personnel.
    e. government officials seeking ADA evidence.
41. If an applicant requests a testing accommodation, you can
    a. deny the request.
    b. demand the person's medical records.
    c. request documentation of the need for accommodation.
    d. delay the test until the next round of interviews.
    e. all of the above.
42. Readily achievable accessibility is *not* based on
    a. the nature and cost of the action.
    b. undue hardship.
    c. the overall financial resources of the facility.
    d. the impact of the action on the operation of the facility.
    e. the financial resources of the parent company.
43. Which of the following can assist in identifying accessibility barriers?
    a. Disabled employees
    b. Architects
    c. Company nurses
    d. Rehabilitation experts
    e. All of the above
44. Which one of the following structural descriptions is *not* required by ADA?
    a. Entry door at least 32 inches wide
    b. All parking spaces at least 96 inches wide
    c. Internal corridors 36 inches wide
    d. Drinking fountains 36 inches high or less
    e. Public telephone cords at least 29 inches long
45. The ADA suggests that employers correct which of the following barriers in existing office buildings?
    a. Lowering all public water fountains and telephones
    b. Widening all office and building doors
    c. Installing elevators in buildings with two or more stories
    d. Updating restrooms
    e. Replacing all stairs with ramps

Answers

True or False Questions

1. F	6. F	11. T	16. F	21. T
2. F	7. F	12. F	17. F	22. F
3. T	8. F	13. T	18. T	23. F
4. T	9. F	14. F	19. T	24. F
5. F	10. F	15. T	20. F	25. F

26. T	31. F	36. F	41. F	46. F
27. F	32. F	37. T	42. F	47. F
28. T	33. F	38. F	43. F	48. T
29. F	34. T	39. F	44. F	49. F
30. F	35. F	40. T	45. T	50. F

Fill-in-the-Blank
Questions

1. 25
2. 15
3. all
4. cannot
5. Rehabilitation
6. 43
7. qualified, essential functions
8. employer
9. consider
10. fundamental
11. with or without
12. essential or nonessential
13. infinite
14. undue hardship
15. recruiting
16. available
17. qualification
18. sign and date
19. essential job functions
20. illegal

21. relevant
22. 20, 80
23. internal
24. stop
25. invisible
26. courtesy, sense
27. hearing
28. discriminatory
29. Do not
30. all
31. consistently
32. documenting
33. can
34. Prepare
35. drug
36. accommodation request
37. architects, contractors
38. difficulty, expense
39. internal, external
40. parking lot, employment office

Multiple-Choice Questions

1. d	10. e	19. c
2. e	11. c	20. e
3. b	12. e	21. c
4. c	13. d	22. e
5. e	14. a	23. d
6. c	15. e	24. d
7. e	16. c	25. b
8. d	17. e	26. b
9. c	18. b	27. c

28. e	34. a	40. a
29. c	35. c	41. c
30. e	36. c	42. b
31. e	37. e	43. e
32. d	38. e	44. c
33. a	39. d	45. d

Appendixes

Appendix A

Interview Question Guidelines: What You Can and Cannot Ask

There are so many leading questions that interviewers ask that are potentially discriminatory. You need to avoid any questions that go beyond exploring the skills and experience required for the job. Whether it is a specific question or an indirect discussion of personal matters, these are potentially illegal conversations. The interviewer must control the interview. Move the discussion back to the job, to the person's abilities to perform the job, and to questions related to the job.

The following are guidelines to help keep you away from those questions that elicit potentially discriminating information.

Name

Can Ask: Have you worked at this company under a different name? (Provides information for reference check.)

Can't Ask: *Questions that would refer to the applicant's national origin or whether she prefers Ms., Miss, or Mrs., which reflect marital status.*

Marital and Family Status

Can Ask: Whether the applicant can work required schedules or if there are commitments creating an attendance conflict.

Can't Ask: *Any inquiry on marital status, number and age of children, child-care arrangements, pregnancy.*

Age

Can Ask: A minor for proof of age, such as a work certificate.

Can't Ask: *Requirement that applicant provide age or birth date or pro-*

vide birth certificate. The Age Discrimination in Employment Act forbids discrimination against persons over the
age of 40.

Sex

Can Ask: Gender for affirmative action purposes, but not for
                employment purposes. Make this inquiry on a form
                separate from the employment application.

Can't Ask: *Sex, height, weight, or any other inquiry that would indi-
                cate sex.*

Race or Color

Can Ask: Race for affirmative action purposes, but not for em-
                ployment purposes. Make this inquiry on a separate
                form from the employment application.

Can't Ask: *Any questions requiring applicant to identify race or color.*

Address or Duration of Residence

Can Ask: Applicant's address, length of stay at current and pre-
                vious address, how long a resident in state or city.

Can't Ask: *Inquiry into a foreign address that would indicate national
                origin, names and relationships of "roommates," or
                whether an applicant owns or rents a home.*

Birthplace

Can Ask: Can you after employment submit a birth certificate
                or other proof of U.S. citizenship?

Can't Ask: *Birthplace of applicant or applicant's relatives; requirement
                that applicant submits a birth certificate before employment
                or any other questions regarding national origin.*

Religion

Can Ask: An applicant can be made aware of the scheduled
                hours required for the job to avoid possible conflict
                with religious observances. The employer is required
                to make reasonable accommodations regarding these
                conflicts.

Can't Ask: *Applicant's religious denomination, church affiliation, reli-
                gious customs, or holiday observance.*

Military Record

Can Ask: Type of education and experience relating to the job.
Can't Ask: *Type of discharge.*

Photograph

Can Ask: After hiring, picture for identification.
Can't Ask: *For optional or required photograph either attached to application or after the interview but before hiring.*

Citizenship

Can Ask   Are you a U.S. citizen? Do you intend to remain in the United States permanently? Are you able to work in the United States? If hired, you may be required to submit proof of citizenship.
Can't Ask: *Of what country are you a citizen? Are you, your parents, or your spouse naturalized or native U.S. citizens? What is the date of your U.S. citizenship? Requirement to produce naturalization papers.*

Ancestry or National Origin

Can Ask: If another language is necessary to perform the job, you can ask what languages the applicant knows.
Can't Ask: *Inquiries into applicant's (parents' or spouse's) natural origin, birthplace, and so on.*

Education

Can Ask: Applicant's academic, vocational, or professional school(s) attended.
Can't Ask: *Nationality, racial, or religious affiliation of the school.*

Conviction, Arrest, and Court Record

Can Ask: Inquiry into actual convictions that relate to fitness to perform a particular function.
Can't Ask: *Any inquiry into arrest, court, or conviction record if not related to the particular job in question.*

Relatives

Can Ask: Name of applicant's relatives already employed by this company. If the applicant is a minor, you can request the name and address of parents or guardian.
Can't Ask: *Name or address of any relative of an adult applicant.*

Organizations

Can Ask: Inquiry into membership of organizations, providing the name of the organization if it does not reflect race, religion, and the like.

Can't Ask: *All organizations, clubs, societies to which you belong.*

References

Can Ask: Names of persons willing to provide professional and character references.

Can't Ask: *For a religious or pastoral reference.*

Miscellaneous

Can Ask: Notice to applicants that any misstatements or omissions of material facts in the application may be cause for dismissal.

Can't Ask: *Any information designed to elicit information regarding race, color, ancestry, age, sex, religion, disability, or arrest and court record unless based on a bona fide occupational qualification.*

Appendix B

Job Requirements:
How to Identify Work Skills

There are many different approaches employers can take to identify, track, and document the physical, mental, and environmental requirements for each position. There are numerous creative job-analysis tools for these purposes. Here are two ways.

Job Analysis 1

A large piece of paper (see Figure B-1) is positioned horizontally (11 inches high × 16 inches wide). Across the top are noted the position title and job summary. The remainder of the front side of the page is marked for vertical columns. The columns are headed as follows:

- Task
- Method/Technique
- Tools/Equipment
- Frequency/Time Required
- Physical Involvement
- Mental Involvement
- Human Relations Involvement
- Notes

The Task is defined by a simple phrase. The Method is a one- to three-sentence description of the effort. The Tools lists each tool used in each task; tools used in multiple tasks are repeated. Frequency and Time are reported in the number of incidences and/or percentages of the work day or week. Physical Involvement includes such specifics as seeing, hearing, keying, and reaching. Mental In-

(Text continues on page 218.)

Figure B-1. Job analysis example 1.

POSITION TITLE:

JOB SUMMARY:

SIDE ONE

Task	Method/ Technique	Tools and Equipment	Frequency/ Time Required	Physical Involvement	Mental Involvement	Human Relations Involvement	Notes

WORK ENVIRONMENT FACTORS

Location:

Mobility Barriers to Access the Work Site:

Climatic and Atmospheric Conditions at the Work Site:

Type and Level of Noise and Vibration:

Potential Health Hazards:

Notes:

volvement includes interpreting and understanding. Human Relations Involvement is supervisory relationships as well as customer relationships. Any requirements that involve essential functions to the job are checked.

The reverse side of the form lists the Work Environment Factors, including:

- Location
- Mobility Barriers to Access the Work Site
- Climatic and Atmospheric Conditions at the Work Site
- Type and Level of Noise and Vibration
- Potential Health Hazards
- Notes

The Location could include specifics such as the warehouse or office address. Mobility Barriers could be entry doors, elevators, or steps. Climate might include outdoor or indoor requirements and temperature levels. Noise and Vibration are rated by a range of low to high, with high levels specified. Potential Hazards can include electrical exposure, repetitive motions, and potential dangers related to equipment or chemicals.

This job-analysis tool can be extremely useful in training and monitoring job responsibilities as well as in accommodating people with disabilities. Industrial situations require more elaborate tracking of work environment factors than office environments. However, it is beneficial to provide a statement about environment in either circumstance.

Job Analysis 2

The job analysis questionnaire (see Figure B-2) can be divided into six components:

- Physical Demands
- Lifting Demands
- Environmental Factors
- Mental and Communication Processes
- Toxic or Irritating Substances or Duties
- Equipment Operation

Each component lists ten to fifteen characteristics or functions. Physical Demands includes standing and sitting. Lifting Demands specifies weight ranges as well as lifting levels (floor to hip, hip to shoulder). Environmental Factors lists temperature, weather, and noise. Mental and Communication Processes includes calculating and speaking. Toxic or Irritating Substances or Duties might mention working with solvents and spray painting. Equipment Operation specifies vehicles and tools.

The unique aspect of this form is its level of evaluation for each function. The functions are listed down the left side of the page, sorted by the six components listed above. Across the page are three columns. Every function is evaluated according to accountability, frequency, and its essential nature.

Accountabilities relate back to the job description, according to the job task number. For each function—for example, sitting—the evaluator circles the corresponding task numbers that require sitting. Then each function is rated on a 0 to 5 frequency scale, from not required to 100 percent of time spent sitting. The evaluator then rates the function as essential or nonessential. With this form, over fifty functions are evaluated to this level of detail. The form is extremely thorough; however, employees or managers who know the jobs are able to complete the task relatively quickly once the job description is up-to-date. The detailed list of functions simplifies the evaluation.

A Job Requirements Checklist

To help you determine the best method of identifying job requirements, use the following list of functions. Select the functions most relevant to your jobs, or use the list as an attachment to your standard form. For the Mental and Communication Functions as well as the Environmental Conditions, specify the weights lifted, the tools used, the items manipulated by hand, what is climbed (stairs, ladders), and so on. Include the frequency of the physical activities and leave space for other physical functions that are unique to a particular job.

Physical Functions

Assemble	Clean
Balance	Climb
Bend	Crawl
Carry	Crouch

(Text continues on page 222.)

Figure B-2. Job analysis example 2.

JOB ANALYSIS QUESTIONNAIRE

Position Title _____ Department _____ Date _____
Analysis By _____ Reviewed By _____

KEY FOR FREQUENCY
0 = Not Required
1 = 1–10% of time
2 = 11–33% of time
3 = 34–66% of time
4 = 67–90% of time
5 = 91–100% of time

PART A: PHYSICAL DEMANDS
The position requires that the incumbent perform physical activity as follows:

FUNCTION	ACCOUNTABILITIES WHERE REQUIRED	FREQUENCY	ESSENTIAL FUNCTION
Standing	0 1 2 3 4 5 6 7 8	0 1 2 3 4 5	Yes No
Sitting	0 1 2 3 4 5 6 7 8	0 1 2 3 4 5	Yes No
Walking	0 1 2 3 4 5 6 7 8	0 1 2 3 4 5	Yes No
Climbing	0 1 2 3 4 5 6 7 8	0 1 2 3 4 5	Yes No
Kneeling, crawling, squatting	0 1 2 3 4 5 6 7 8	0 1 2 3 4 5	Yes No
Bending, twisting body	0 1 2 3 4 5 6 7 8	0 1 2 3 4 5	Yes No
Gripping, grasping, wrist turning	0 1 2 3 4 5 6 7 8	0 1 2 3 4 5	Yes No
Reaching, stretching	0 1 2 3 4 5 6 7 8	0 1 2 3 4 5	Yes No
Pushing and pulling	0 1 2 3 4 5 6 7 8	0 1 2 3 4 5	Yes No
Typing, keyboard	0 1 2 3 4 5 6 7 8	0 1 2 3 4 5	Yes No
Filing	0 1 2 3 4 5 6 7 8	0 1 2 3 4 5	Yes No
Other	0 1 2 3 4 5 6 7 8	0 1 2 3 4 5	Yes No

PART B: LIFTING DEMANDS
The position requires that the incumbent must be able to lift as follows:

FUNCTION	ACCOUNTABILITIES WHERE REQUIRED	FREQUENCY	ESSENTIAL FUNCTION
At floor to knuckle height the lifting of a weight from:			
0–15 lbs	0 1 2 3 4 5 6 7 8	0 1 2 3 4 5	Yes No
15–35 lbs	0 1 2 3 4 5 6 7 8	0 1 2 3 4 5	Yes No
35–55 lbs	0 1 2 3 4 5 6 7 8	0 1 2 3 4 5	Yes No
55 + lbs	0 1 2 3 4 5 6 7 8	0 1 2 3 4 5	Yes No
At knuckle to shoulder height the lifting of a weight from:			
0–15 lbs	0 1 2 3 4 5 6 7 8	0 1 2 3 4 5	Yes No
15–35 lbs	0 1 2 3 4 5 6 7 8	0 1 2 3 4 5	Yes No
35–55 lbs	0 1 2 3 4 5 6 7 8	0 1 2 3 4 5	Yes No
55 + lbs	0 1 2 3 4 5 6 7 8	0 1 2 3 4 5	Yes No
At shoulder height to over head the lifting of a weight from:			
0–15 lbs	0 1 2 3 4 5 6 7 8	0 1 2 3 4 5	Yes No
15–35 lbs	0 1 2 3 4 5 6 7 8	0 1 2 3 4 5	Yes No
35–55 lbs	0 1 2 3 4 5 6 7 8	0 1 2 3 4 5	Yes No
55 + lbs	0 1 2 3 4 5 6 7 8	0 1 2 3 4 5	Yes No

PART C: ENVIRONMENTAL FACTORS
The position requires that the incumbent will be exposed to the following external conditions:

FUNCTION	ACCOUNTABILITIES WHERE REQUIRED	FREQUENCY	ESSENTIAL FUNCTION
Acute vision for distance	0 1 2 3 4 5 6 7 8	0 1 2 3 4 5	Yes No
Vision for close work	0 1 2 3 4 5 6 7 8	0 1 2 3 4 5	Yes No
Color perception	0 1 2 3 4 5 6 7 8	0 1 2 3 4 5	Yes No
Work in 90 degrees or more	0 1 2 3 4 5 6 7 8	0 1 2 3 4 5	Yes No
Work in 50 degrees or less	0 1 2 3 4 5 6 7 8	0 1 2 3 4 5	Yes No
Outdoors work	0 1 2 3 4 5 6 7 8	0 1 2 3 4 5	Yes No

FUNCTION	ACCOUNTABILITIES WHERE REQUIRED		FREQUENCY	ESSENTIAL FUNCTION	
Work in confined spaces	0 1 2 3 4 5 6 7 8		0 1 2 3 4 5	Yes	No
Working overhead (roofs, etc.)	0 1 2 3 4 5 6 7 8		0 1 2 3 4 5	Yes	No
Working in a wet environment	0 1 2 3 4 5 6 7 8		0 1 2 3 4 5	Yes	No
Work where noise is + 80 db	0 1 2 3 4 5 6 7 8		0 1 2 3 4 5	Yes	No
Travel by public airlines	0 1 2 3 4 5 6 7 8		0 1 2 3 4 5	Yes	No

PART D: MENTAL AND COMMUNICATION PROCESSES
The position requires that the incumbent may be expected to perform the following mental & communication processes:

FUNCTION	ACCOUNTABILITIES WHERE REQUIRED		FREQUENCY	ESSENTIAL FUNCTION	
Reasoning	0 1 2 3 4 5 6 7 8		0 1 2 3 4 5	Yes	No
Remembering	0 1 2 3 4 5 6 7 8		0 1 2 3 4 5	Yes	No
Comparing	0 1 2 3 4 5 6 7 8		0 1 2 3 4 5	Yes	No
Evaluating	0 1 2 3 4 5 6 7 8		0 1 2 3 4 5	Yes	No
Calculating	0 1 2 3 4 5 6 7 8		0 1 2 3 4 5	Yes	No
Interpreting	0 1 2 3 4 5 6 7 8		0 1 2 3 4 5	Yes	No
Editing	0 1 2 3 4 5 6 7 8		0 1 2 3 4 5	Yes	No
Instructing	0 1 2 3 4 5 6 7 8		0 1 2 3 4 5	Yes	No
Reading	0 1 2 3 4 5 6 7 8		0 1 2 3 4 5	Yes	No
Writing	0 1 2 3 4 5 6 7 8		0 1 2 3 4 5	Yes	No
Speaking	0 1 2 3 4 5 6 7 8		0 1 2 3 4 5	Yes	No

PART E: TOXIC OR IRRITATING SUBSTANCES/DUTIES
The position requires that the incumbent may be exposed to the following toxic or irritating substances:

FUNCTION	ACCOUNTABILITIES WHERE REQUIRED		FREQUENCY	ESSENTIAL FUNCTION	
Work with solvents	0 1 2 3 4 5 6 7 8		0 1 2 3 4 5	Yes	No
Work with acids, corrosives	0 1 2 3 4 5 6 7 8		0 1 2 3 4 5	Yes	No
Work with epoxies	0 1 2 3 4 5 6 7 8		0 1 2 3 4 5	Yes	No
Work with cutting oils	0 1 2 3 4 5 6 7 8		0 1 2 3 4 5	Yes	No
Soldering	0 1 2 3 4 5 6 7 8		0 1 2 3 4 5	Yes	No
Brazing and welding	0 1 2 3 4 5 6 7 8		0 1 2 3 4 5	Yes	No
Spray painting	0 1 2 3 4 5 6 7 8		0 1 2 3 4 5	Yes	No
Dusty work	0 1 2 3 4 5 6 7 8		0 1 2 3 4 5	Yes	No
Other _____	0 1 2 3 4 5 6 7 8		0 1 2 3 4 5	Yes	No
Other _____	0 1 2 3 4 5 6 7 8		0 1 2 3 4 5	Yes	No
Other _____	0 1 2 3 4 5 6 7 8		0 1 2 3 4 5	Yes	No
Other _____	0 1 2 3 4 5 6 7 8		0 1 2 3 4 5	Yes	No

PART F: EQUIPMENT OPERATION
The position requires the incumbent to operate various types of equipment, including:

FUNCTION	ACCOUNTABILITIES WHERE REQUIRED		FREQUENCY	ESSENTIAL FUNCTION	
Driving cars and light trucks	0 1 2 3 4 5 6 7 8		0 1 2 3 4 5	Yes	No
Driving heavy trucks or vans	0 1 2 3 4 5 6 7 8		0 1 2 3 4 5	Yes	No
Driving trucks over two axles	0 1 2 3 4 5 6 7 8		0 1 2 3 4 5	Yes	No
Operating forklifts, stackers	0 1 2 3 4 5 6 7 8		0 1 2 3 4 5	Yes	No
Operating hoisting equipment	0 1 2 3 4 5 6 7 8		0 1 2 3 4 5	Yes	No
Operating battery powered carts	0 1 2 3 4 5 6 7 8		0 1 2 3 4 5	Yes	No
Operating power presses, shears	0 1 2 3 4 5 6 7 8		0 1 2 3 4 5	Yes	No
Operating machine tools	0 1 2 3 4 5 6 7 8		0 1 2 3 4 5	Yes	No
Operating power saws	0 1 2 3 4 5 6 7 8		0 1 2 3 4 5	Yes	No
Operating power hand tools	0 1 2 3 4 5 6 7 8		0 1 2 3 4 5	Yes	No
Operating non-power hand tools	0 1 2 3 4 5 6 7 8		0 1 2 3 4 5	Yes	No
Other _____	0 1 2 3 4 5 6 7 8		0 1 2 3 4 5	Yes	No
Other _____	0 1 2 3 4 5 6 7 8		0 1 2 3 4 5	Yes	No
Other _____	0 1 2 3 4 5 6 7 8		0 1 2 3 4 5	Yes	No
Other _____	0 1 2 3 4 5 6 7 8		0 1 2 3 4 5	Yes	No

Draw   Read
Drive   Recline
File   Sit
Fold   Stamp
Hand manipulation   Stand
Handle   Stoop
Kneel   Twist
Lift   Type/keyboard
Load   Unload
Polish   Use Tools
Pour   Walk
Pull   Write
Push   Other
Reach

Mental and Communication Functions

Advise   Memorize
Analyze   Negotiate
Calculate   Organize
Compare   Plan
Concentrate   Present
Coordinate   Problem solve
Copy   Reason
Diagnose   Record
Edit   Remember
Evaluate   Sell
Influence   Sequence
Inspect   Solicit
Instruct   Speak
Interact   Supervise
Interpret   Work independently
Make decisions   Other
Measure

Environmental Conditions

Dry/humid/wet conditions   Mechanical hazards
Dust/fumes/odors/gases   Noise levels
Electrical hazards   Outdoor work
Exposure to varying   Radiation
  temperatures   Toxic or caustic chemicals
Indoor work   Ventilation/air pressure
Lighting levels   Vibration levels

Appendix C

Training Outlines

The following outlines will help managers train individuals to better understand the basics of the ADA-essential functions, disability awareness, effective interviewing techniques, and selection decision making. These outlines can be used as a training guide, as an outline for conducting presentations, or as visual aids in the training sessions.

Outlines in this Appendix

1. The Five Titles of the Americans with Disabilities Act
2. Title I—Employment
3. How the ADA Defines *Disabled* and *Qualified*
4. Essential Functions Are the Core of ADA Compliance
5. Essential Functions as the Core of Effective Employment
6. Identifying Essential Functions
7. Components of Compliant Job Descriptions
8. Components of Compliant Employment Ads
9. Application and Resumé Screening Tips
10. Interview Preparation
11. Tips for Developing Interview Questions
12. Components of an Effective Interview
13. Disability-Awareness Discussion Topics
14. Disability Awareness and Interviewing
15. Interview Evaluation
16. Candidate Selection

Outline 1

The Five Titles Of
The Americans with Disabilities Act

■ Title I—Employment

    ☐ Effective July 26, 1992, for employers with 25 or more employees

    ☐ Effective July 26, 1994, for employers with 15 or more employees

■ Title II—Public Services

■ Title III—Public Accommodations

■ Title IV—Telecommunications

■ Title V—Miscellaneous

Outline 2

Title I—Employment

"Equal employment opportunities for qualified individuals with disabilities"

Who is protected by ADA?

An individual with a disability who can perform the essential functions of the job in question with or without accommodation, unless the accommodation presents an undue hardship to the employer.

It is illegal to discriminate against qualified individuals with disabilities in all terms and conditions of employment, including:

☐ Recruiting methods and tools
☐ Selection
☐ Training
☐ Compensation
☐ Benefits
☐ Promotion
☐ Termination

Outline 3

How the ADA Defines *Disabled* and *Qualified*

■ A person is protected under ADA as ***disabled*** if he or she:

    ☐ has a physical or mental impairment that substantially limits one or more major life activity

    ☐ has a record of such an impairment

    ☐ is regarded as having an impairment

    ☐ associates with someone with a disability

■ A person is ***qualified*** according to ADA if he or she:

    ☐ can perform the essential functions of the job with or without accommodation

    ☐ can meet the job qualifications established by the employer, such as:

        ■ education requirements

        ■ work experience

        ■ training levels

        ■ job skills

Outline 4

Essential Functions Are the Core Of ADA Compliance

Essential functions are the primary responsibilities of a position

Identifying essential functions benefits all employee-management issues:

- Position opening
- Update job description
- Advertise jobs
- Screen applications
- Select candidates
- Interview candidates
- Make the hiring decision
- Orient new employee
- Train new employee
- Develop performance criteria
- Supervise employee
- Evaluate employee performance
- Determine new opportunities for employee
- Promote employee

Outline 5

Essential Functions as the Core Of Effective Employment

Utilize essential functions to:

☐ Determine the need to hire

☐ Identify hiring criteria

☐ Create the job advertisement

☐ Screen applications and resumés

☐ Select qualified candidates

☐ Develop interview questions

☐ Conduct interviews

☐ Evaluate final candidates

☐ Make the hiring decision

☐ Extend the job offer

Outline 6

Identifying Essential Functions

1. Are employees performing the task?
2. Did previous employees perform the task?
3. Does the position exist to perform the function?
4. How much time does the employee spend performing the function?
5. Are there a limited number of other employees available to perform the function or among whom to distribute the function?
6. Are there peak work periods that would prevent the transfer of responsibilities to others in the department?
7. Is the function so highly specialized that the person is hired for his or her special expertise or ability to perform the function?
8. Would there be serious consequences if the employee is not required to perform the function?

Outline 7

Components of Compliant Job Descriptions

■ Job Identification Header
  ☐ Title
  ☐ Reporting and work relationships
  ☐ Revision date

■ Job Function Statement
  ☐ Overall job purpose and benefit to the operation

■ Major Tasks
  ☐ Specify tasks: what, when, how often
  ☐ Differentiate essential and nonessential job functions
  ☐ Include percentages of time spent performing each function

■ Job Qualifications
  ☐ Knowledge, skills, experience, education, abilities
  ☐ Physical and mental requirements
  ☐ Tools and equipment

■ Work Conditions
  ☐ Safety and hazards
  ☐ Work site layout
  ☐ General environment

■ Attendance and Other Work Requirements
  ☐ Work schedule
  ☐ Travel
  ☐ Overtime

Outline 8

Components of Compliant Employment Ads

Advertising Objective: to produce a qualified pool of applicants

■ Base advertising on essential functions
■ Focus on the most important responsibilities, the screening criteria
■ Identify the key skills, experience, and education
■ State qualification requirements as minimums
■ Avoid nonessential function references
■ Emphasize "have to have" criteria over "nice to have" criteria
■ Include special physical or mental requirements
■ Include unique or demanding scheduling requirements
■ Include licensing or special skill requirements
■ Identify and use ad locations with proven recruiting results
■ Evaluate internal job-posting methods
■ Develop an advertising success tracking system

Outline 9

Application and Resumé Screening Tips

Review the essential functions of the job—keep them
"fresh in your mind"

■ Identify the screening criteria for the position:

    ☐ Focus on the overall job objective
    ☐ Outline key qualifications
    ☐ List primary skills
    ☐ Create a list of buzzwords to locate in the resumé
    ☐ Develop a checklist of screening criteria
    ☐ Highlight key criteria on the job description

■ Prioritize the criteria you use to screen applicants

■ Develop a screening and sorting method

■ Consider 3-pile sorting method:

    1. Underqualified
    2. Overqualified
    3. Needs further consideration

■ Match no. 3 above to screening list

■ Prioritize applications based on match with required criteria

Outline 10

Interview Preparation

■ Prepare the interview setting
  ☐ Schedule sufficient time for a thorough interview
  ☐ Locate interview in private location
  ☐ Eliminate all possible interruptions
  ☐ Remove desktop distractions

■ Prepare the interview substance
  ☐ Create a list of questions particular to the candidate
  ☐ Create a list of questions particular to the position

■ Develop a note-taking tool

■ Reread each candidate's resumé just prior to the interview as a refresher

■ Commit yourself to:
  ☐ Remember to listen at least 80 percent of the interview period
  ☐ Remember to listen to:
  —what they say
  —how they say it
  —how their answers relate to your hiring needs
  ☐ Stick to your list of questions for fair and equitable interviewing

Outline 11

Tips for Developing Interview Questions

☐ Start with easier questions
☐ Don't repeat obvious resumé questions
☐ Avoid close-ended questions requiring yes and no answers *(is, can, did?)*
☐ Ask explorative questions *(how, why, when, describe)*
☐ Follow up key explorative questions to target your needs
☐ Probe for facts, opinions, and ideas
☐ Ask candidates to describe situations and how they handled them
☐ Ask questions that help you evaluate how the candidate thinks
☐ Create mini-cases based on true job events
☐ Probe the candidate's expertise—don't assume knowledge or skills
☐ Have the candidate clarify incomplete or unclear statements
☐ Don't ask typical questions
☐ Ask questions that show the difference between candidates
☐ Avoid long questions
☐ Ask the same questions of all candidates
☐ Only pursue areas that are relevant to the job
☐ Don't assume tenure is synonymous with achievement
☐ Study how each candidate answers a question, not merely what the person says
☐ Listen without interruption
☐ Direct and guide the conversation to acquire the best job-related information

Outline 12

Components of an Effective Interview

☑ Introductory conversation
☑ Brief introduction of company and position
☑ Review of candidate's education
☑ Overview of work history
☑ Technical abilities and job knowledge
☑ Work-related personality traits
☑ Interpersonal skills
☑ Managerial abilities
☑ Motivational characteristics and work objectives
☑ More complete review of company and position
☑ Open discussion for candidate's questions
☑ Interview closure

Outline 13

Disability-Awareness Discussion Topics

☐ Invisible and visible disabilities
☐ Review who is disabled according to the ADA
☐ True equal opportunity
☐ Practice common courtesy and common sense
☐ Eliminate common myths and misconceptions
☐ Use respectful terminology:
  ▪ Don't use *handicapped*
  ▪ Replace "he is disabled" with "he has a disability"
  ▪ Replace generalization: "the blind, the deaf" with "she has a visual impairment"
☐ Don't prejudge abilities or inabilities based on your perception of a disability
☐ Give every candidate the opportunity to portray his or her on-the-job capabilities
☐ Consider different disabilities and appropriate etiquette:
  ▪ Visual impairments
  ▪ Mobility impairments
  ▪ Hearing impairments
  ▪ Speech impairments
  ▪ Manual impairments
  ▪ Mental retardation
  ▪ Learning disabilities
☐ Take the "discrimination test"

Outline 14

Disability Awareness and Interviewing

Remember the objective of selection: hiring the most qualified candidate for the job without discriminating

- Merge the essential functions of the job into the interviewing process
- Structure the interview
- Focus on essential functions throughout the interview
- Prepare conscientiously for the interview
- Interview consistently
- Take usable notes

<u>Don't</u> ask about:

- ☒ a current or previous disability
- ☒ how a disability occurred or changed
- ☒ the severity or prognosis of a disability
- ☒ absences due to illness
- ☒ the disability of a friend or relative
- ☒ workers' compensation experiences
- ☒ disabled veteran status
- ☒ why the person cannot perform a function
- ☒ why the person requires an accommodation
- ☒ drug or alcohol problems

Outline 15

Interview Evaluation

■ Evaluate each candidate's qualifications and abilities against the job's key components

■ Develop a job-specific, essential function–based evaluation form

■ Compare candidates on:
  - [ ] education
  - [ ] experience level
  - [ ] ability to perform job duties
  - [ ] possession of job qualifications
  - [ ] overall candidate assessment
  - [ ] post-interview hiring recommendation

■ Use the evaluation form consistently for all interviewed candidates

Outline 16

Candidate Selection

☑ Determine or confirm the primary decision maker
☑ Include and welcome input from all interviewers
☑ Conduct a thorough candidate evaluation meeting
☑ Merge multiple inteview evaluation forms for each candidate
☑ Compare all candidates fairly and completely
☑ Rank candidates according to qualifications and skills
☑ Conduct reference checks on top candidates
☑ Make a final hiring decision
☑ Document the reason for selecting the final candidate
☑ Document the reason for rejecting the interviewed candidates

Appendix D

Regulations for Implementing the Equal Employment Provisions of the ADA

PART 1630—REGULATIONS TO IMPLEMENT THE EQUAL EMPLOYMENT PROVISIONS OF THE AMERICANS WITH DISABILITIES ACT

Appendix to Part 1630—Interpretive Guidance on Title I of the Americans with Disabilities Act

Authority: 42 U.S.C. 12116.

§ 1630.1 Purpose, applicability, and construction.

(a) *Purpose.* The purpose of this part is to implement title I of the Americans with Disabilities Act (42 U.S.C. 12101, *et seq.*) (ADA), requiring equal employment opportunities for qualified individuals with disabilities, and sections 3(2), 3(3), 501, 503, 506(e), 508, 510, and 511 of the ADA as those sections pertain to the employment of qualified individuals with disabilities.

(b) *Applicability.* This part applies to "covered entities" as defined at § 1630.2(b).

(c) *Construction.*—(1) *In general.* Except as otherwise provided in this part, this part does not apply a lesser standard than the standards applied under title V of the Rehabilitation Act of 1973 (29 U.S.C. 790–794a), or the regulations issued by Federal agencies pursuant to that title.

(2) *Relationship to other laws.* This part does not invalidate or limit the remedies, rights, and procedures

From the *Federal Register* 56 (144), July 26, 1991.

of any Federal law or law of any State or political subdivision of any State or jurisdiction that provides greater or equal protection for the rights of individuals with disabilities than are afforded by this part.

§ 1630.2 Definitions.

(a) *Commission* means the Equal Employment Opportunity Commission established by section 705 of the Civil Rights Act of 1964 (42 U.S.C. 2000e–4).

(b) *Covered entity* means an employer, employment agency, labor organization, or joint labor management committee.

(c) *Person, labor organization, employment agency, commerce and industry affecting commerce* shall have the same meaning given those terms in section 701 of the Civil Rights Act of 1964 (42 U.S.C. 2000e).

(d) *State* means each of the several States, the District of Columbia, the Commonwealth of Puerto Rico, Guam, American Samoa, the Virgin Islands, the Trust Territory of the Pacific Islands, and the Commonwealth of the Northern Mariana Islands.

(e) *Employer.*—(1) *In general.* The term employer means a person engaged in an industry affecting commerce who has 15 or more employees for each working day in each of 20 or more calendar weeks in the current or preceding calendar year, and any agent of such person, except that, from July 26, 1992 through July 25, 1994, an employer means a person engaged in an industry affecting commerce who has 25 or more employees for each working day in each of 20 or more calendar weeks in the current or preceding year and any agent of such person.

(2) *Exceptions.* The term *employer* does not include—

(i) The United States, a corporation wholly owned by the government of the United States, or an Indian tribe; or

(ii) A bona fide private membership club (other than a labor organization) that is exempt from taxation under section 501(c) of the Internal Revenue Code of 1986.

(f) *Employee* means an individual employed by an employer.

(g) *Disability* means, with respect to an individual—

(1) A physical or mental impairment that substantially limits one or more of the major life activities of such individual;

(2) A record of such an impairment; or

(3) Being regarded as having such an impairment. (See § 1630.3 for exceptions to this definition.)

(h) *Physical or mental impairment* means:

(1) Any physiological disorder, or condition, cosmetic disfigurement, or anatomical loss affecting one or more of the following body systems: neurological, musculoskeletal, special sense organs, respiratory (including speech organs), cardiovascular, reproductive, digestive, genito-urinary, hemic and lymphatic, skin, and endocrine; or

(2) Any mental or psychological disorder, such as mental retardation, organic brain syndrome, emotional or mental illness, and specific learning disabilities.

(i) *Major life activities* means functions such as caring for oneself, performing manual tasks, walking, seeing, hearing, speaking, breathing, learning, and working.

(j) *Substantially limits*—(1) The term *substantially limits* means:

(i) Unable to perform a major life activity that the average person in the general population can perform; or

(ii) Significantly restricted as to the condition, manner or duration under which an individual can perform a particular major life activity as compared to the condition, manner, or duration under which the average person in the general population can perform that same major life activity.

(2) The following factors should be considered in determining whether an individual is substantially limited in a major life activity:

(i) The nature and severity of the impairment;

(ii) The duration or expected duration of the impairment; and

(iii) The permanent or long-term impact, or the expected permanent or long-term impact of or resulting from the impairment.

(3) With respect to the major life activity of *working*—

(i) The term *substantially limits* means significantly restricted in the ability to perform either a class of jobs or a broad range of jobs in various classes as compared to the average person having comparable training, skills and abilities. The inability to perform a single, particular job does not constitute a substantial limitation in the major life activity of working.

(ii) In addition to the factors listed in paragraph (j)(2) of this section, the following factors may be considered in determining whether an individual is substantially limited in the major life activity of "working":

(A) The geographical area to which the individual has reasonable access;

(B) The job from which the individual has been disqualified because of an impairment, and the number and types of jobs utilizing similar training, knowledge, skills or abilities, within that geographical area, from which the individual is also disqualified because of the impairment (class of jobs); and/or

(C) The job from which the individual has been disqualified because of an impairment, and the number and types of other jobs not utilizing similar training, knowledge, skills or abilities, within that geographical area, from which the individual is also disqualified because of the impairment (broad range of jobs in various classes).

(k) *Has a record of such impairment* means has a history of, or has been misclassified as having, a mental or physical impairment that substantially limits one or more major life activities.

(l) *Is regarded as having such an impairment* means:

(1) Has a physical or mental impairment that does not substantially limit major life activities but is treated by a covered entity as constituting such limitation;

(2) Has a physical or mental impairment that substantially limits major life activities only as a result of the attitudes of others toward such impairment; or

(3) Has none of the impairments defined in paragraphs (h) (1) or (2) of this section but is treated by a covered entity as having a substantially limiting impairment.

(m) *Qualified individual with a disability* means an individual with a disability who satisfies the requisite skill, experience, education and other job-related requirements of the employment position such individual holds or desires, and who, with or without reasonable accommodation, can perform the essential functions of such position. (See § 1630.3 for exceptions to this definition).

(n) *Essential functions.*—(1) *In general.* The term *essential functions* means the fundamental job duties of the employment position the individual with a disability holds or desires. The term "essential functions" does not include the marginal functions of the position.

(2) A job function may be considered essential for any of several reasons, including but not limited to the following:

(i) The function may be essential because the reason the position exists is to perform that function;

(ii) The function may be essential because of the limited number of employees available among whom the performance of that job function can be distributed; and/or

(iii) The function may be highly specialized so that the incumbent in the position is hired for his or her expertise or ability to perform the particular function.

(3) Evidence of whether a particular function is essential includes, but is not limited to:

(i) The employer's judgment as to which functions are essential;

(ii) Written job descriptions prepared before advertising or interviewing applicants for the job;

(iii) The amount of time spent on the job performing the function;

(iv) The consequences of not requiring the incumbent to perform the function;

(v) The terms of a collective bargaining agreement;

(vi) The work experience of past incumbents in the job; and/or

(vii) The current work experience of incumbents in similar jobs.

(o) *Reasonable accommodation.* (1) The term *reasonable accommodation* means:

(i) Modifications or adjustments to a job application process that enable a qualified applicant with a disability to be considered for the position such qualified applicant desires; or

(ii) Modifications or adjustments to the work environment, or to the manner or circumstances under which the position held or desired is customarily performed, that enable a qualified individual with a disability to perform the essential functions of that position; or

(iii) Modifications or adjustments that enable a covered entity's employee with a disability to enjoy equal benefits and privileges of employment as are enjoyed by its other similarly situated employees without disabilities.

(2) *Reasonable accommodation* may include but is not limited to:

(i) Making existing facilities used by employees readily accessible to and usable by individuals with disabilities; and

(ii) Job restructuring; part-time or modified work schedules; reassignment to a vacant position; acquisition or modifications of equipment or devices; appropriate adjustment or modifications of examinations, training materials, or policies; the provision of qualified readers or interpreters; and other similar accommodations for individuals with disabilities.

(3) To determine the appropriate reasonable accommodation it may be necessary for the covered entity to initiate an informal, interactive process

with the qualified individual with a disability in need of the accommodation. This process should identify the precise limitations resulting from the disability and potential reasonable accommodations that could overcome those limitations.

(p) *Undue hardship*—(1) *In general. Undue hardship* means, with respect to the provision of an accommodation, significant difficulty or expense incurred by a covered entity, when considered in light of the factors set forth in paragraph (p)(2) of this section.

(2) *Factors to be considered.* In determining whether an accommodation would impose an undue hardship on a covered entity, factors to be considered include:

(i) The nature and net cost of the accommodation needed under this part, taking into consideration the availability of tax credits and deductions, and/or outside funding;

(ii) The overall financial resources of the facility or facilities involved in the provision of the reasonable accommodation, the number of persons employed at such facility, and the effect on expenses and resources;

(iii) The overall financial resources of the covered entity, the overall size of the business of the covered entity with respect to the number of its employees, and the number, type and location of its facilities;

(iv) The type of operation or operations of the covered entity, including the composition, structure and functions of the workforce of such entity, and the geographic separateness and administrative or fiscal relationship of the facility or facilities in question to the covered entity; and

(v) The impact of the accommodation upon the operation of the facility, including the impact on the ability of other employees to perform their duties and the impact on the facility's ability to conduct business.

(q) *Qualification standards* means the personal and professional attributes including the skill, experience, education, physical, medical, safety and other requirements established by a covered entity as requirements which an individual must meet in order to be eligible for the position held or desired.

(r) *Direct threat* means a significant risk of substantial harm to the health or safety of the individual or others that cannot be eliminated or reduced by reasonable accommodation. The determination that an individual poses a "direct threat" shall be based on an individualized assessment of the individual's present ability to safely perform the essential functions of the job. This assessment shall be based on a reasonable medical judgment that relies on the most current medical knowledge and/or on the best available objective evidence. In determining whether an individual would pose a direct threat, the factors to be considered include:

(1) The duration of the risk;

(2) The nature and severity of the potential harm;

(3) The likelihood that the potential harm will occur; and

(4) The imminence of the potential harm.

§ 1630.3   Exceptions to the definitions of "Disability" and "Qualified Individual with a Disability."

(a) The terms *disability* and *qualified individual with a disability* do not include individuals currently engaging in the illegal use of drugs, when the covered entity acts on the basis of such use.

(1) *Drug* means a controlled substance, as defined in schedules I through V of Section 202 of the Controlled Substances Act (21 U.S.C. 812)

(2) *Illegal use of drugs* means the use of drugs the possession or distribution of which is unlawful under the Controlled Substances Act, as periodically updated by the Food and Drug Administration. This term does not include the use of a drug taken under the supervision of a licensed health care professional, or other uses authorized by the Controlled Substances Act or other provisions of Federal law.

(b) However, the terms *disability* and *qualified* individual with a disability may not exclude an individual who:

(1) Has successfully completed a supervised drug rehabilitation program and is no longer engaging in the illegal use of drugs, or has otherwise been rehabilitated successfully and is no longer engaging in the illegal use of drugs; or

(2) Is participating in a supervised rehabilitation program and is no longer engaging in such use; or

(3) Is erroneously regarded as engaging in such use, but is not engaging in such use.

(c) It shall not be a violation of this part for a covered entity to adopt or administer reasonable policies or procedures, including but not limited to drug testing, designed to ensure that an individual described in paragraph (b) (1) or (2) of this section is no longer engaging in the illegal use of drugs. (See § 1630.16(c) Drug testing).

(d) *Disability* does not include:

(1) Transvestism, transsexualism, pedophilia, exhibitionism, voyeurism, gender identity disorders not resulting from physical impairments, or other sexual behavior disorders;

(2) Compulsive gambling, kleptomania, or pyromania; or

(3) Psychoactive substance use disorders resulting from current illegal use of drugs.

(e) *Homosexuality and bisexuality* are not impairments and so are not disabilities as defined in this part.

§ 1630.4   Discrimination prohibited.

It is unlawful for a covered entity to discriminate on the basis of disability against a qualified individual with a disability in regard to:

(a) Recruitment, advertising, and job application procedures;

(b) Hiring, upgrading, promotion, award of tenure, demotion, transfer, layoff, termination, right of return from layoff, and rehiring;

(c) Rates of pay or any other form of compensation and changes in compensation;

(d) Job assignments, job classifications, organizational structures, position descriptions, lines of progression, and seniority lists;

(e) Leaves of absence, sick leave, or any other leave;

(f) Fringe benefits available by virtue of employment, whether or not administered by the covered entity;

(g) Selection and financial support for training, including: apprenticeships, professional meetings, conferences and other related activities, and selection for leaves of absence to pursue training;

(h) Activities sponsored by a covered entity including social and recreational programs; and

(i) Any other term, condition, or privilege of employment. The term *discrimination* includes, but is not limited to, the acts described in §§ 1630.5 through 1630.13 of this part.

§ 1630.5 Limiting, segregating, and classifying.

It is unlawful for a covered entity to limit, segregate, or classify a job applicant or employee in a way that adversely affects his or her employment opportunities or status on the basis of disability.

§ 1630.6 Contractual or other arrangements.

(a) *In general.* It is unlawful for a covered entity to participate in a contractual or other arrangement or relationship that has the effect of subjecting the covered entity's own qualified applicant or employee with a disability to the discrimination prohibited by this part.

(b) *Contractual or other arrangement defined.* The phrase *contractual or other arrangement or relationship* includes, but is not limited to, a relationship with an employment or referral agency; labor union, including collective bargaining agreements; an organization providing fringe benefits to an employee of the covered entity; or an organization providing training and apprenticeship programs.

(c) *Application.* This section applies to a covered entity, with respect to its own applicants or employees, whether the entity offered the contract or initiated the relationship, or whether the entity accepted the contract or acceded to the relationship. A covered entity is not liable for the actions of the other party or parties to the contract which only affect that other party's employees or applicants.

§ 1630.7 Standards, criteria, or methods of administration.

It is unlawful for a covered entity to use standards, criteria, or methods of administration, which are not job-related and consistent with business necessity, and:

(a) That have the effect of discriminating on the basis of disability; or

(b) That perpetuate the discrimination of others who are subject to common administrative control.

§ 1630.8 Relationship or association with an individual with a disability.

It is unlawful for a covered entity to exclude or deny equal jobs or benefits to, or otherwise discriminate against, a qualified individual because of the known disability of an individual with whom the qualified individual is known to have a family, business, social or other relationship or association.

§ 1630.9 Not making reasonable accommodation.

(a) It is unlawful for a covered entity not to make reasonable accommodation to the known physical or mental limitations of an otherwise qualified applicant or employee with a disability, unless such covered entity can demonstrate that the accommodation would impose an undue hardship on the operation of its business.

(b) It is unlawful for a covered entity to deny employment opportunities to an otherwise qualified job applicant or employee with a disability based on the need of such covered entity to make reasonable accommodation to such individual's physical or mental impairments.

(c) A covered entity shall not be excused from the requirements of this part because of any failure to receive technical assistance authorized by section 506 of the ADA, including any failure in the development or dissemination of any technical assistance manual authorized by that Act.

(d) A qualified individual with a disability is not required to accept an accommodation, aid, service, opportunity or benefit which such qualified individual chooses not to accept. However, if such individual rejects a reasonable accommodation, aid, service, opportunity or benefit that is necessary to enable the individual to perform the essential functions of the position held or desired, and cannot, as a result of that rejection, perform the essential functions of the position, the individual will not be considered a qualified individual with a disability.

§ 1630.10 Qualification standards, tests, and other selection criteria.

It is unlawful for a covered entity to use qualification standards, employment tests or other selection criteria that screen out or tend to screen out an individual with a disability or a class of individuals with disabilities, on the basis of disability, unless the standard, test or other selection criteria, as used by the covered entity, is shown to be job-related for the position in question and is consistent with business necessity.

§ 1630.11 Administration of tests.

It is unlawful for a covered entity to fail to select and administer tests concerning employment in the most effective manner to ensure that, when a test is administered to a job applicant or employee who has a disability that impairs sensory, manual or speaking skills, the test results accurately reflect the skills, aptitude, or whatever other factor of the applicant or employee that the test purports to measure, rather than reflecting the impaired sensory, manual, or speaking skills of such employee or applicant (except where such skills are the factors that the test purports to measure).

§ 1630.12 Retaliation and coercion.

(a) *Retaliation.* It is unlawful to discriminate against any individual because that individual has opposed any act or practice made unlawful by this part or because that individual made a charge, testified, assisted, or participated in any manner in an investigation, proceeding, or hearing to enforce any provision contained in this part.

(b) *Coercion, interference or intimidation.* It is unlawful to coerce, intimidate, threaten, harass or interfere with any individual in the exercise or enjoyment of, or because that individual aided or encouraged any other individual in the exercise of, any right granted or protected by this part.

§ 1630.13 Prohibited medical examinations and inquiries.

(a) *Pre-employment examination or inquiry.* Except as permitted by § 1630.14, it is unlawful for a covered entity to conduct a medical examination of an applicant or to make inquiries as to whether an applicant is an individual with a disability or as to the nature or severity of such disability.

(b) *Examination or inquiry of employees.* Except as permitted by § 1630.14, it is unlawful for a covered entity to require a medical examination of an employee or to make inquiries as to whether an employee is an individual with a disability or as to the nature or severity of such disability.

§ 1630.14 Medical examinations and inquiries specifically permitted.

(a) *Acceptable pre-employment inquiry.* A covered entity may make pre-employment inquiries into the ability of an applicant to perform job-related functions, and/or may ask an applicant to describe or to demonstrate how, with or without reasonable accommodation, the applicant will be able to perform job-related functions.

(b) *Employment entrance examination.* A covered entity may require a medical examination (and/or inquiry) after making an offer of employment to a job applicant and before the applicant begins his or her employment duties, and may condition an offer of employment on the results of such examination (and/or inquiry), if all entering employees in the same job category are subjected to such an examination (and/or inquiry) regardless of disability.

(1) Information obtained under paragraph (b) of this section regarding the medical condition or history of the applicant shall be collected and maintained on separate forms and in separate medical files and be treated as a confidential medical record, except that:

(i) Supervisors and managers may be informed regarding necessary restrictions on the work or duties of the employee and necessary accommodations;

(ii) First aid and safety personnel may be informed, when appropriate, if the disability might require emergency treatment; and

(iii) Government officials investigating compliance with this part shall be provided relevant information on request.

(2) The results of such examination shall not be used for any purpose inconsistent with this part.

(3) Medical examinations conducted in accordance with this section do not have to be job-related and consistent with business necessity. However, if certain criteria are used to screen out an employee or employees with disabilities as a result of such an examination or inquiry, the exclusionary criteria must be job-related and consistent with business necessity, and performance of the essential job functions cannot be accomplished with

reasonable accommodation as required in this part. (See § 1630.15(b) Defenses to charges of discriminatory application of selection criteria.)

(c) *Examination of employees.* A covered entity may require a medical examination (and/or inquiry) of an employee that is job-related and consistent with business necessity. A covered entity may make inquiries into the ability of an employee to perform job-related functions.

(1) Information obtained under paragraph (c) of this section regarding the medical condition or history of any employee shall be collected and maintained on separate forms and in separate medical files and be treated as a confidential medical record, except that:

(i) Supervisors and managers may be informed regarding necessary restrictions on the work or duties of the employee and necessary accommodations;

(ii) First aid and safety personnel may be informed, when appropriate, if the disability might require emergency treatment; and

(iii) Government officials investigating compliance with this part shall be provided relevant information on request.

(2) Information obtained under paragraph (c) of this section regarding the medical condition or history of any employee shall not be used for any purpose inconsistent with this part.

(d) *Other acceptable examinations and inquiries.* A covered entity may conduct voluntary medical examinations and activities, including voluntary medical histories, which are part of an employee health program available to employees at the work site.

(1) Information obtained under paragraph (d) of this section regarding the medical condition or history of any employee shall be collected and maintained on separate forms and in separate medical files and be treated as a confidential medical record, except that:

(i) Supervisors and managers may be informed regarding necessary restrictions on the work or duties of the employee and necessary accommodations;

(ii) First aid and safety personnel may be informed, when appropriate, if the disability might require emergency treatment; and

(iii) Government officials investigating compliance with this part shall be provided relevant information on request.

(2) Information obtained under paragraph (d) of this section regarding the medical condition or history of any employee shall not be used for any purpose inconsistent with this part.

§ 1630.15 Defenses.

Defenses to an allegation of discrimination under this part may include, but are not limited to, the following:

(a) *Disparate treatment charges.* It may be a defense to a charge of disparate treatment brought under §§ 1630.4 through 1630.8 and 1630.11 through 1630.12 that the challenged action is justified by a legitimate, nondiscriminatory reason.

(b) *Charges of discriminatory application of selection criteria—(1) In general.* It may be a defense to a charge of discrimination, as described in § 1630.10, that an alleged application of qualification standards, tests, or selection criteria that screens out or tends to screen out or otherwise denies a job or benefit to an individual with a disability has been shown to be job-related and consistent with business necessity, and such performance cannot be accomplished with reasonable accommodation, as required in this part.

(2) *Direct threat as a qualification standard.* The term "qualification standard" may include a requirement that an individual shall not pose a direct threat to the health or safety of the individual or others in the workplace. (See § 1630.2(r) defining direct threat.)

(c) *Other disparate impact charges.* It may be a defense to a charge of discrimination brought under this part that a uniformly applied standard, criterion, or policy has a disparate impact on an individual with a disability or a class of individuals with disabilities that the challenged standard, criterion or policy has been shown to be job-related and consistent with business necessity, and such performance cannot be accomplished with reasonable accommodation, as required in this part.

(d) *Charges of not making reasonable accommodation.* It may be a defense to a charge of discrimination, as described in § 1630.9, that a requested or necessary accommodation would impose an undue hardship on the operation of the covered entity's business.

(e) *Conflict with other federal laws.* It may be a defense to a charge of discrimination under this part that a challenged action is required or necessitated by another Federal law or regulation, or that another Federal law or regulation prohibits an action (including the provision of a particular reasonable accommodation) that would otherwise be required by this part.

(f) *Additional defenses.* It may be a defense to a charge of discrimination under this part that the alleged discriminatory action is specifically permitted by §§ 1630.14 or 1630.16.

§ 1630.16 Specific activities permitted.

(a) *Religious entities.* A religious corporation, association, educational institution, or society is permitted to give preference in employment to individuals of a particular religion to perform work connected with the carrying on by that corporation, association, educational institution, or society of its activities. A religious entity may require that all applicants and employees conform to the religious tenets of such organization. However, a religious entity may not discriminate against a qualified individual, who satisfies the permitted religious criteria, because of his or her disability.

(b) *Regulation of alcohol and drugs.* A covered entity:

(1) May prohibit the illegal use of drugs and the use of alcohol at the workplace by all employees;

(2) May require that employees not be under the influence of alcohol or be engaging in the illegal use of drugs at the workplace;

(3) May require that all employees behave in conformance with the requirements established under the Drug-Free Workplace Act of 1988 (41 U.S.C. 701 et seq.);

(4) May hold an employee who engages in the illegal use of drugs or who is an alcoholic to the same qualification standards for employment or job performance and behavior to which the entity holds its other employees, even if any unsatisfactory performance or behavior is related to the employee's drug use or alcoholism;

(5) May require that its employees employed in an industry subject to such regulations comply with the standards established in the regulations (if any) of the Departments of Defense and Transportation, and of the Nuclear Regulatory Commission, regarding alcohol and the illegal use of drugs; and

(6) May require that employees employed in sensitive positions comply with the regulations (if any) of the Departments of Defense and Transportation and of the Nuclear Regulatory Commission that apply to employment in sensitive positions subject to such regulations.

(c) *Drug testing*—(1) *General policy.* For purposes of this part, a test to determine the illegal use of drugs is not considered a medical examination. Thus, the administration of such drug tests by a covered entity to its job applicants or employees is not a violation of § 1630.13 of this part. However, this part does not encourage, prohibit, or authorize a covered entity to conduct drug tests of job applicants or employees to determine the illegal use of drugs or to make employment decisions based on such test results.

(2) *Transportation employees.* This part does not encourage, prohibit, or authorize the otherwise lawful exercise by entities subject to the jurisdic-

tion of the Department of Transportation of authority to:

(i) Test employees of entities in, and applicants for, positions involving safety sensitive duties for the illegal use of drugs or for on-duty impairment by alcohol; and

(ii) Remove from safety-sensitive positions persons who test positive for illegal use of drugs or on-duty impairment by alcohol pursuant to paragraph (c)(2)(i) of this section.

(3) *Confidentiality.* Any information regarding the medical condition or history of any employee or applicant obtained from a test to determine the illegal use of drugs, except information regarding the illegal use of drugs, is subject to the requirements of § 1630.14(b) (2) and (3) of this part.

(d) *Regulation of smoking.* A covered entity may prohibit or impose restrictions on smoking in places of employment. Such restrictions do not violate any provision of this part.

(e) *Infectious and communicable diseases; food handling jobs*—(1) *In general.* Under title I of the ADA, section 103(d)(1), the Secretary of Health and Human Services is to prepare a list, to be updated annually, of infectious and communicable diseases which are transmitted through the handling of food. (Copies may be obtained from Center for Infectious Diseases, Centers for Disease Control, 1600 Clifton Road, N.E., Mailstop C09, Atlanta, GA 30333.) If an individual with a disability is disabled by one of the infectious or communicable diseases included on this list, and if the risk of transmitting the disease associated with the handling of food cannot be eliminated by reasonable accommodation, a covered entity may refuse to assign or continue to assign such individual to a job involving food handling. However, if the individual with a disability is a current employee, the employer must consider whether he or she can be accommodated by reassignment to a vacant position not involving food handling.

(2) *Effect on state or other laws.* This part does not preempt, modify, or

amend any State, county, or local law, ordinance or regulation applicable to food handling which:

(i) Is in accordance with the list, referred to in paragraph (e)(1) of this section, of infectious or communicable diseases and the modes of transmissibility published by the Secretary of Health and Human Services; and

(ii) Is designed to protect the public health from individuals who pose a significant risk to the health or safety of others, where that risk cannot be eliminated by reasonable accommodation.

(f) *Health insurance, life insurance, and other benefit plans*—(1) An insurer, hospital, or medical service company, health maintenance organization, or any agent or entity that administers benefit plans, or similar organizations may underwrite risks, classify risks, or administer such risks that are based on or not inconsistent with State law.

(2) A covered entity may establish, sponsor, observe or administer the terms of a bona fide benefit plan that are based on underwriting risks, classifying risks, or administering such risks that are based on or not inconsistent with State law.

(3) A covered entity may establish, sponsor, observe, or administer the terms of a bona fide benefit plan that is not subject to State laws that regulate insurance.

(4) The activities described in paragraphs (f) (1), (2), and (3) of this section are permitted unless these activities are being used as a subterfuge to evade the purposes of this part.

Appendix to Part 1630—Interpretive Guidance on Title I of the Americans with Disabilities Act

Background

The ADA is a federal antidiscrimination statute designed to remove barriers which prevent qualified individuals with disabilities from enjoying the same employment opportunities that are available to persons without disabilities.

Like the Civil Rights Act of 1964 that prohibits discrimination on the bases of race, color, religion, national origin, and sex, the ADA seeks to ensure access to equal employment opportunities based on merit. It does not guarantee equal results, establish quotas, or require preferences favoring individuals with disabilities over those without disabilities.

However, while the Civil Rights Act of 1964 prohibits any consideration of personal characteristics such as race or national origin, the ADA necessarily takes a different approach. When an individual's disability creates a barrier to employment opportunities, the ADA requires employers to consider whether reasonable accommodation could remove the barrier.

The ADA thus establishes a process in which the employer must assess a disabled individual's ability to perform the essential functions of the specific job held or desired. While the ADA focuses on eradicating barriers, the ADA does not relieve a disabled employee or applicant from the obligation to perform the essential functions of the job. To the contrary, the ADA is intended to enable disabled persons to compete in the workplace based on the same performance standards and requirements that employers expect of persons who are not disabled.

However, where that individual's functional limitation impedes such job performance, an employer must take steps to reasonably accommodate, and thus help overcome the particular impediment, unless to do so would impose an undue hardship. Such accommodations usually take the form of adjustments to the way a job customarily is performed, or to the work environment itself.

Appendix E

Examples of Reasonable Accommodations

The first six examples were provided by TransCen, Inc., of Rockville, Maryland, a firm specializing in effective employment of people with disabilities.

Office Clerk

Primary Duties: Sorting and delivering office mail throughout a large division office. Photocopying and procuring supplies at the supply store.

Employee Characteristics: Employee has spina bifida. He uses both a manual wheelchair and an electric wheelchair for mobility on the job. He drives his own adapted car.

Accommodations: The mailboxes into which he sorts mail were lowered to arm reach from his wheelchair. At work, he substitutes the use of his manual wheelchair with his electric wheelchair, both of which he owned prior to his employment. A wire mesh basket was added to his electric wheelchair, thus enabling him to deliver the various mail and photocopy items from floor to floor throughout the building. Furniture and boxes were removed from his path to allow for wider wheelchair access. A short wooden dowel gives him the added arm reach he sometimes needs to engage rear photocopy buttons.

Cost to Employer: Less than $150.

Food Preparation Worker

Primary Duties: Preparing and mixing pizza dough at a large national franchise restaurant, placing the dough in the oven to "proof," and adding the pizza sauce.

Reprinted with the permission of the publisher from *The Americans with Disabilities Act: A Review of Best Practices*, © 1993 AMA Membership Publications Division, American Management Association.

Employee Characteristics: Employee is moderately mentally retarded and visually impaired.

Accommodations: To accommodate her visual impairment, a thick line of dark indelible ink was marked on the measuring cup at the level to which the cup needs to be filled. An indelible ink mark also has been made on the oven dial to enable her to see where to set the dial for correct temperatures. Initial on-the-job training was provided by her job coach, employed by a local rehabilitation agency.

Cost to Employer: $0.

Sales Associate

Primary Duties: Initiating customer contact via telephone and written correspondence, answering customer inquiries orders, and tabulating daily quotas.

Employee Characteristics: Employee has quadriplegia. He uses a wheelchair for mobility and requires typing splints for his fingers to compensate for limited digital dexterity. He has a bachelor's degree in business administration.

Accommodations: His desk was raised with wood blocks to allow for space for the wheelchair to fit under. A small attachment to the telephone receiver allows easier handling of the telephone. A slightly "flexed" schedule eases transportation and attendant care arrangements.

Cost to Employer: $40 for the telephone attachment and wood blocks.

Assistant Store Manager

Primary Duties: Assisting the manager, tracking convenience store inventory, ordering the necessary items, overseeing the vending of hot food, operating the cash register when necessary, and supervising part-time store clerks.

Employee Characteristics: Employee has specific learning disabilities, including dyslexia.

Accommodations: Since the employee had worked as a full-time clerk for over a year, he knew all aspects of his job well. Due to his reading difficulties, however, he was unable to pass the written exam needed for promotion to assistant store manager in the standard allotment of time. The company arranged for the exam monitor to read him the questions so that he could respond more quickly. After scoring one of the highest marks ever achieved on the test, he was immediately promoted to assistant store manager.

Cost to Employer: $0.

Receptionist

Primary Duties: Interacting with the public entering a busy university office. Responding to requests for transcripts, schedules, registration, and grade inquiries.

Employee Characteristics: Employee uses a wheelchair for mobility and has limited arm reach.

Accommodations: To allow the employee to reach the computer keyboard used to answer student requests, a semi-circle was cut out of the front receptionist counter, enabling the employee to be closer to the keyboard and to better access the counter space without having to move her wheelchair.

Cost to Employer: $200 for carpentry work.

Stock Clerk

Primary Duties: Stocking and cleaning the showroom of a large retail store.

Employee Characteristics: Employee has a learning disability that makes it difficult for her to process oral directions.

Accommodations: A chart was posted in a convenient location, listing the sequence of duties. This list is organized on a daily basis with a specified time allotment for each task. The list provides the employee with the structure to move independently from one job function to the next, and has actually decreased the amount of supervisory time needed.

Cost to Employer: $0.

Examples of Equipment Modifications or Devices

The EEOC has given the following examples of ways in which an employer could reasonably accommodate an individual with a disability by modifying standard equipment:

- A telephone amplifier designed to work with a hearing aid allowed a plant worker to retain his job and avoid transfer to a lower paying job. Cost: $24;
- A blind receptionist was provided a light probe that allowed her to determine which lines on the switchboard were ringing, on hold, or in use. (A light probe gives an audible signal when held over an illuminated source.) Cost: $50–$100;
- A person working in the food service position, who had use

of only one hand, could perform all tasks except opening cans. She was provided with an electric can opener. Cost: $35;

- Purchase of a lightweight mop and a smaller broom enabled an employee with Down's syndrome and congenital heart problems to do his job with minimal strain. Cost: under $40;
- A truck driver had carpal tunnel syndrome, which limited his wrist movement and caused extreme discomfort in cold weather. A special wrist splint used with a glove designed for skin divers made it possible for him to drive even in extreme weather conditions. Cost: $55;
- A phone headset allowed an insurance salesman with cerebral palsy to write while talking to clients. Rental cost: $6 per month;
- A simple cardboard form, called a "jog," made it possible for a person with mental retardation to properly fold jeans as a stock clerk in a retail store. Cost: $0;
- A timer with an indicator light allowed a medical technician who was deaf to perform laboratory tests. Cost: $27;
- A clerk with limited use of her hands was provided a "lazy susan" file holder that enabled her to reach all materials needed for her job. Cost: $85;
- A groundskeeper who had limited use of one arm was provided a detachable extension arm for a rake. This enabled him to grasp the handle on the extension with the impaired hand and control the rake with the functional arm. Cost: $20;
- A desk layout was changed from the right to the left side to enable a data entry operator who is visually impaired to perform her job. Cost: $0.

Other Examples

A major insurance company reports these accommodations:

- Providing a drafting table, page turner, and pressure-sensitive tape recorder for a sales agent paralyzed from a broken neck ($300).
- Supplying a telephone amplifier for a computer programmer with a hearing impairment ($56).
- Enlarging toilet facilities and installing a hand rail for employees who use wheelchairs ($500).
- Removing turnstiles in the cafeteria and installing lighter weight doors—as part of a general renovation—and having

the cafeteria deliver lunch to a payroll technician disabled from polio ($40 per month).
- Providing a special chair to alleviate back pain for a district sales agent affected by vertebra surgery ($400).

Reasonable Accommodations for People With Psychiatric Disabilities

Following is a list of reasonable accommodations that individuals with psychiatric disabilities involved in the Community Support Program demonstration projects, self-help programs, and supported employment services have found helpful.

Human Assistance

Just as a sign language interpreter or personal care attendant might be provided for a person with a hearing impairment or a physical disability, people with psychiatric disabilities may benefit from the provision of human assistance, such as:

- A job coach to help a worker apply interpersonal or time management skills on the job;
- Additional individualized training on specific job tasks or methods;
- Designation of a coworker to serve as a peer support and/or advocate through regularly scheduled appointments or as needed; and
- Pairing workers with mentors (who may or may not have a disability).

Changes in Workplace Policies

Flexibility in enforcing traditional policies can create helpful, relatively inexpensive accommodations such as:

- Permitting telephone calls during work hours to friends or other supportive individuals;
- Allowing people to work at home;
- Allowing use of sick leave for emotional as well as physical illness; and
- Reserving an enclosed office for an entry-level worker who loses concentration and accuracy amid distractions.

Because of the episodic nature of mental disorders, flexible scheduling can be an essential accommodation for individuals with psychiatric disabilities. Specific strategies include the following:

- Allowing workers to shift work hours for medical appointments or emotional needs;
- Advancing additional paid or unpaid leave during a hospitalization;
- Creating a job-sharing policy;
- Keeping a job open and/or providing backup coverage during a period of extended leave; and
- Permitting a self-paced workload.

Supervision

Good supervision improves anyone's work situation, but it may be critical to the success of workers with psychiatric disabilities. Supervisory accommodations include the following:

- Assigning or reassigning the worker to a supervisor who is supportive and has good listening skills;
- Offering management training to all supervisors to improve their ability to provide clear direction and constructive feedback;
- Educating managers about the ADA so they can have frank discussions with applicants and/or workers about known disabilities and desirable accommodations;
- Training supervisors to offer praise and positive reinforcement;
- Instructing supervisors to provide detailed explanations of job duties, responsibilities, and expectations; and
- Establishing written agreements between workers and supervisors for short-term performance indicators, work flow management, and handling crises.

Shaping Coworkers' Attitudes

Proactive strategies for making a workplace "emotionally accessible" include the following:

- Sensitivity training for coworkers about disabilities;
- Staging open discussions involving disabled and nondisabled workers to air feelings;

A Quick Look at How Title I of the ADA Protects People With Psychiatric Disabilities

It is now illegal for employers to:

- Ask job applicants about psychiatric treatment—past or present;
- Deny a job to someone with the necessary experience and skills because of the person's past or current psychiatric treatment or possible future treatment;
- Deny a job or promotion because of a belief that a person with a mental disability won't be able to "handle" the job;
- Refuse to make reasonable modifications in workplace rules, schedules, policies, or procedures that would help a person with a mental disability perform the job;
- Force an employee with mental disabilities to accept a workplace modification;
- Contract with other organizations and individuals that discriminate against people with mental disabilities; or
- Retaliate against people with mental disabilities for asserting their rights.

- Orienting coworkers as to why people with disabilities receive accommodations; and
- Dispelling myths by educating staff about the causes, treatment, and personal experience of mental illness.

Guiding Principles for Providing Reasonable Accommodations

Providing reasonable accommodations in a manner that empowers rather than stigmatizes the individual includes the following:

- Recognizing the individual's strengths and potential contributions to the organization;
- Being willing to engage in joint problem solving;
- Involving the individual in all decision making related to restructuring a job and developing reasonable accommodations;
- Making only voluntary reasonable accommodations; and
- Providing an environment in which disclosure is not punished, but conversely the individual's desire for confidentiality is respected.

Bibliography

Akabas, Sheila H., Lauren B. Gates, and Donald E. Galvin. *Disability Management*. New York: AMACOM, 1992.

Arthur, Diane. *Recruiting, Interviewing, Selecting, and Orienting New Employees*, 2nd ed. New York: AMACOM, 1991.

————. *Workplace Testing*. New York: AMACOM, 1994.

Bolles, Richard Nelson. *Job Hunting Tips for the So-Called Handicapped or People Who Have Disabilities*. Berkeley, Calif.: Ten Speed Press, 1991.

Bozza, Linda. *Ready, Willing & Able: What You Should Know about Workers with Disabilities*. New York: Industry Labor Council, 1985.

Byham, William C. *Targeted Selection: A Behavioral Approach to Improved Hiring Decisions* (Monograph XIV). Pittsburgh: Development Dimensions International Press, 19XX.

Drake, John D. *The Effective Interviewer: A Guide for Managers*. New York: AMACOM, 1972.

Equal Employment Opportunity Commission, *A Technical Assistance Manual on the Employment Provisions (Title I) of the Americans with Disabilities Act*. Washington, D.C.: Government Printing Office, January 1992.

Fritz, Rumpel, ed. *Planning Reasonable Accommodations: A Cost-Effective Approach in a Legal Framework*. Washington, D.C.: Mainstream Inc., 1990.

Grant, Philip C. *Multiple Use Job Descriptions*. New York: Quorum Books, 1989.

Haegstedt, Ted C. "How to Effectively Answer Unexpected Interview Questions," *National Employment Business Weekly*, August 14–20 (1992), pp. 5–6.

Keck, Mahin & Cate. *Personnel Selection under the ADA*. Rosemont, Illinois: London House/SRA, 1992.

McCray, Paul M. *The Job Accommodation Handbook*. Tucson: RPM Press, 1987.

Morrisey, Patricia. *Disability Etiquette in the Workplace*. Washington, D.C.: Employment Policy Foundation, 1991.

National Easter Seal Society. *The Americans With Disabilities Act: An Easy Checklist*. Chicago: National Easter Seal Society, 1990.

Plachy, Roger J., and Sandra J. Plachy. *Results-Oriented Job Descriptions*. New York: AMACOM, 1993.

President's Committee on Employment of People with Disabilities. *People with Disabilities: Working for You in the Insurance Industry*. Washington, D.C.: Government Printing Office, 1991.

Smart, Bradford D. *The Smart Interviewer: Tools & Techniques for Hiring the Best*. New York: John Wiley & Sons, 1989.

Swan, William S. *Swan's Hot to Pick the Right People Program*. New York: John Wiley & Sons, 1989.

Uris, Auren. *88 Mistakes Interviewers Make . . . And How to Avoid Them*. New York: AMACOM, 1989.

Vernon-Oehmke, Arlene. *Manager's Guide: The Americans with Disabilities Act: A Practical Approach*. Atlanta: LOMA (Life Office Management Association), 1992.

———. *The Human Resource Manager's Guide to ADA Compliance*. Atlanta: LOMA (Life Office Management Association), 1992.

Witt, Melanie Astaire. *Job Strategies for People with Disabilities: Enable Yourself for Today's Job Market*. Princeton, N.J.: Peterson's Guides, 1992.

Yate, Martin John. *Hiring the Best: A Manager's Guide to Effective Interviewing*. Holbrook, Mass.: Bob Adams, 1987.

Index